D1624477

Mainstreaming the Exceptional Child: A Bibliography

MAINSTREAMING THE EXCEPTIONAL CHILD: A BIBLIOGRAPHY

Compiled by Mary Cervantes Clarkson

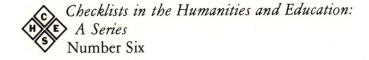

Checklists in the Humanities and Education:
A Series
Number Six

Trinity University Press
San Antonio

Checklists in the Humanities and Education: a Series

Harry B. Caldwell, Trinity University, General Editor

As a continuing endeavor, *Checklists in the Humanities and Education: a Series* provides essential bibliographical information on important scholarly subjects not readily available in composite form. The series emphasizes careful selection of both primary and secondary works, providing a practical and convenient research tool. This compilation, number six in the Series, is, therefore, not exhaustive but will serve as the single most complete checklist to date for materials on mainstreaming the exceptional child into the regular classroom. It is intended to help the professional educator and administrator as well as students and scholars to locate information on this important issue in American education.

Other volumes in the Series

English Tragedy, 1370-1600: Fifty Years of Criticism. Harry B. Caldwell and David L. Middleton.

Twentieth-Century Criticism of English Masques, Pageants, and Entertainments: 1558-1642. David M. Bergeron.

Religion in Contemporary Fiction: Criticism from 1945 to the Present. George N. Boyd and Lois A. Boyd. (Out of Print.)

A Bibliography of Modern Irish and Anglo-Irish Literature. Frank L. Kersnowski, C. W. Spinks, and Laird Loomis.

Mannerism in Art, Literature, and Music: A Bibliography. Richard Studing and Elizabeth Kruz.

© Copyright 1982 Mary Cervantes Clarkson
Library of Congress Catalog Card Number 81-84656
SBN 911536-92-2
All Rights Reserved

Printed by Best Printing Company
Bound by Custom Bookbinders

Printed in the United States of America

LC
3965
C53
1982

CONTENTS

189120

WITHDRAWN

EMORY & HENRY LIBRARY

WITHDRAWN

INTRODUCTION

The enactment of the Education for All Handicapped Children Act of 1975 (Public Law 94-142) mandates a national commitment to educate all handicapped children. The law has determined that handicapped children have the same rights as other children to receive an education according to their needs at public expense, and that public schools must change to accommodate this principle. This development is commonly known as "mainstreaming."

"Mainstreaming," according to the Council for Exceptional Children (1975),

- provides the most appropriate education for each child in the least restrictive setting.
- looks at the educational needs of children instead of clinical or diagnostic labels such as mentally handicapped, learning disabled, physically handicapped, hearing impaired, or gifted.
- searches for and creates alternatives that will help general educators serve children with learning or adjustment problems in the regular setting. Some approaches being used to help achieve this are consulting teachers, methods and materials specialists, itinerant teachers and resource room teachers.
- unites the skills of general education and special education so that all children may have equal educational opportunity.

Mainstreaming is not:
- returning all exceptional children in special classes to regular classes.
- permitting children with special needs to remain in regular classrooms without the support services that they need.
- ignoring the needs of some children for a more specialized program than can be provided in the general education program.
- less costly than serving children in special self-contained classrooms.*

*(From *Exceptional Children*, 1975, 42: 174.)

Mainstreaming is a controversial issue that has caused concern to many educators. There are those educators who fear that the law demands that education of all handicapped children will fall on teachers and regular students or that special education classes will be completely eliminated. Other educators, however, believe that certain handicapped children may profit from learning with regular students in regular classes without detriment to either group. Nonetheless, state and the individual school districts must adhere to stipulations in the law. One stipulation is that the handicapped child should be placed in the "least restrictive environment" in which his or her educational or related needs can be satisfactorily met. Another requirement is that there will be an "individualized education program" for each handicapped child, a written statement developed by a qualified school official, the child's teachers and the child's parents or guardians as to how to best meet the educational needs of the child.

Such questions regarding the definition of mainstreaming, the legal history of mainstreaming, the implementation of mainstreaming programs, the attitudes of teachers, administrators, students, and parents toward mainstreaming, and case studies involving mainstreaming have led college and university departments of education and local public school administrators to implement teacher inservice training programs for their faculty in order to introduce them to the new legislation and its effect on public education. Literature on the subject, however, has been scattered and, in many cases, unobtainable. State education agencies designed and made available some teacher training packets. Many individual school districts devised their own implementation programs. A computerized search of the ERIC and the Exceptional Child Education Resources databases would have yielded helpful information, but many educators are unaware of this valuable reference tool. The term "mainstreaming" was not a valid controlled subject term in these databases until 1978, so the descriptor "regular classroom placement" had to be used in manual and computer searches in conjunction with other descriptors and identifiers such as "least restrictive environment, individualized education programs, Public Law 94-142, and The Education for All Handicapped Children Act of 1975." Even Education Index, a most popular education reference tool, did not use the subject heading "mainstreaming" until 1975. To use this index one used the broad subject headings of "Deaf—Education—Public Schools, Handicapped—Public Schools, Mentally Handicapped—Public Schools, or Mentally Handicapped Children—Public Schools."

This bibliography consists of books, journal articles, ERIC documents, theses, dissertations, government documents, proceedings, pamphlets, and other materials dating as far back as 1964. Specific bibliographies on mainstreaming discovered in searching the literature were consulted and included. Mention should be made of R. L. Peterson's *Mainstreaming: A Working Bibliography* (1976) and T. M. Stephens' *A Comprehensive Bibliography on Mainstreaming* (1976). The ERIC database was searched using controlled vocabulary, free term vocabulary, and all possible identifiers from 1966 to present.

The work is divided into eight areas of exceptionality with the majority of the references falling in the general category. Citations dealing with three or fewer handicaps are repeated in each category. The gifted child is considered an exceptional child and therefore merits a section of its own. Because references dealing with the emotionally disturbed child often treat the learning disabled also, these two disabilities have been combined in one section.

The Supplement contains citations discovered and acquired while the main section was in production. It also is arranged by General and Disability categories.

The subject index is arranged so that by selecting the subject heading needed, the disability category can be determined by the citation number given. For example, if one wishes information on mainstreaming the preschool hearing impaired child, by searching under the subject term "preschool education" in the subject index, all referred references which fall between the numbers 1617 and 2021 treat that topic.

I hope that this bibliography will be used in the following ways: 1) as a reference tool for the public, academic, or school librarian who is the professional consulted when research material is needed, 2) as a guide for the administrator searching for information on mainstreaming for inservice training or program implementation, 3) as a helpful device for the teacher who wants background information on mainstreaming or teaching techniques to use in the classroom, 4) and as an aid for the education student researching any aspect of mainstreaming.

This bibliography is a culmination of four years' work. It would not have been possible without the encouragement of my colleagues at the Reference Department of Trinity University Library, Craig Likness, Norma Carmack, Jane Mackay, and Kathy Malanga. Special thanks go to Louise Frye, a graduate student in education who took time from her studies to help me verify sources. Most of all I dedicate this book to my family; my daughters, Laura and Jennifer, and my husband, Bill.

MARY CERVANTES CLARKSON

I. GENERAL

1. Abbruzzese, J. A., Jr. *The administrative aspects of P.L. 94-142: Dealing with federal mandates and compliances.* Paper presented at the 112th Annual Meeting of the American Association of School Administrators, Anaheim, CA, February 1980. (ERIC Document Reproduction Service No. ED 184 240)

2. Abel, C. B. Recycling old spaces; remodeling a school for the handicapped. *Design*, 1976, 78(2), 12-15.

3. Abelson, A. B. Measuring preschools' readiness to mainstream handicapped children. *Child Welfare*, 1976, 55, 216-220.

4. Abeson, A. The educational least restrictive alternative. *Amicus*, 1977, 2(4), 23-26.

5. _____. The logic and the law for parent participation in the education of handicapped students. *Journal of Career Education*, 1978, 5, 35-43.

6. _____. Movement and momentum: Government and the education of handicapped children. *Exceptional Children*, 1972, 39, 63-66.

7. _____. Movement and momentum: Government and the education of handicapped children—II. *Exceptional Children*, 1974, 41, 109-115.

8. _____. Right to education. *Mental Hygiene*, 1973, 57, 34-37.

9. _____. (Ed.). *A continuing summary of pending and completed litigation regarding the education of handicapped children.* Reston, VA: The Council for Exceptional Children, 1973. (ERIC Document Reproduction Service No. ED 085 930)

10. _____, & Blacklow, J. *Environmental design: New relevance for special education.* Reston, VA: The Council for Exceptional Children, 1971. (ERIC Document Reproduction Service No. ED 055 404)

11. _____, Bolick, N., & Hass, J. Education decision for handicapped children. *Education and Training of the Mentally Retarded*, 1976, 11, 287-289.

12. _____, Bolick, N., & Hass, J. A primer on due process: Education decisions for handicapped children. *Exceptional Children*, 1975, 42, 68-74.

13. _____, & Trudeau, E. Handicapped children redefined—legal eligibility for services expanded. *Exceptional Children*, 1970, 37, 305-311.

14. _____, & Zettel, J. The end of the quiet revolution: The Education for All Handicapped Children Act of 1975. *Exceptional Children*, 1977, *44*, 114-128.

15. Abeson, A. R., & Weintraub, F. J. Appropriate education for all handicapped children: A growing issue. *Syracuse Law Review*, 1972, *23*, 1037-1058.

16. Adams, A., & Coble, C. *Mainstreaming science and mathematics.* Santa Monica, CA: Goodyear, 1977.

17. _____, Coble, C. R., & Hounshell, P. B. *Mainstreaming language arts and social studies: Special activities for the whole class.* Santa Monica, CA: Goodyear, 1977.

18. Adamson, G., & Everett, J. *Upgrading special education in the regular classroom.* Paper presented at the Special Study Institute, Washington, D.C., October 1971. (ERIC Document Reproduction Service No. ED 060 609)

19. _____, & Van Etten, G. Zero reject model revisited: A workable alternative. *Exceptional Children*, 1972, *38*, 735-738.

20. Adcock, D. C. Media services for exceptional children: Some current practices in Illinois. *Illinois Libraries*, 1979, *59*, 477-479.

21. Ade, W., & Hoot, J. L. Parent involvement: Motivation vs. alienation. *Day Care and Early Education*, 1976, *4*(2), 19-20.

22. Adelman, H. S. *A competency based model training program.* Paper presented at the Special Study Institute, Washington, D.C., October 1971. (ERIC Document Reproduction Service No. ED 060 609)

23. _____. *Learning problems and classroom instruction.* Washington, D.C.: Office of Education, Bureau of Education for the Handicapped, Division of Training Programs, 1973. (ERIC Document Reproduction Service No. ED 090 744)

24. _____. The resource concept: Bigger than a room! *Journal of Special Education*, 1972, *6*, 361-367.

25. Adkins, P. G., & Walker, C. A call for early learning centers. *Academic Therapy*, 1972, *7*, 447-451.

26. *Administration of mainstreaming. The best of ERIC on educational management, number 49.* Eugene, OR: University of Oregon, ERIC Clearinghouse on Educational Management, 1980. (ERIC Document Reproduction Service No. ED 182 800)

27. Affleck, J. Q., Lehning, T. W., & Brow, K. D. Expanding the resource concept: The resource school. *Exceptional Children*, 1973, *39*, 446-453.

28. AFT Council urges teachers to demand improvements in new handicapped law. *American Teacher*, January 1977, p. 9.

29. Agard, J. A. *The classroom ecological structure: An approach to the specification of the treatment problem.* Paper presented at the Meeting of the American Educational Research Association, Washington, D.C., March-April 1975. (ERIC Document Reproduction Service No. ED 112 568)

30. Aid for education of the handicapped. *American Education*, 1974, *10*(6), 29-32.

31. Aiello, B. *Mainstreaming: Teacher training workshops on individualized instruction.* Reston, VA: The Council for Exceptional Children, 1975. (ERIC Document Reproduction Service No. ED 107 091)

32. _____ (Ed.). *Making it work: Practical ideas for integrating exceptional children into regular classes.* Reston, VA: The Council for Exceptional Children, 1975. (ERIC Document Reproduction Service No. ED 116 372)

33. _____ (Ed.). *Places and spaces: Facility planning for handicapped children.* Reston, VA: The Council for Exceptional Children, 1976. (ERIC Document Reproduction Service No. ED 123 838)

34. Aksamit, D., Johnson, J., & Vasa, S. *A vehicle for serving handicapped students in Nebraska.* Lincoln, NB: University of Nebraska, Department of Education, 1976.

35. Alberto, P. A., Castricone, N. R., & Cohen, S. B. Mainstreaming—implications for training regular class teachers. *Education & Training of the Mentally Retarded*, 1978, *13*, 90-92.

36. Albright, L. *Assessing vocational skill development. Instructor's guide 6.* Urbana, IL: University of Illinois, Bureau of Educational Research, 1978. (ERIC Document Reproduction Service No. ED 165 403)

37. _____. *Conducting employer follow-up. Instructor's guide 9.* Urbana, IL: University of Illinois, Bureau of Educational Research, 1978. (ERIC Document Reproduction Service No. ED 165 406)

38. _____. *Monitoring the student's individualized vocational plan. Instructor's guide 7.* Urbana, IL: University of Illinois, Bureau of Educational Research, 1978. (ERIC Document Reproduction Service No. ED 165 404)

39. _____. *Preparing an individualized vocational plan. Instructor's guide 4.* Urbana, IL: University of Illinois, Bureau of Educational Research, 1978. (ERIC Document Reproduction Service No. ED 165 401)

40.   _____. *Procedures for identifying students with special needs. Instructor's guide 2.* Urbana, IL: University of Illinois, Bureau of Educational Research, 1978. (ERIC Document Reproduction Service No. ED 165 399)

41.   _____. *Strategies for assessing the student's present level(s) of performance. Instructor's guide 3.* Urbana, IL: University of Illinois, Bureau of Educational Research, 1978. (ERIC Document Reproduction Service No. ED 165 400)

42.   _____, & Fabac, J. *Conducting student follow-up. Instructor's guide 8.* Urbana, IL: University of Illinois, Bureau of Educational Research, 1978. (ERIC Document Reproduction Service No. ED 165 405)

43.   _____, & Fabac, J. *Introduction to the identification and assessment system. Instructor's guide 1.* Urbana, IL: University of Illinois, Bureau of Educational Research, 1978. (ERIC Document Reproduction Service No. ED 165 398)

44.   _____, & Fabac, J. *The use of the training plan in concurrent work-education programs. Instructor's guide 5.* Urbana, IL: University of Illinois, Bureau of Education Research, 1978. (ERIC Document Reproduction Service No. ED 165 402)

45.   Alexander, J., Bond, D., & Soffer, R. M. *The impact of P. L. 94-142 on collective bargaining at the local school district level.* Paper presented at the 57th Annual International Convention of The Council for Exceptional Children, Dallas, TX, April 1979. (ERIC Document Reproduction Service No. ED 171 101)

46.   Alexander, M. Let me learn with the other kids. *Learning,* 1973, *1*(3), 18-21.

47.   Allard, W. G., Dodd, J. M., & Foos, R. B. Helping teachers work with "unteachable" children. *Children Today,* 1975, 4(5), 15-16.

48.   Allen, J. Y. A study to compare the belief systems and attitudes of selected preservice teachers toward the handicapped and mainstreaming. (Doctoral dissertation, The University of Toledo, 1978). *Dissertation Abstracts International,* 1978, *39,* 3510A. (University Microfilms No. 78-24513)

49.   Allen, K. E. *Early intervention and integration: Implications for research.* Paper presented at the First World Congress on Future Special Education, Stirling, Scotland, June-July 1978. (ERIC Document Reproduction Service No. ED 157 306)

50.   _____. *Mainstreaming in early childhood education.* Albany, NY: Delmar, 1980.

51.   _____. Research in review. Mainstreaming: What have we learned. *Young Children,* 1980, *35*(5), 54-63.

52. _____, Benning, P. M., & Drummond, T. W. Integration of normal and handicapped children in a behavioral modification preschool: A case study. In G. Semb (Ed.), *Behavior analysis and education*. Lawrence, KS: University of Kansas Press, 1972.

53. _____, Ruggles, T., & LeBlanc, J. M. *Analysis of teacher-child interaction patterns in the preschool setting*. Paper presented at the Conference on "Serving Young Handicapped Children—Issues and Research in Honor of Alice H. Hayden," Seattle, WA, February 1980.

54. Allen, K. W., & Frazer, G. Providing mediated services for the handicapped—a community college learning resources center perspective. *Illinois Libraries*, 1977, *59*, 500-503.

55. Alschuler, J. N. Education for the handicapped. *Journal of Law and Education*, 1978, *7*, 523-538.

56. Alson, M. L. Into the mainstream. *Instructor*, 1977, *87*(2), 222-224.

57. Alvir, H. P. *Mainstreaming the handicapped. 1. Overview; 2. Special support services; 3. Teacher roles*. Unpublished manuscript, 1978. (ERIC Document Reproduction Service No. ED 163 703)

58. _____. *Professional training activities as a part of mainstreaming the handicapped: An analytical survey of the literature. (Intensive courses for in-service staff development)*. Unpublished manuscript, 1978. (ERIC Document Reproduction Service No. ED 168 254)

59. American Alliance for Health, Physical Education and Recreation. *Integrating persons with handicapping conditions into regular physical education and recreation programs*. Washington, D.C.: Author, 1974.

60. _____. Tips on mainstreaming: Do's and don'ts in activity programs. Washington, D.C.: Author, 1978. (ERIC Document Reproduction Service No. ED 165 437)

61. _____. Information and Research Utilization Center. *Individual education programs: Assessment and evaluation in physical education*. Washington, D.C.: Author, 1978. (ERIC Document Reproduction Service No. 165 436)

62. _____. Information and Research Utilization Center. *Individualized education programs*. Washington, D.C.: Author, 1977. (ERIC Document Reproduction Service No. ED 160 584)

63. _____. Information and Research Utilization Center. *Individualized education programs: Methods for individualizing physical education*. Washington, D.C.: Author, 1977. (ERIC Document Reproduction Service No. ED 160 585)

64. _____. Information and Research Utilization Center. *Involving impaired, disabled, and handicapped persons in regular camp programs.* Washington, D.C.: Author, 1976. (ERIC Document Reproduction Service No. ED 154 549)

65. American Association of Elementary/Kindergarten/Nursery Educators. Children with special needs. *Educating Children: Early and Middle Years,* 1975, *20*(1), 3-31.

66. American Association of School Administrators. Court reinforces mainstream concept. *The School Administrator,* 1976, *33*(6), 12.

67. Ameruoso, F. A. *Concordance for the implementation of P.L. 94-142.* Pittsburgh, PA: Allegheny Intermediate Unit, 1978. (ERIC Document Reproduction Service No. ED 155 847)

68. Amos, N. G., & Moody, L. *Comparisons among principals, regular classroom teachers and special education teachers of their perceptions of the extent of implementation of administrative practices pertaining to mainstreaming mildly handicapped students.* Unpublished manuscript, 1977. (ERIC Document Reproduction Service No. ED 168 241)

69. Anastasiow, N. Strategies and models for early childhood intervention programs in integrated settings. In M. J. Guralnick (Ed.), *Early intervention and the integration of handicapped and nonhandicapped children.* Baltimore, MD: University Park Press, 1978.

70. Andelman, F. Mainstreaming in Massachusetts under Law 766. *Today's Education,* 1976, *65*(2), 20-22.

71. Anderson, B. R. Mainstreaming is the name for a new idea. *School Management,* 1973, *17*(7), 28-30, 52.

72. Anderson, E. M. *The disabled school child: A study of integration in primary schools.* London: Methuen & Co., 1973.

73. _____. Special schools or special schooling for the handicapped child? The debate in perspective. *Journal of Child Psychology and Psychiatry and Allied Disciplines,* 1976, *17*, 151-155.

74. Anderson, F. E. Mainstreaming art as well as children. *Art Education,* 1975, *28*, 26-27.

75. Anderson, R. D. A staff development program for mainstreaming secondary handicapped students (Doctoral dissertation, Arizona State University, 1976). *Dissertation Abstracts International,* 1976, *37*, 759A. (University Microfilms No. 76-18577)

76. Anderson, R. M., & Schifani, J. W. Exemplary generic programs to prepare teachers of the handicapped. In J. W. Schifani (Ed.), *Contemporary issues in mainstreaming.* Dubuque, IA: Kendall/Hunt Pub., 1976.

77. Andrews, R. J., & Schonell, E. Rehabilitation international and special education in Australia. *Slow Learning Child,* 1972, *19*(3), 131-137.

78. Anthony, W. A. The effects of contact on an individual's attitude towards disabled persons. *Rehabilitation Counseling Bulletin,* 1969, *12,* 168-170.

79. Apffel, J. Significant trends in special education. *Educational Perspectives,* 1974, *13*(3), 2-3.

80. Apolloni, T., & Cooke, T. P. Integrated programming at the infant, toddler and preschool levels. In M. J. Guralnick (Ed.), *Early intervention and the integration of handicapped and nonhandicapped children.* Baltimore, MD: University Park Press, 1978.

81. Appell, L. S. Enhancing learning and enriching lives: Arts in the education of handicapped children. *Teaching Exceptional Children,* 1979, *11,* 74-76.

82. Apter, S. J. Applications of ecological theory: Toward a community special education model. *Exceptional Children,* 1977, *43,* 366-373.

83. Ardi, D., & Palmer, G. U. *Access to higher education: Mainstreaming on the campus.* Paper presented at the 57th Annual International Convention of the Council for Exceptional Children, Dallas, TX, April 1979. (ERIC Document Reproduction Service No. ED 171 031)

84. Arena, J. *How to write an I.E.P.* Novato, CA: Academic Therapy Pub., 1978.

85. Arent, R. P. *Stretching strategies: Individualized learning for successful mainstreaming.* Paper presented at the 54th Annual International Meeting of the Council for Exceptional Children, Chicago, IL, April 1976. (ERIC Document Reproduction Service No. ED 122 478)

86. Armstrong, J. R. Individually guided education (IGE): One model for mainstreaming. *Focus on Exceptional Children,* 1976, 8(7), 1-11.

87. ———. Teaching—an ongoing process of assessing, selecting, developing, generalizing, applying, and reassessing. In J. W. Schifani (Ed.), *Contemporary issues in mainstreaming handicapped citizens.* Dubuque, IA: Kendall/Hunt Pub., 1976.

88. Arneklev, B. L. *A program to assist educational personnel to teach students of wide variability in regular classrooms. Director's annual progress report.* Logan, UT: Utah State University, 1972. (ERIC Document Reproduction Service No. ED 068 443)

89.   _____, & Pugmire, D. J. *A program to assist educational personnel to teach students of wide variability in regular classrooms. Director's final report (July 1, 1970 to July 30, 1973).* Logan, UT: Utah State University, College of Education, 1973. (ERIC Document Reproduction Service No. ED 083 198)

90.   Arnold, L. E. Is this label necessary? *Journal of School Health,* 1973, *43,* 510-514.

91.   *Arts and the handicapped—an issue of access.* New York, NY: Educational Facilities Laboratories, 1976. (ERIC Document Reproduction Service No. ED 117 829)

92.   Artuso, A. A., Taylor, F. D., & Hewett, F. M. The Madison plan really swings. *Today's Education,* 1970, *59*(8), 14-17.

93.   Ascione, F. R., & Borg, W. R. Effects of a training program on teacher behavior and handicapped children's self-concept. *Journal of Psychology,* 1980, *104,* 53-65.

94.   Ashcroft, S. C. The handicapped in the regular classroom. *Today's Education,* 1967, *56*(8), 33-48.

95.   Ashley, J. G. Mainstreaming: One step forward, two steps back. *American Educator,* 1977, *6,* 3-7.

96.   Awen, E., Haynes, A. B., & Post, L. *Minimum conflict mainstreaming.* Paper presented at the 54th Annual International Convention of the Council for Exceptional Children, Chicago, IL, April 1976. (ERIC Document Reproduction Service No. ED 122 477)

97.   Babcock, E. V. A special education mainstreaming process (Doctoral dissertation, Saint Louis University, 1977). *Dissertation Abstracts International,* 1977, *38,* 5389A. (University Microfilms No. 78-00470)

98.   Baker, B. A. *Movement education for students with special needs in physical education.* Arlington, VA: Arlington County Public Schools, 1973. (ERIC Document Reproduction Service No. ED 113 898)

99.   Baker, C. D. *The preparation of regular classroom teachers to work with students with special learning problems: A preservice training project.* Greeley, CO: University of Northern Colorado, Department of Special Education and Rehabilitation, 1976.

100.   _____. Special education preservice training of general educators. *Colorado Journal of Educational Research,* 1976, *15*(2), 14-16.

101.   Baker, D. P. Mediacentric: An idea whose time has come. *Wilson Library Bulletin,* 1978, *53,* 174-175.

102. Baldwin, C. P., & Baldwin, A. L. *Personality and social development of handicapped children.* Ithaca, NY: Cornell University, 1972. (ERIC Document Reproduction Service No. ED 079 895)

103. Ballard, J. *Public Law 94-142 and Section 504—understanding what they are and are not.* Reston, VA: The Council for Exceptional Children, 1977. (ERIC Document Reproduction Service No. ED 146 764)

104. _____, Nazarro, J. N., & Weintraub, F. J. *The Education for All Handicapped Children Act of 1975.* Reston, VA: The Council for Exceptional Children, 1976.

105. _____, & Zettel, J. J. Law review: Fiscal arrangements of Public Law 94-142. *Exceptional Children,* 1978, *44,* 333-337.

106. _____, & Zettel, J. J. Law review: The managerial aspects of Public Law 94-142. *Exceptional Children,* 1978, *44,* 457-462.

107. _____, & Zettel, J. J. Public Law 94-142 and Section 504—what they say about rights and protections. *Exceptional Children,* 1977, *44,* 177-184.

108. Balow, B., & Reynolds, M. C. Categories and variables in special education. *Exceptional Children,* 1972, *38,* 357-366.

109. Bancroft, R. Special education: Legal aspects. In P. A. O'Donnell & R. H. Bradfield (Eds.), *Mainstreaming: Controversy and consensus.* San Rafael, CA: Academic Therapy Pub., 1976.

110. Banks, S. L., & Harris, J. L. Blacks and handicapped students in our public schools: A bicentennial challenge. *Negro History Bulletin,* 1976, *39,* 580-581.

111. Barbacovi, D. R., & Clelland, R. W. *Public Law 94-142: Special education in transition.* Arlington, VA: American Association of School Administrators, 1978. (ERIC Document Reproduction Service No. ED 172 412)

112. Bardon, J. I. Overview of the issue—implications for future trends in school psychology. *Journal of School Psychology,* 1972, *10,* 207-211.

113. Barnes, E. B. *Children learn together: The integration of handicapped children into schools.* Syracuse, NY: Human Policy Press, 1974.

114. Barngrover, E. Clearinghouse: A study of educators' preferences in special education programs. *Exceptional Children,* 1971, *37,* 754-755.

115. Bartlett, J. E. Diary of a mainstreaming teacher. *Early Years,* 1978, *8,* 64-65.

116.   Bartlett, R. H. Politics, litigation and mainstreaming: Special education's demise. *Mental Retardation,* 1977, *15,* 24-26.

117.   Barton, S. Promoting, respecting and positively coping with diversity. *Teaching Exceptional Children,* 1976, *8,* 150-152.

118.   Bateman, B., & Frankel, H. Special education and the pediatrician. *Journal of Learning Disabilities,* 1972, *5,* 178-186.

119.   Bates, P., West, T. L., & Schmerl, R. B. (Eds.). *Mainstreaming: Problems, potentials, and perspectives.* Ann Arbor, MI: University of Michigan, School of Education, 1977. (ERIC Document Reproduction Service No. ED 163 671)

120.   Bates, R. D. To meet the unique needs of a handicapped child. *Journal of School Health,* 1980, *50,* 171-172.

121.   Batsche, C. J. *Barriers to vocational education of the handicapped.* Paper presented at the 57th Annual International Convention of the Council for Exceptional Children, Dallas, TX, April 1979. (ERIC Document Reproduction Service No. ED 171 089)

122.   _____. *Mainstreaming the handicapped in vocational education.* Paper presented at the 56th Annual International Convention of the Council for Exceptional Children, Kansas City, MO, May 1978. (ERIC Document Reproduction Service No. ED 153 421)

123.   Battaglia, M. *Mainstreaming from plan to program: From the perspective of the regular classroom teacher.* Paper presented at the 55th Annual International Convention of the Council for Exceptional Children, Atlanta, GA, April 1977. (ERIC Document Reproduction Service No. ED 139 230)

124.   Bauer, H. Resource teacher; a teacher consultant: Helping special students integrated in the mainstream. *Academic Therapy,* 1975, *10,* 299-304.

125.   Beatty, L. F. Impact of Public Law 94-142 on the preparation of school media coordinators. *Educational Technology,* 1978, *18*(11), 44-46.

126.   Beeler, A. Integrating exceptional children in preschool classrooms. *BAYEC Reports,* 1973, *15*(2), 33-41.

127.   Beery, K. E. Mainstreaming: A problem and an opportunity for general education. *Focus on Exceptional Children,* 1974, *6*(6), 1-7).

128.   _____. *Models for mainstreaming.* San Rafael, CA: Dimensions, 1972.

129.   _____. *Project Catalyst: Final program performance report.* San Rafael, CA: Institute for Independent Educational Research, 1975. (ERIC Document Reproduction Service No. ED 129 036)

130. Behrend, M. W., & Shimkus, J. P. Considerations of the implementation of P.L. 94-142 in the state of Georgia. *Journal of International Association of Pupil Personnel Workers,* 1978, *22,* 204-236.

131. Belli, K. Should handicapped students be mainstreamed? *Journal of Business Education,* 1978, *54,* 58-60.

132. Benefield, G., Jr. An exploratory study of the administrative perceptions of the state of affairs of mainstream programs in effect in school districts for two years or more (Doctoral dissertation, The University of Michigan, 1976). *Dissertation Abstracts International,* 1976, *37,* 702A. (University Microfilms No. 76-19082)

133. Bennett, L. M., & Henson, F. O. *Keeping in touch with parents.* Austin, TX: Learning Concepts, 1977.

134. Bensky, J. M., Shaw, S. F., Gouse, A. S., Bates, H., & Dixon, B. *P.L. 94-142 and stress: An analysis and direction for the future.* Paper presented at the 57th Annual International Convention of the Council for Exceptional Children, Dallas, TX, April 1979. (ERIC Document Reproduction Service No. ED 171 028)

135. Bernstein, C. D., Hartman, W. T., Kirst, M. W., & Marshall, R. S. *Financing educational services for the handicapped: An analysis of current research and practices.* Reston, VA: The Council for Exceptional Children, 1976. (ERIC Document Reproduction Service No. ED 116 402)

136. Berry, M. F. The federal role in education for the handicapped. *Exceptional Parent,* 1977, 7(5), 6-7.

137. Berry, S. R. *Legal considerations in the education of the handicapped: An annotated bibliography for the school administrators.* Washington, D.C.: National Association of State Directors of Special Education, 1978.

138. Berryman, J. D. The validation of a scale to measure attitudes toward the classroom integration of disabled students. *Journal of Educational Research,* 1980, *73,* 199-203.

139. Bertness, H. J. Progressive inclusion: The mainstream movement in Tacoma. In M. C. Reynolds (Ed.), *Mainstreaming: Origins and implications.* Reston, VA: The Council for Exceptional Children, 1976.

140. Beseler, Y. M. The principal and parents of the handicapped. *National Elementary Principal,* 1978, *58*(1), 39-42.

141. Bessant, H. P. (Ed.). *Norfolk State College. Education Professions Development Act Project. A final report, 1969-75.* Norfolk, VA: Norfolk State College, 1975. (ERIC Document Reproduction Service No. ED 113 916)

142.   Best, G. A. Mainstreaming in education: Implications in higher education for preservice and inservice training. In P. H. Mann (Ed.), *Shared responsibility for handicapped students. Advocacy and programming.* Coral Gables, FL: University of Miami, Training and Technical Assistance Center, 1976. (ERIC Document Reproduction Service No. ED 132 136)

143.   Beyond the mandate: The professional imperative. Educating professionals for educating the handicapped. *Journal of Teacher Education,* 1978, *29*(6), 44-46.

144.   *Beyond the mandate: The professional imperative. Educating professionals for educating the handicapped.* Washington, D.C.: American Association of Colleges for Teacher Education, 1978. (ERIC Document Reproduction Service No. ED 160 553)

145.   Bhaerman, R. D. *Career and vocational development of handicapped learners: An annotated bibliography. Information Series No. 134.* Columbus, OH: ERIC Clearinghouse on Adult, Career, and Vocational Education, 1978. (ERIC Document Reproduction Services No. ED 166 418)

146.   Bies, J. D. Serving students with special needs. *Journal of Epsilon Pi Tau,* 1977, *3*(2), 39-47.

147.   Big package for education for the handicapped. *American Education,* 1972, *8*(4), 39.

148.   Biklen, D. Exclusion. *Peabody Journal of Education,* 1973, *50,* 226-234.

149.   _____. *Let our children go; an organizing manual for advocates and parents.* Syracuse, NY: Human Policy Press, 1974.

150.   Birch, J. W. Mainstreaming that works in elementary and secondary schools. *Journal of Teacher Education,* 1978, *29*(6), 18-21.

151.   _____. *The myth of individualization, or beyond lip service in colleges of education.* Paper presented at the 4th Annual Invitational Special Education Leadership Conference, Minneapolis, MN, December 1974. Also in R. A. Johnson, R. F. Weatherman, & A. M. Rehman (Eds.), *Special education leadership series. Vol. IV: Handicapped youth and the mainstream educator.* Minneapolis, MN; Audio Visual Extension Service, University of Minnesota, 1975.

152.   _____. Special education for exceptional children through regular school personnel and programs. In J. W. Schifani (Ed.), *Contemporary issues in mainstreaming handicapped citizens.* Dubuque, IA: Kendall/Hunt Pubs., 1976.

153.   _____, & Johnstone, B. K. *Designing schools and schooling for the handicapped.* Springfield, IL: C. C. Thomas, 1975.

154.   _____, & Johnstone, B. K. *Mainstreaming—a new public policy in education.* Paper presented at the 107th Annual Convention of the American Association of School Administrators, Dallas, TX, February 1975. (ERIC Document Reproduction Service No. ED 109 740)

155.   Bird, P. J., & Gansneder, B. M. Preparation of physical education teachers as required under Public Law 94-142. *Exceptional Children*, 1979, *45*, 464-466.

156.   Bishop, L. *Individualizing educational systems: The elementary and secondary school.* New York, NY: Harper & Row, 1971.

157.   Bitter, G. B. From conflict to coalition: Disability groups, parents, professionals. *Volta Review*, 1977, *79*, 317-326.

158.   _____, & Johnston, K. A. Bibliography of references on integration. In W. Northcott (Ed.), *The hearing impaired child in a regular classroom: Preschool, elementary, and secondary years.* Washington, D.C.: Alexander G. Bell Association for the Deaf, 1973.

159.   _____, & Johnston, K. A. *Review of literature: Integration of exceptional children into regular classes.* Rev. ed. Salt Lake City, UT: University of Special Education, University of Utah, 1973.

160.   _____. & Johnston, K. A. *A review of the literature pertaining to the integration of exceptional children into regular public school classes.* Salt Lake City, UT: University of Utah, Department of Special Education, 1972.

161.   Blacher-Dixon, J. *Preschool mainstreaming: Current state of the art.* Paper presented at the 57th Annual International Convention of the Council for Exceptional Children, Dallas, TX, April 1979. (ERIC Document Reproduction Service No. ED 171 087)

162.   Black, J. Integrating the handicapped into the college community. *Journal of College Student Personnel*, 1977, *18*, 68.

163.   Blackhurst, A. E., Cross, D. P., Nelson, C. M., & Tawny, J. W. Approximating noncategorical teacher education. *Exceptional Children*, 1973, *39*, 284-288.

164.   Blackman, L. S. Research and the classroom: Mahomat and the mountain revisited. *Exceptional Children*, 1972, *39*, 181-191.

165.   Blackwell, R. B., & Joynt, R. R. *Mainstreaming, what to expect . . . what to do.* Johnstown, PA: Mafex Assoc., 1979.

166.   Blake, T. E. Friends and hobbies. *Volta Review*, 1967, *69*, 264-266.

167.   Bland, E. L. Learning resource services for the handicapped. *Exceptional Children*, 1976, *43*, 161-163.

168. Blankenship, C. S. *Illinois interim resource manual for preparing individualized education programs.* Springfield, IL: Illinois State Department of Education, Division of Specialized Education Services, 1977. (ERIC Document Reproduction Service No. ED 150 814)

169. Blatt, B. The integration-segregation issue: Some questions, assumptions, and facts. *Family Involvement,* 1975, *8* (2), 10-14.

170. _____. Mainstreaming: Does it matter? *Exceptional Parent,* 1976, *6*(1), 11-12.

171. _____. Public policy and the education of children with special needs. *Exceptional Children,* 1972, *38,* 537-545.

172. Blum, E. R. The now way to know: The Madison plan as an alternative to special class placement: An interview with Frank Hewett. *Education and Training of the Mentally Retarded,* 1971, *6,* 29-42.

173. Board members are well informed on issues involving P. L. 94-142. *American School Board Journal,* 1980, *167*(1), 28-29.

174. Boardman, S. G. (Ed.). *Inservice programs for helping regular classroom teachers implement Public Law 94-142.* Washington, D.C.: ERIC Clearinghouse on Teacher Education, 1980. (ERIC Document Reproduction Service No. ED 181 024)

175. Bobbitt, F. Mainstreaming disadvantaged and handicapped students. *Agricultural Education,* 1975, *47,* 250.

176. Bodley, D., Nordlinger, J., Orr, R., & Trollope, J. *Physical education guide for the exceptional child.* Ann Arbor, MI: Ann Arbor Public Schools, 1970. (ERIC Document Reproduction Service No. ED 061 683)

177. Boland, S. K. Integration: Parent alliance. *In-Service Consultor,* 1974, *1*(1), 7.

178. Bond, R., & Weisgerber, R. *Mainstreaming the handicapped in vocational education. Developing a positive attitude.* Palo Alto, CA: American Institute for Research in the Behavioral Sciences, 1977. (ERIC Document Reproduction Service No. ED 142 768)

179. Bookbinder, S. What every child needs to know. *Exceptional Parent,* 1977, *7*(4), 31-35. Update: *Exceptional Parent,* 1978, *8*(4), 48-49.

180. Boote, K. S. Principal and teacher perceptions of special education inservice programs for regular elementary teachers (Doctoral dissertation, Temple University, 1976). *Dissertation Abstracts International,* 1976, *37,* 217A. (University Microfilms No. 76-15830)

181.   Boothroyd, A., Gatty, J. C., & Poland, N. *Mainstream services and the role of the special school.* Paper presented at the Alexander Graham Bell Association for the Deaf National Convention, St. Louis, MO, June 1978.

182.   Bornstein, L., & Lowry, A. Mainstreaming atypical students within a MUS/E organizational framework. *Research Bulletin,* 1974, *19*(3), 20-22.

183.   Boston, B. O. *Education policy and the Education for all Handicapped Children Act (P.L. 94-142). A report on regional conferences, January-April 1977.* Denver, CO: Education Commission of the States, 1977. (ERIC Document Reproduction Service No. ED 150 800)

184.   _____. *A resource directory on P.L. 94-142: The Education for all Handicapped Children Act.* Washington, D.C.: George Washington University, 1977.

185.   Bowden, M. G., & Otto, H. J. *The education of the exceptional child in Casis School.* Austin, TX: University of Texas Press, 1964.

186.   Bowman, L. Guess who's coming to class. *Early Years,* 1977, 7, 38-40, 62-63.

187.   _____. TLC; teens loving children. *Early Years,* 1978, 9, 45-49.

188.   Boyd, F. M., & Jiggetts, J. The mainstreaming of special and regular education teachers through inservice workshops. *Education,* 1977, *98,* 165-167.

189.   Boyer, E. L. *Keynote address of Ernest L. Boyer, United States Commissioner of Education.* Paper presented at the 56th Annual International Convention of the Council for Exceptional Children, Kansas City, MO, May 1978. (ERIC Document Reproduction Service No. ED 153 383)

190.   _____. Public Law 94-142: A promising start? *Educational Leadership,* 1979, *36,* 298-301.

191.   Boylan, W. S. Mainstreaming: The effects on the academic achievement of special education and regular students (Doctoral dissertation, California School of Professional Psychology, San Francisco, 1976). *Dissertation Abstracts International,* 1976, *37,* 3546A. (University Microfilms No. 76-28124)

192.   Bradfield, R. H. How to fail in mainstreaming without really trying. In P. A. O'Donnell, & R. H. Bradfield (Eds.), *Mainstreaming: Controversy and consensus.* San Rafael, CA: Academic Therapy, 1976.

193.   _____ & Brown, J. *Model instructional program for handicapped children: North Sacramento School District.* Tallahassee, FL: Florida State University, College of Education, 1972. (ERIC Document Reproduction Service No. ED 060 609)

194.   Bransford, L. A. Social issues in special education. *Phi Delta Kappan,* 1974, *55,* 530-532.

195.   Brault, D. *Expanding physical education services to pupils with handicapping conditions: Summary report.* Madison, WI: Madison Public Schools, Wisconsin Department of Specialized Educational Services, 1974. (ERIC Document Reproduction Service No. ED 113 903)

196.   Braun, S. J. *Are you ready to mainstream: Helping preschoolers with learning and behavior problems.* Columbus, OH: C. E. Merrill, 1978.

197.   _____, & Lasher, M. G. Can programs for special needs preschoolers thrive in public schools? *Behavioral Disorders,* 1978, *3,* 160-167.

198.   Brekke, B. How can teachers begin to meet the special needs of mainstreamed children in the regular classroom? *Delta Kappa Gamma Bulletin,* 1975, *42,* 49-51.

199.   Brenton, M. Mainstreaming the handicapped. *Today's Education,* 1974, *63*(2), 20-25.

200.   Breuning, S. E., & Regan, J. T. Teaching regular class material to special education students. *Exceptional Children,* 1978, *45,* 180-187.

201.   Bricker, D. A rationale for the integration of handicapped and nonhandicapped preschool children. In M. J. Guralnick (Ed.), *Early intervention and the integration of handicapped and nonhandicapped children.* Baltimore, MD: University Park Press, 1978.

202.   Bricker, D. D., & Bricker, W. A. *Non-categorical education for the preschool child.* Miami, FL: Mailman Center for Child Development, University of Miami, 1975. (ERIC Document Reproduction Service No. ED 112 558)

203.   Brinegar, L. *The principle of the least restrictive environment and the schools.* Sacramento, CA: Office of Special Education, Sacramento City Unified District, 1978. (ERIC Document Reproduction Service No. ED 162 445)

204.   Brody, C., Plutchik, R., Reilly, E., & Peterson, M. Personality and problem behavior of third-grade children in regular classes. *Psychology in the Schools,* 1973, *10,* 196-199.

205.   Brolin, D. E. Vocational evaluation—special education's responsi-
       bility. In J. W. Schifani (Ed.), *Contemporary issues in mainstream-
       ing handicapped citizens.* Dubuque, IA: Kendall/Hunt Pub.,
       1976.

206.   _____. Inservice training of educators for special needs students:
       The price model. *Career Education Quarterly,* 1977, *2*(1), 6-17.

207.   _____, Magnuson, C., Schneider, C., & West, L. *Mainstreaming
       (handicapped) students in vocational education: A resource guide
       for vocational educators.* Jefferson City, MO: Missouri State
       Department of Elementary and Secondary Education, and Colum-
       bia, MO: University of Missouri, Department of Counseling and
       Personnel Services, 1978. (ERIC Document Reproduction Service
       No. ED 170 452)

208.   _____, Magnuson, C., Schneider, C., & West, L. *Mainstreaming
       (handicapped) students in vocational education: An administrator's
       guide.* Jefferson City, MO: Missouri State Department of Elemen-
       tary and Secondary Education, and Columbia, MO: University of
       Missouri, Department of Counseling and Personnel Services, 1978.
       (ERIC Document Reproduction Service No. ED 170 451)

209.   Brooke, E. P.L. 94-142—getting the money to make it work.
       Today's Education, 1977, *66*(4), 50-52.

210.   Brooks, B. L., & Bransford, L. A. Clearinghouse: Modification of
       teachers' attitudes toward exceptional children. *Exceptional Chil-
       dren,* 1971, *38,* 259-260.

211.   Brown, J. A. Keeping a professional perspective. *Elementary
       School Guidance and Counseling,* 1979, *13,* 222-228.

212.   Brown, J. H., & Brown, C. S. Concomitants of social acceptance:
       Exploratory research and implications for treatment. *American
       Journal of Orthopsychiatry,* 1976, *46,* 470-476.

213.   Brown, J. M., & Peak, L. M. *Determining the need for vocational
       special needs inservice training for vocational educators.* Paper pre-
       sented at the Annual Meeting of the American Educational
       Research Association, Boston, MA, April 1980. (ERIC Document
       Reproduction Service No. ED 183 881)

214.   Brown, L., Scheuerman, N., Cartwright, S., & York, R. *The design
       and implementation of an empirically based instructional program
       for severely handicapped students: Toward the rejection of the
       exclusion principle. Vol. III.* Madison, WI: Madison Public
       Schools, 1973. (ERIC Document Reproduction Service No. ED 100
       100)

215.   _____, Williams, W., & Crowner, T. *A collection of papers and programs related to public school services for severely handicapped students. Vol. IV.* Madison, WI: Madison Public Schools, 1974. (ERIC Document Reproduction Service No. ED 100 101)

216.   Brown, M.D. An investigation of academic achievement of handicapped children in mainstream education (Doctoral dissertation, East Texas State University, 1976). *Dissertation Abstracts International,* 1976, *37,* 2781A. (University Microfilms No. 76-24527)

217.   Brown, M. S. Is mainstreaming fair to kids? *Instructor,* 1976, *87*(7), 38, 40.

218.   Brownsmith, K, Field, D., & Guskin, S. *Description and evaluation of the mainstreaming modules. Final report 48.3.* Bloomington, IN: Indiana University, Bloomington, Center for Innovation in Teaching the Handicapped, 1976. (ERIC Document Reproduction Service No. ED 162 463)

219.   Bruce, W. T. Academic mainsteaming: How to determine when. Paper presented at the National Convention of the Alexander Graham Bell Association for the Deaf, Boston, MA, June 1976.

220.   _____. Trends in education. *Volta Review,* 1976, *78,* 318-323.

221.   Bryan, W. A., & Becker, K. M. Student services for the handicapped student. *New Directions for Student Services,* 1980, *1*(10), 9-21.

222.   Budoff, M. *Comments on providing special education without special classes. Studies in Learning Potential, Vol. 2, No. 25, 1971.* Cambridge, MA: Research Institute for Educational Problems, 1971. (ERIC Document Reproduction Service No. ED 058 707)

223.   _____. Engendering change in special education practices. *Harvard Educational Review,* 1975, *45,* 507-526.

224.   _____. Providing special education without special classes. *Journal of School Psychology,* 1972, *10,* 199-205.

225.   _____, Mitchell, S., & Kotin, L. *Procedural due process: Its application to special education and its implications for teacher training.* Cambridge, MA: Research Institute for Educational Problems, 1976. (ERIC Document Reproduction Service No. ED 131 626)

226.   Buell, C. *Bibliography on physical education, 1974.* Philadelphia, PA: Association for Education of the Visually Handicapped, 1974. (ERIC Document Reproduction Service No. ED 100 092)

227. Buffmire, J. A. *Special education delivery alternatives: Changes over time in teacher ratings, self-image, perceived classroom climate and academic achievement among handicapped and non-handicapped children.* Revised. Salt Lake City, UT: Southwest Regional Resource Center, 1977. (ERIC Document Reproduction Service No. ED 140 565)

228. *Building foundations for educational change: Wisconsin Title III, ESEA, 1975.* Madison, WI: State Department of Public Instruction, 1974. (ERIC Document Reproduction Service No. ED 110 573)

229. Bullock, L. M. An inquiry into the special education training of elementary school administrators. *Exceptional Children,* 1970, *36,* 770-771.

230. Bundschuh, E. L. *Approaches to mainstreaming.* Paper presented at the National Convention of the American Alliance for Health, Physical Education and Recreation, Atlantic City, NJ, March 1975. (ERIC Document Reproduction Service No. ED 109 052)

231. Burgdorf, R. The doctrine of the least restrictive alternative. In R. A. Johnson, R. F. Weatherman, & A. M. Rehman (Eds.), *Special education leadership series. Vol. IV: Handicapped youth and the mainstream educator.* Minneapolis, MN: Audio Visual Extension Service, University of Minnesota, 1975.

232. Burgess, J. M., Schilmoeller, G. L., & Peters, D. L. *Social interaction in developmentally integrated preschool classrooms.* Unpublished manuscript, 1980.

233. Burggraf, M. Z. Consulting with parents of handicapped children. *Elementary School Guidance and Counseling,* 1979, *13,* 214-221.

234. Burke, P. J. Personnel preparation: Historical perspective. *Exceptional Children,* 1976, *43,* 144-147.

235. _____, & Sage, D. D. The unorthodox use of a simulation instrument. *Simulation and Games,* 1970, *1,* 155-171.

236. Burns, H. P. Educating handicapped children: Whose responsibility? *Momentum,* 1977, *59*(3), 21-25.

237. Burns, M. A. *Mainstreaming: A one-room country schoolhouse in a modern public school.* Paper presented at the Alexander Graham Bell Association for the Deaf National Convention, St. Louis, MO, June 1978.

238. Burnstein, M. A curricular program using group processes to facilitate mainstreaming (Doctoral dissertation, Case Western Reserve University, 1978). *Dissertation Abstracts International,* 1978, *39,* 1469A. (University Microfilms No. 78-16451)

239. Burrello, L. C., & Baker, K. T. Developing a CSPD through a peer planning and dissemination network. *Teacher Education and Special Education,* 1980, *3*(1), 5-10.

240. ———, Tracy, M. L., & Schultz, E. W. Special education as experimental education: A new conceptualization. *Exceptional Children,* 1973, *40,* 29-34.

241. Bursor, D. E., & Hosie, T. W. Sex education: A reality in mainstreaming. *Humanist Educator,* 1980, *18,* 135-143.

242. Butler, D. J. A study of teacher training programs for the regular and handicapped child-assessment (Doctoral dissertation, Saint Louis University, 1973). *Dissertation Abstracts International,* 1973, *35,* 2820A. (University Microfilms No. 74-24055)

243. Butler, M. J. Responses to P.L. 94-142: Institutional changes for pre-service teacher preparation. *Journal of Teacher Education,* 1978, *29*(6), 77-79.

244. Buttery, T. J. Affective response to exceptional children by students preparing to be teachers. *Perceptual and Motor Skills,* 1978, *46,* 288-90.

245. Byford, E. M. A descriptive study of teacher-training programs at institutions of higher education for regular classroom personnel involved in mainstreaming mildly educationally handicapped pupils (Doctoral dissertation, The American University, 1977). *Dissertation Abstracts International,* 1977, *38,* 197A. (University Microfilms No. 77-14612)

246. Cain, L. F. Emerging placement alternatives: Implications for teacher-training programs. In P. A. O'Donnell, & R. H. Bradfield (Eds.), *Mainstreaming: Controversy and consensus.* San Rafael, CA: Academic Therapy, 1976.

247. ———. Special education moves ahead: A comment on the education of teachers. *Exceptional Children,* 1964, *30,* 211-217.

248. Caldwell, B. M. The rationale for early intervention. *Exceptional Children,* 1970, *36,* 717-725.

249. Calhoun, G., Jr. A comparison of regular and integrated special education pupils in achievement, behavior and self-esteem (Doctoral dissertation, University of Michigan, 1973). *Dissertation Abstracts International,* 1973, *35,* 93A. (University Microfilms No. 74-15680)

250. Calovini, G. Implications of Public Law 94-142. *Illinois Libraries,* 1977, *59,* 468-469.

251. Cameron, S. Define a perfect pupil. *Times Educational Supplement (London),* March 29, 1974, no. 3070, p. 17.

252. Candor-Chandler, C. Charleston, W. Va.: Competency require-
     ments for special education students. *Phi Delta Kappan*, 1978, *59*,
     611-612.

253. Cantrell, R. P., & Cantrell, M. L. Preventive mainstreaming:
     Impact of a supportive services program on pupils. *Exceptional
     Children*, 1976, *42*, 381-386.

254. Carlson, L. B., & Potter, R. E. Training classroom teachers to pro-
     vide in-class educational services for exceptional children in rural
     areas. *Journal of School Psychology*, 1972, *10*, 147-151.

255. Carlson, R. E. Legislation and special needs teacher education: the
     vocational amendments of 1976 (P.L. 94-482). *Journal of Industrial
     Teacher Education*, 1977, *14*(4), 19-22.

256. Carpenter, B. W. Selected educators' perceptions toward the study
     of mainstreaming in home economics programs (Doctoral disserta-
     tions, Kansas State University, 1978). *Dissertation Abstracts Inter-
     national*, 1978, *39*, 2789A. (University Microfilms No. 78-21859)

257. Carpenter, R. Get everyone involved when you mainstream your
     children. *Instructor*, 1975, *85*(1), 181-182, 188.

258. Carpenter, R. D. A followup study of selected Illinois Public School
     principals' attitudes and knowledges of mainstreaming handi-
     capped children (Doctoral dissertation, Southern Illinois Univer-
     sity, 1976). *Dissertation Abstracts International*, 1976, *37*, 3547A.
     (University Microfilms No. 76-28731)

259. Carroll, A., & Purdy, J. *Inservice program development to assist
     teachers to effectively service students with exceptional needs in the
     mainstream. Final report.* Goleta, CA: Santa Barbara County
     Schools, 1978. (ERIC Document Reproduction Service No. ED 162
     453)

260. Carroll, A. W. *Personalizing education in the classroom.* Denver,
     CO: Love Pub., 1975.

261. Carter, B. Y. *Mainstreaming: The effects on social interaction
     among preschoolers.* Unpublished manuscript, 1977. (ERIC Docu-
     ment Reproduction Service No. ED 157 634)

262. Cartwright, G. P., & Cartwright, C. A. Gilding the Lilly: Com-
     ments on the training based model. *Exceptional Children*, 1972,
     39, 231-234.

263. _____, Cartwright, C. A., & Ysseldyke, J. E. Two decision
     models: Identification and diagnostic teaching of handicapped
     children in the regular classroom. *Psychology in the Schools*, 1973,
     10, 4-11.

264.   *Case study of the implementation of P.L. 94-142: Preliminary find-ings summary.* Washington, D.C.: Education Turnkey Systems, 1978. (ERIC Document Reproduction Service No. ED 173 470)

265.   Caster, J. What is mainstreaming? *Exceptional Children,* 1975, *42,* 174.

266.   _____. *Writing a personnel development plan: Guidelines and resources.* Des Moines, IA: Drake University, Midwest Regional Resource Center, 1977. (ERIC Document Reproduction Service No. ED 163 705)

267.   Castleberry, M., & Gazvoda, M. *Complementary teacher training program: Academic year 1973-1974; three year report 1971-1974.* Washington, D.C.: George Washington University, School of Education, 1974. (ERIC Document Reproduction Service No. ED 112 537)

268.   _____, & Sobel, N. (Ed.). *Handbook for complementary teachers.* Washington, D.C.: George Washington University, 1974.

269.   Castricone, N., Alberto, P., & Cohen, S. *Opinions of regular class teachers on mainstreaming.* Atlanta, GA: Georgia State University, 1974.

270.   Cawley, J., Korba, W. L., & Pappanikou, A. J. *Special education placement: Issues and alternatives—a decision-making module.* Reston, VA: The Council for Exceptional Children, 1976. (ERIC Document Reproduction Service No. ED 121 020)

271.   Cejka, J. M., & Needham, F. (Eds.). *Approaches to mainstreaming: Teaching the special child in the regular classroom.* Boston, MA: Teaching Resources Corp., 1976.

272.   Chaffin, J. D., & Geer, F. *The Pinckney Project: An innovative approach to mainstreaming exceptional children.* Lawrence, KS: Kansas State University, Department of Education, n.d.

273.   Chalfant, J. C., & Van Dusen, M. *The compliance manual.* New Rochelle, NY: Pem Press, 1980.

274.   Challenge of mainstreaming; excerpt from Mainstreaming: Helping teachers meet the challenge. *Education Digest,* 1976, *42*(3), 6-9.

275.   A challenge to teachers from handicapped scientists. Statements from four members of AAAS. *Science and Children,* 1976, *13*(6), 15-16.

276.   *Change in education: Three policy papers on the implementation of the Education for All Handicapped Children Act, P.L. 94-142.* Washington, D.C.: Educational Testing Service, Educational Policy Research Institute, 1976. (ERIC Document Reproduction Service No. ED 121 012)

277. Chapin, R. C. The legal rights of children with handicapping conditions and the process of mainstreaming. *Peabody Journal of Education*, 1978, *56*, 18-23.

278. Charles, C. M. *Individualizing instruction*. St. Louis, MO: C. V. Mosby, 1976.

279. Chiba, C., & Semmel, M. Due process and least restrictive alternative: New emphasis on parental participation. *Viewpoint*, 1977, *53*, 17-29.

280. *Children with special needs in day care: A guide to integration (A guide for integrating developmentally delayed children into regular day care services)*. Toronto, Ontario, Canada: National Institute on Mental Retardation, 1978. (ERIC Document Reproduction Service No. ED 167 243)

281. Childs, R. E. A second look at resource room instruction by a resource teacher. *Education and Training of the Mentally Retarded*, 1975, *10*, 288-289.

282. Chow, S. H. L., Rice, C. F., & Whitmore, L. A. *Effects of a mediated training course on teachers and students in mainstreaming programs*. Paper presented at the Annual Meeting of the Far West Lab for Educational Research and Development, San Francisco, CA, April 1976. (ERIC Document Reproduction Service No. ED 123 822)

283. Christensen, G. The circle of human needs. *Instructor*, 1976, *85*(7), 103-106.

284. Christenson, G. Walden-in-the-woods. *Communicator*, 1977, *9*(1), 15-21.

285. Christie, L. S., & McKenzie, H. S. *Minimum objectives: A measurement system to provide evaluation of special education in regular classrooms*. Burlington, VT: University of Vermont, College of Education and Social Services, 1974. (ERIC Document Reproduction Service No. ED 102 786)

286. _____, McKenzie, H. S., & Burdett, C. The consulting teacher approach to special education: Inservice training for regular teachers. In E. L. Meyen, G. A. Vergason, & R. J. Whelan (Eds.), *Alternatives for teaching exceptional children*. Denver, CO: Love Pub., 1975.

287. Christopherson, J. The special child in the "regular" preschool: Some administrative notes. *Childhood Education*, 1972, *49*, 138-140.

288. Christoplos, F. Keeping exceptional children in regular classes. *Exceptional Children*, 1973, *39*, 569-572.

289.   _____, & Renz, P. A critical examination of special education programs. *The Journal of Special Education*, 1969, *3*, 371-379.

290.   Clark, E. A. Teacher attitudes toward integration of children with handicaps. *Education and Training of the Mentally Retarded*, 1976, *11*, 333-335.

291.   Clark, M. M. Why remedial? Implications of using the concept of remedial education. *Remedial Education*, 1976, *11*(1), 5-8.

292.   Clark, O. C. *Mainstreaming. Special education is a part of, not a part from, regular education, Background and guidelines.* Waupun, WI: CESA, 1978. (ERIC Document Reproduction Service No. ED 169 717)

293.   Clay, J. E. *Similarities in the Education for All Handicapped Children Act of 1975 and the Vocational Rehabilitation Act of 1973.* Normal, AL: Alabama A&M University, 1977. (ERIC Document Reproduction Service No. ED 165 369)

294.   Cleary, M. F. Helping children understand the child with special needs. *Children Today*, 1976, *5*(4), 6-10.

295.   Clelland, R. *Comprehensive system of personnel development and the implementation of P.L. 94-142: Issues and problems.* Paper presented at the 32nd Annual Meeting of the Association for Supervision and Curriculum Development, Houston, TX, March 1977. (ERIC Document Reproduction Service No. ED 140 556)

296.   Cochrane, P. V., & Marini, B. Mainstreaming exceptional children: The counselor's role. *School Counselor*, 1977, *25*(1), 17-22.

297.   _____, & Westling, D. L. Principal and mainstreaming: Ten suggestions for success. *Educational Leadership*, 1977, *34*, 506-510.

298.   Cohen, J. S., & DeYoung, H. The role of litigation in the improvement of programming for the handicapped. In L. Mann, & D. A. Sabatino (Eds.), *The first review of special education.* Philadelphia, PA: JSE Press, 1973.

299.   Cohen, M. Fiasco. *Mathematics Teaching*, 1978, *83*, 21-25.

300.   Cohen, S. Fostering positive attitudes toward the handicapped: A new curriculum. *Children Today*, 1977, *6*(6), 7-12.

301.   _____. Improving attitudes toward the handicapped: preparation for mainstreaming. *Educational Forum*, 1977, *42*, 9-20. Also in *Education Digest*, 1978, *43*(7), 16-19.

302.   _____. Integrating children with handicaps into early childhood education programs. *Children Today*, 1975, *4*(1), 15-17.

303.   _____, Semmes, M., & Guralnick, M. J. Public Law 94-142 and the education of preschool handicapped children. *Exceptional Children*, 1979, *45*, 279-285.

304. Coinstruction of normal and handicapped children. *School & Society,* 1970, *98,* 463.

305. Cole, H. P. *Growth of attitudes, knowledge, and skill required by P.L. 94-142 among preservice teachers.* Paper presented at the First Behavioral Studies Conference, St. Louis, MO, October, 1978. (ERIC Document Reproduction Service No. ED 161 845)

306. Cole, P. G. Parents and teachers' estimates of the social competence of handicapped and normal children. *Australian Journal of Mental Retardation,* 1976, *4*(4), 1-8.

307. Cole, R. W., & Dunn, R. A new lease on life for education of the handicapped: Ohio copes with 94-142. *Phi Delta Kappan,* 1977, *59,* 3-6, 10, 22.

308. Colella, H. V., & Foster, H. BOCES: A delivery system for special education, *Phi Delta Kappan,* 1974, *55,* 544-545.

309. Collins, E. C. Validation of selected instructional objectives for regular educators teaching children with special needs (Doctoral dissertation, Bowling Green State University, 1975). *Dissertation Abstracts International,* 1975, *36,* 5205A. (University Microfilms No. 76-02746)

310. Collins, J. F., & Calevro, M. J. *Mainstreaming special education using a peer tutoring system and a minimum objective curriculum for nine eighth grade students.* Barre Town, VT: Orange Washington Supervisory Union, Barre Town Elementary School, 1974. (ERIC Document Reproduction Service No. ED 102 788)

311. _____, & Mercurio, J. A. (Eds.). *Meeting the special needs of students in regular classrooms.* Syracuse, NY: National Dissemination Center, Syracuse University, n.d.

312. Combs, R. H., & Harper, J. L. Effects of labels on attitudes of educators towards handicapped children. *Exceptional Children,* 1967, *33,* 399-403.

313. *Comprehensive services for children: Third year evaluation report. Dothan City (Ala) Schools Title III Project.* Dothan, AL: Human Resources Research Organization, Division 6, 1974. (ERIC Document Reproduction Service No. ED 104 068)

314. *A comprehensive study into the effects and changes upon professional staff of Montgomery County Intermediate Unit 23 as a result of IEP implementation.* Blue Bell, PA: Montgomery County Intermediate Unit 23, 1978. (ERIC Document Reproduction Service No. ED 166 910)

315. *Comprehensive system of personnel development.* Baltimore, MD: Maryland State Department of Education, Office of Special Education, 1978. (ERIC Document Reproduction Service No. ED 169 741)

316.   Conine, T. A. Acceptance or rejection of disabled persons by teachers. *Journal of School Health,* 1969, *39,* 278-281.

317.   Cook, P. F. *Research and development recommendations related to vocational training and placement of the severely handicapped and mainstreaming handicapped students into vocational training programs.* Paper presented at the 55th Annual International Convention of the Council for Exceptional Children, Atlanta, GA, April 1977. (ERIC Document Reproduction Service No. ED 139 178)

318.   Coons, D. E. *Staff development in the mainstream: A mutual support model.* Paper presented at the 57th Annual International Convention of the Council for Exceptional Children, Dallas, TX, April 1979. (ERIC Document Reproduction Service No. ED 171 091)

319.   Cooper, N. E. Vocational reintegration of handicapped workers with assistive devices. *International Labour Review,* 1977, *115,* 343-352.

320.   Corrigan, D. C. Political and moral contexts that produced P.L. 94-142. *Journal of Teacher Education,* 1978, *29*(6), 10-14.

321.   *Costs in serving handicapped children in Head Start: An analysis of methods and cost estimates. Final report.* Syracuse, NY: Syracuse University, Division of Special Education and Rehabilitation, 1974. (ERIC Document Reproduction Service No. ED 108 443)

322.   Council for Exceptional Children. *Mainstreaming: Program descriptions in areas of exceptionality; a selective bibliography. Exceptional Child Bibliography Series No. 623.* Reston, VA: Author, 1975. (ERIC Document Reproduction Service No. ED 102 808)

323.   _____. *Regular class placement/special classes: A selective bibliography.* Reston, VA: Author, 1972. (ERIC Document Reproduction Service No. ED 065 967)

324.   _____. *Selected readings in early education of handicapped children.* Reston, VA: Author, 1974. (ERIC Document Reproduction Service No. ED 091 884)

325.   Coursen, D. *Administrative implications of mainstreaming. NAESP School Leadership Digest Second Series, Number 7. ERIC/CEM Research Analysis Series, Number 22.* Washington, D.C.: National Association for Elementary School Principals, 1976. (ERIC Document Reproduction Service No. ED 120 899).

326.   Coy, M. N. *The effects of integrating young severely handicapped children into regular preschool headstart and child development programs.* Merced, CA: Merced County Schools, 1977. (ERIC Document Reproduction Service No. ED 149 498)

327. Craig, O. L., & Risner, E. *The teen-age years: A time to declare independence.* Paper presented at the 55th Annual International Convention of the Council for Exceptional Children, Atlanta, GA, April 1977. (ERIC Document Reproduction Service No. ED 140 576)

328. Crisler, J. R. Utilizaton of a team approach in implementing Public Law 94-142. *Journal of Research and Development in Education,* 1979, *12*(4), 101-108.

329. Cristiani, T., & Sommers, P. The school counselor's role in mainstreaming the handicapped. *Viewpoints in Teaching and Learning,* 1978, *54*(1), 20-28.

330. Crockett, R. E. The relationship of "mainstreaming" to self-concept and academic achievement of the upper elementary special education pupils in a large mid-West middle school (Doctoral dissertation, Indiana University, 1977). *Dissertation Abstracts International,* 1977, *39,* 5233A. (University Microfilms No. 78-01011)

331. Cromwell, R. Ethics, umbrage, and the ABCDs. In M. C. Reynolds (Ed.), *Mainstreaming: Origins and implications.* Reston, VA: The Council for Exceptional Children, 1976.

332. Cruickshank, W. M. The false hope of integration. *The Slow Learning Child,* 1974, *21*(2), 67-83.

333. _____. Least-restrictive placement: Administrative wishful thinking. *Journal of Learning Disabilities,* 1977, *10,* 193-194.

334. Csapo, M. Being "sorted out" for what? The myth of "special education." *British Columbia Journal of Special Education,* 1978, *2,* 321-330.

335. _____, & Webster, J. Guidelines to evaluating special education programs. *British Columbia Journal of Special Education,* 1978, *2,* 131-138.

336. Culbertson, J. *Administrator training and mainstreaming of the handicapped.* Paper presented at the 4th Annual Invitational Special Education Leadership Conference, Minneapolis, MN, December 1974. Also in R. A. Johnson, R. F. Weatherman, & A. M. Rehman (Eds.), *Special education leadership series. Vol. IV: Handicapped youth and the mainstream educator.* Minneapolis, MN: Audio Visual Extension Service, University of Minnesota, 1975.

337. Dabney, M. G. Curriculum building and implementation in mainstream settings: Some concepts and propositions. In R. L. Jones, & Wilderson, F. B. (Eds.), *Mainstreaming and the minority child.* Reston, VA: The Council for Exceptional Children, 1976. (ERIC Document Reproduction Service No. ED 133 941)

338. Dahl, P. R. *The nature of barriers and strategies for overcoming them.* Paper presented at the 55th Annual International Convention of the Council for Exceptional Children, Atlanta, GA, April 1977. (ERIC Document Reproduction Service No. ED 139 179)

339. _____, Appleby, J. A., & Lipe, D. *Mainstreaming guidebook for vocational educators: Teaching the handicapped.* Salt Lake City, UT: Olympus Pub., 1978.

340. _____, & Lipe, D. *Overcoming barriers to mainstreaming: A problem-solving approach. Final report.* Palo Alto, CA: American Institutes for Research in the Behavioral Sciences, 1978. (ERIC Document Reproduction Service No. ED 164 914)

341. Dailey, R. F. Dimensions and issues in '74: Tapping into the special education grapevine. *Exceptional Children,* 1974, *40,* 503-506.

342. D'Alonzo, B. J., D'Alonzo, R. L., & Mauser, A. J. Developing resource rooms for the handicapped. *Teaching Exceptional Children,* 1979, *11,* 91-96.

343. Dapper, G. *Educating children with special needs: Current trends in school policies and programs.* Arlington, VA: National School Public Relations Assoc., 1974. (ERIC Document Reproduction Service No. ED 093 134)

344. D'Audney, W. (Ed.). *Giving a head start to parents of the handicapped.* Omaha, NB: University of Nebraska Medical Center, Meyer Children's Rehabilitation Institute, 1976. (ERIC Document Reproduction Service No. ED 119 434)

345. Daugherty, D., & Mertens, D. M. *A summative evaluation of teaching the young handicapped child.* Lexington, KY: Appalachian Education Satellite Project, 1978. (ERIC Document Reproduction Service No. ED 165 810)

346. Davis, E. D. *Promising practices in mainstreaming for the secondary school principal.* Dallas, TX: Southern Methodist University, 1977. (ERIC Document Reproduction Service No. ED 161 189)

347. D-day for the disabled; Education for All Handicapped Children Act. *Time,* May 30, 1977, p. 44.

348. Decker, K. N. A comparison of the abilities of teachers prepared to teach special classes and regular elementary classes to identify children's problems and to choose appropriate remediation techniques (Doctoral dissertation, Indiana State University, 1975). *Dissertation Abstracts International,* 1975, *36,* 4398A. (University Microfilms No. 75-29875)

349. Deever, R. M. *Staff development program for mainstreaming secondary handicapped.* Tempe, AZ: Arizona State University, Bureau of Educational Research and Services, 1977.

350. Deleo, A. V. The attitudes of public school administrators and teachers toward the integration of children with special needs into regular education programs (Doctoral dissertation, Boston College, 1976). *Dissertation Abstracts International,* 1976, *37*, 915A. (University Microfilms No. 76-06078)

351. Delgado, G. L., & Shellem, G. W. *Mainstreaming professional personnel—where are we going?* Paper presented at the First World Congress on Future Special Education, Stirling, Scotland, June-July 1978. (ERIC Document Reproduction Service No. ED 158 466)

352. Delon, F. G. *Litigation on rights of the handicapped in education.* Paper presented at the Inter-University Conference, Columbia, MO, February 1979. (ERIC Document Reproduction Service No. ED 168 138)

353. Delp, H. A., & Boote, K. Mainstreaming of the exceptional: In the future or now? *The School Administrator,* February 1975, pp. 18-19.

354. Dembinski, R. J. Mainstreaming: We may be lost but we're making excellent time. *Journal of the Association for the Study of Perception,* 1977, *12*, 6-13.

355. Deno, E. N. Special education as developmental capital. *Exceptional Children,* 1970, *37*, 229-237.

356. _____. (Ed.). *Instructional alternatives for exceptional children.* Washington, D.C.: The Council for Exceptional Children, Information Center on Exceptional Children, 1973. (ERIC Document Reproduction Service No. ED 074 678)

357. Dente, R. A. A survey of selected teacher preparation programs concerning the concept of mainstreaming (Doctoral dissertation, University of Cincinnati, 1976). *Dissertation Abstracts International,* 1976, *37*, 3548A. (University Microfilms No. 76-27998)

358. Depatie, R., Lefebvre, Y., & Parent, C. *Identification of the schools in which a considerable proportion of the students come from disadvantaged areas. Report on disadvantaged schools on the Island of Montreal.* Quebec: Island of Montreal School Council, 1975. (ERIC Document Reproduction Service No. ED 129 953)

359. DeRenzis, J. S. *Individually prescribed instruction: Background information and research.* Paper presented at the Meeting of the International Reading Association, Atlantic City, NJ, April 1971. (ERIC Document Reproduction Service No. ED 051 974)

360. Devoney, C., Guralnick, M. J., & Rubin, H. Integrating handicapped and non-handicapped preschool children: Effects on social play. *Childhood Education*, 1974, *50*, 360-364.

361. Dexter, B. L. *Special education and the classroom teacher: Concepts, perspectives and strategies.* Springfield, IL: C. C. Thomas, 1977.

362. _____. *Teach unto teachers as you would have them teach unto children.* Paper presented at the 1st World Congress on Future Special Education, Stirling, Scotland, June-July 1978. (ERIC Document Reproduction Service No. ED 157 340)

363. Dickerson, J. R. A comparison of observable items of interpersonal relations between special education and regular classrooms in the state of Idaho (Doctoral dissertation, University of Idaho, 1972). *Dissertation Abstracts International*, 1972, *33*, 2198A. (University Microfilms No. 72-30491)

364. Dickerson, M. G., & Davis, M. D. Implications of P.L. 94-142 for developmental early childhood teachers. *Young Children*, 1979, *34*(2), 28-36.

365. Dietrich, W. L., & Anderson, R. M. Exceptional children in our schools—a new direction. In J. W. Schifani (Ed.), *Contemporary issues in mainstreaming handicapped citizens.* Dubuque, IA: Kendall/Hunt Pub., 1976.

366. *Directory and abstracts for "deans' grants projects" training programs for educators to accommodate handicapped children in regular class settings.* Minneapolis, MN: Leadership Training Institute/Special Education, University of Minnesota, 1976.

367. Dirksen, J. *Teachers prepare for regular class placement of handicapped students. Briefly on . . . regular class placement No. 2.* Washington, D.C.: ERIC Clearinghouse on Teacher Education, 1978. (ERIC Document Reproduction Service No. ED 170 292)

368. Dirr, P. J., & Laughlin, C. A. *Individualizing instruction for handicapped children.* Unpublished manuscript, 1974. (ERIC Document Reproduction Service No. ED 105 675)

369. Divorky, D. Mainstreaming: Moving special ed out of the basement. *Compact*, 1976, *10*(1), 2-5.

370. Dixon, B., Shaw, S., & Bensky, J. *The administrator's role in fostering the mental health of special services personnel.* Paper presented at the 57th Annual International Convention of the Council for Exceptional Children, Dallas, TX, April 1979. (ERIC Document Reproduction Service No. ED 171 086)

371. Dixon, C. C. Integrating . . . a positive note. *Hearing and Speech News*, 1968, *36*, 16, 18.

372. Doll, G. F. Classroom integration: Concerns and cautions. *Mental Retardation Bulletin*, 1974/75, *2*(3), 108-111.

373. _____. An investigation of factors identified by regular classroom teachers as contributors in the process of integrating mildly handicapped children into regular classes (Doctoral dissertation, University of Oregon, 1972). *Dissertation Abstracts International*, 1972, *33*, 2198A. (University Microfilms No. 72-28132)

374. Dollar, B. *Learning opportunities for teachers (L.O.F.T.)*. New Brighton, MN: Accelerated Learning Systems, 1976.

375. Donahue, G., & Rainear, A. *Resource room approach to mainstreaming: Survey of literature*. Pitman, NJ: Educational Improvement Center, n.d. (ERIC Document Reproduction Service No. ED 111 122)

376. _____, & Rainear, A. *Resource room approach to mainstreaming: Survey of program planning*. Pitman, NJ: Educational Improvement Center, n.d. (ERIC Document Reproduction Service No. ED 111 123)

377. Donohue, K. Career education for the handicapped: The vocational school psychologist as consultant. *School Psychology Digest*, 1977, *7*, 55-59.

378. Dopheide, W. R., & Dalenger, J. Improving remedial speech and language services through clinician-teacher in-service interaction. *Language, Speech and Hearing Services in Schools*, 1975, *6*, 196-205.

379. Doran, B. Into the mainstream. *Nation's Schools and Colleges*, 1975, *2*(3), 33-41.

380. Dory, F. J., & Pickett, A. L. *Task analysis for paraprofessionals working with severely/profoundly handicapped children and in "mainstream" classrooms and career ladders and lattices for paraprofessionals in special education*. New York: City University of New York, New York Center for Advanced Study in Education, n.d. (ERIC Document Reproduction Service No. ED 148 089)

381. Dowling, R. J. Legal remedies in education and employment. *Volta Review*, 1977, *79*, 327-334.

382. Doyle, P. B., Chafetz, M., Lutz, C. H., & Proger, B. B. *Project MITER: Montgomery Inservice Training and Educational Resources. Final report*. Blue Bell, PA: Montgomery County Intermediate Unit 23, 1978. (ERIC Document Reproduction Service No. ED 159 842)

383. Dresang, E. T. There are no other children; special children in the library media center. *School Library Journal*, 1977, *24*, 19-23.

384. Drummer, G. M., & Semmel, M. I. In physical education programs: The implications of mainstreaming handicapped children. *Viewpoints*, 1977, *53*, 89-102.

385. Duclos, C., Litwin, B., Meyers, R., & Ullrich, H. *Mainstreaming exceptional children: A guideline for the principal.* Urbana, IL: University of Illinois, Urbana-Champaign, and Gurney, IL: Lake County Special Education District, 1977. (ERIC Document Reproduction Service No. ED 151 991)

386. Dunlop, K. H. Mainstreaming: Valuing diversity in children. *Young Children*, 1977, *32*(4), 26-32.

387. Dunn, L. M. (Ed.). *Exceptional children in the schools: Special education in transition.* New York, NY: Holt, Rinehart & Winston, 1973.

388. Dunn, R. S., & Cole, R. W. Inviting malpractice through mainstreaming. *Educational Leadership*, 1979, *36*, 302-306.

389. Dunst, C. J. Attitudes of parents with children in contrasting early education programs. *Mental Retardation Bulletin*, 1976, *4*, 120-132.

390. Dutt, S., & Forte, S. *A reference system to published IEP resources for educational assessment and programming.* Lancaster, PA: Lancaster-Lebanon Intermediate Unit 13, 1978. (ERIC Document Reproduction Service No. ED 159 846)

391. Eads, F. D., & Gill, D. H. Prescriptive teaching for handicapped students. Vocational education awareness program, Georgia. *American Vocational Journal*, 1975, *50*, 52-56.

392. East, L. Mainstreaming success story. *Today's Education*, 1976, *65*(4), 71.

393. (Editorial). Integration or mainstreaming. *American Annals of the Deaf*, 1975, *120*, 15.

394. Edmonds, M. Accountability for all children in the regular classroom. *Language Arts*, 1976, *53*, 425-427.

395. *Educating exceptional children 79/80.* Guilford, CT: Dushkin Pub., 1980.

396. *Education for All Handicapped Children: Consensus, Conflict, and Challenge.* Washington, D.C.: National Education Association, Teacher Rights Division, 1978. (ERIC Document Reproduction Service No. ED 157 214)

397. *Education for All Handicapped Children Act. Hearings before the Subcommittee on Select Education of the Committee on Education and Labor, House of Representatives, 95th Congress, 1st Session, September 26-27, 1977.* Washington, D.C.: Government Printing Office, 1977. (ERIC Document Reproduction Service No. ED 155 845)

398. *The education for all handicapped children act: P.L. 94-142.* Reston, VA: The Council for Exceptional Children, 1976.

399. *Education for all handicapped children 1975: Hearings before the Subcommittee on the Handicapped of the Committee on Labor and Public Welfare, U.S. Senate, 94th Congress, 1st Session on S6; to provide financial assistance to the states for improved educational services to handicapped children (April 8, 9, 15, 1975).* Washington, D.C.: Government Printing Office, 1975. (ERIC Document Reproduction Service No. ED 116 399)

400. Education for the handicapped. *Education Digest,* 1978, *43*(7), 12-15.

401. *Education for the handicapped: Part I.* Washington, D.C.: George Washington University, Institute for Educational Leadership and the National Public Radio, 1976. (ERIC Document Reproduction Service No. ED 131 646)

402. *Education for the handicapped: Part II. Transcripts of National Public Radio's Options in Education, broadcasted in July 1976.* Washington, D.C.: George Washington University, Institute for Educational Leadership and the National Public Radio, 1976. (ERIC Document Reproduction Service No. ED 131 647)

403. Education of handicapped adolescents. *OECD Observer,* 1978, *94,* 15-16.

404. *An educational needs study report related to incidence of exceptionality; a prelude to planning special education services in New Mexico.* Santa Fe, MN: New Mexico State Department of Education/Division of Special Education, 1973. (ERIC Document Reproduction Service No. ED 087 165)

405. *The educational rights of your handicapped child.* Austin, TX: Texas Education Agency, Division of Special Education, 1979. (ERIC Document Reproduction Service No. ED 168 272)

406. Edwards, E., & Motemurro, T. J. *The behavior of preschool handicapped children and their interaction with model children.* Paper presented at the 57th Annual International Convention of the Council for Exceptional Children, Dallas, TX, April 1979. (ERIC Document Reproduction Service No. ED 171 046)

407. Edwards, E. A., & Hagen, J. M. *A Piagetian approach to a main-streamed preschool.* Paper presented at the 10th Annual Interdisciplinary UAP-USC International Conference on Piagetian Theory and the Helping Professions, Los Angeles, CA, February 1980. (ERIC Document Reproduction Service No. ED 186 113)

408. Edwards, R. Children with special needs in the secondary school. *Aspects of Education,* 1975, *20,* 39-47.

409. Egan, Y. M. Portland's gypsies see school in their future. *American Education,* 1980, *16*(2), 20-24.

410. Egner, A. *The challenge of special education in regular high school classrooms: Applications of the behavioral model.* Burlington, VT: University of Vermont, College of Education and Social Services, 1974. (ERIC Document Reproduction Services No. ED 102 790)

411. Egner, A. N. *EPDA 1970-71 yearly report, Chittenden Central School District.* Essex Junction, VT: Chittenden Central School District, Montpelier, VT: Vermont State Department of Education, Burlington, VT: University of Vermont, College of Education and Social Services, 1971. (ERIC Document Reproduction Services No. ED 098 749)

412. _____ (Ed.). *Individualizing junior and senior high school instruction to provide special education within regular classrooms; the 1972-73 research service reports of the Secondary Special Education Project.* Burlington, VT: University of Vermont, College of Education and Social Services, 1973. (ERIC Document Reproduction Services No. ED 095 688)

413. _____, & Paolucci, P. *For the sake of the children—some thoughts on the rights of teachers who provide special education within regular classrooms.* Paper given at the 4th Annual Invitational Special Education Leadership Conference, Minneapolis, MN, December 1974.

414. Ehret, R. C. Them as can, does. *Illinois Libraries,* 1977, *59,* 489-494.

415. Eigeman, E. G. (Ed.). *Vocational programs in Indiana for the disadvantaged and handicapped. Technical Report Series 2.* Bloomington, IN: University of Indiana, Department of Vocational Education, 1977. (ERIC Document Reproduction Service No. ED 141 643)

416. Enos, D. F. *Meeting children's needs: A field centered curriculum for mainstreaming.* Paper presented at the 54th Annual International Convention of the Council for Exceptional Children, Chicago, IL, April 1976. (ERIC Document Reproduction Service No. ED 126 638)

417.   Enright, R. D., & Sutterfield, S. J. Treating the regular class child
       in the mainstreaming process: Increasing social cognitive develop-
       ment. *Psychology in the Schools,* 1979, *16,* 110-118.

418.   Ensher, G. L. Mainstreaming: Yes. *Exceptional Parent,* 1976, *6*(1),
       6-8.

419.   Erickson, J. G. *Social relationships and communication interactions
       of mainstreamed communication handicapped preschool children:
       A pilot study.* Urbana, IL: University of Illinois at Urbana-Cham-
       paign, 1976. (ERIC Document Reproduction Service No. ED 129
       043)

420.   Estle, M. S., & Christensen, C. R. Teacher centers and P.L. 94-142:
       A unique opportunity for cooperation and resource utilization. *Illi-
       nois Libraries,* 1977, *59,* 486-488.

421.   *Evaluation of the process of mainstreaming handicapped children
       into Project Head Start. Phase I. Executive summary.* Silver Spring,
       MD: Applied Management Sciences, 1978. (ERIC Document
       Reproduction Service No. ED 168 236)

422.   *Evaluation of the process of mainstreaming handicapped children
       into Project Head Start. Phase II. Executive Summary.* Silver
       Spring, MD: Applied Management Sciences, 1978. (ERIC Docu-
       ment Reproduction Services No. ED 168 291)

423.   *Evaluation of the process of mainstreaming handicapped children
       into Project Head Start. Phase II. Interim report.* Silver Spring,
       MD: Applied Management Sciences, 1978. (ERIC Document
       Reproduction Services No. ED 168 238)

424.   *Evaluation of the process of mainstreaming handicapped children
       into Project Head Start. Program efforts to ensure post-enrollment
       service continuity for handicapped children in Project Head Start.
       Final report.* Silver Spring, MD: Applied Management Sciences,
       1978. (ERIC Document Reproduction Services No. ED 168 237)

425.   Evans, J. S. *Ability development project for five-year-olds. Final
       report.* Austin, TX: Southwest Educational Development Labora-
       tory, 1977. (ERIC Document Reproduction Services No. ED 154
       577)

426.   _____. *Identification and supplementary instruction for handi-
       capped children in a regular bilingual program.* Austin, TX:
       Southwest Educational Development Laboratory, 1976. (ERIC
       Document Reproduction Services No. ED 123 891)

427.   Evans, T. Teaching children of mixed ability. *Special Educa-
       tion/Forward Trends,* 1976, *3*(3), 8-11.

428. *Facilities for mainstreaming the handicapped. Educational Facilities Digest 13.* Columbus, OH: Council of Educational Facility Planners, 1977. (ERIC Document Reproduction Services No. ED 132 643)

429. Fact sheet on the Education for All Handicapped Children Act of 1975. *Today's Education,* 1977, 66(3), 26.

430. Fairchild, T. N. An analysis of perceived importance ratings of generic teaching competencies: A survey of special education teachers, regular class teachers, and teacher consultants in the elementary grades (Doctoral dissertation, University of Iowa, 1974). *Dissertation Abstracts International,* 1975, *35,* 7768A. (University Microfilms No. 75-13746)

431. _____. *Counseling exceptional children.* Austin, TX: Learning Concepts, 1977.

432. _____, & Henson, F. *Mainstreaming exceptional children.* Austin, TX: Learning Concepts, 1976.

433. Farrer, K., & Guest, E. *A cooperative instructional services program for improving educational personnel to teach special education students in the regular classroom. Director's final report.* Logan, UT: Utah State University, College of Education, 1970. (ERIC Document Reproduction Services No. ED 043 598)

434. *Federal direction needed for educating handicapped children in state schools: Report to the Congress:* Washington, D.C.: Comptroller General of the U.S., 1978. (ERIC Document Reproduction Services No. ED 166 883)

435. Federlin, A. C. *Play in preschool mainstreamed and handicapped settings.* Saratoga, CA: Century Twenty-One Pub., 1981.

436. Feudo, R. A. *A resource center program (a model for mainstreaming and serving children with special needs).* Ft. Lauderdale, FL: Nova University, 1976. (ERIC Document Reproduction Services No. ED 132 748)

437. *Final report on assessment of the handicapped effort in experimental regular Head Start and selected other exemplary preschool programs serving the handicapped.* Syracuse, NY: Syracuse University, Division of Special Education and Rehabilitation, 1974. (ERIC Document Reproduction Services No. ED 108 440)

438. *Final report on assessment of the handicapped effort in experimental regular Head Start and selected other exemplary preschool programs serving the handicapped. Vol. II.* Syracuse, NY: Syracuse University, Division of Special Education and Rehabilitation, 1974. (ERIC Document Reproduction Services No. ED 108 441)

439. *Final report on costs in serving handicapped children in Head Start: An analysis of methods and cost estimates.* Syracuse, NY: Syracuse University, Division of Special Education and Rehabilitation, 1974. (ERIC Document Reproduction Services No. ED 108 443)

440. Fiorentino, M., Jr. A study of the effects of a short-term inservice education program on regular classroom teachers' attitude towards and knowledge of mainstreaming (Doctoral dissertation, University of Massachusetts, 1978). *Dissertation Abstracts International,* 1978, *39,* 220A. (University Microfilms No. 78-10714)

441. *Fiscal year 1979 Maryland amended annual program under Part B of the Education of the Handicapped Act as amended by Public Law 94-142.* Baltimore, MD: Maryland State Department of Education, Office of Special Education, 1978. (ERIC Document Reproduction Services No. ED 169 740)

442. Fisher, G. Integration at the Pingle School. *Special Education/Forward Trends,* 1977, *4,* 8-11.

443. Fitzpatrick, J. L., & Beavers, A. *An inservice course on mainstreaming: An innovative media approach.* Paper presented at the Annual Meeting of the American Educational Research Association, Toronto, Ontario, Canada, March 1978. (ERIC Document Reproduction Services No. ED 154 556)

444. _____, & Beavers, A. *Mainstreaming and the handicapped: Teacher, administrator, and community attitudes.* Paper presented at the Annual Meeting of the American Educational Research Association, Toronto, Ontario, Canada, March 1978. (ERIC Document Reproduction Services No. ED 154 555)

445. Flynn, J. R., Gacka, R. C., & Sundean, D. A. Are classroom teachers prepared for mainstreaming? *Phi Delta Kappan,* 1978, *59,* 562.

446. Folman, R., & Budoff, M. *Attitudes toward school of special and regular class adolescents. Studies in learning potential, v. 2, no. 32.* Cambridge, MA: Research Institute for Educational Problems, 1972. (ERIC Document Reproduction Services No. ED 085 971)

447. _____, & Budoff, M. *Social interests and activities of special and regular class adolescents and compared by learning potential status, vol. 2, no. 36.* Cambridge, MA: Research Institute for Educational Problems, 1972. (ERIC Document Reproduction Services No. 062 752)

448. *For parents only . . . practical advice to parents on special education.* Des Moines, IA: Drake University, Midwest Regional Resource Center, 1979. (ERIC Document Reproduction Services No. ED 169 711)

449.   For the handicapped, new help in schools. *U.S. News & World Report*, June 16, 1975, pp. 40-41.

450.   Forehand, R., & Smith, G. M. Classroom conflict between teacher and student—an intervention technique. In J. W. Schifani (Ed.), *Contemporary issues in mainstreaming handicapped citizens.* Dubuque, IA: Kendall/Hunt Pub. Co., 1976.

451.   Foreman, E. Y. *A study of the attitudes of elementary school principals toward mainstreaming of exceptional children into regular classes.* Unpublished doctoral dissertation, Atlanta University, 1975.

452.   Forness, S. R. Behavioristic orientation to categorical labels. *Journals of School Psychology,* 1976, *14*(2), 90-96.

453.   _____. Implications of recent trends in educational labeling. *Journal of Learning Disabilities,* 1974, *7*, 445-449.

454.   Forsberg, S. J. A program for transfer of learning within a mainstream preschool setting (Doctoral dissertation, Pennsylvania State University, 1977). *Dissertation Abstracts International,* 1977, *39*, 87A. (University Microfilms No. 78-08359)

455.   Forum: Some responses to our coverage of mainstreaming. *Teacher,* 1977, *95*(4), 16-22.

456.   Foster, C. G., & Gable, E. *The Indian child in special education: Two person's perceptions.* Unpublished manuscript, 1980. (ERIC Document Reproduction Service No. ED 188 837)

457.   Fountain Valley School District, California. *Affective instruments used in the evaluation of the 'Handicapped children in the regular classroom,' an ESEA Title III project.* Fountain Valley, CA: Author, n.d. (ERIC Document Reproduction Services No. 096 805)

458.   _____. *Handicapped children in the regular classroom.* Fountain Valley, CA: Author, 1972. (ERIC Document Reproduction Service No. ED 073 592)

459.   _____. *Handicapped children in the regular classroom; Project 1232, 1972-73. (End of Budget Period Report). Title III, ESEA.* Fountain Valley, CA: Author, 1973. (ERIC Document Reproduction Service No. ED 097 784)

460.   Fournier-Negroni, Y. A framework for policy analysis: An application to mainstreaming handicapped children (Doctoral dissertation, Memphis State University, 1978). *Dissertation Abstracts International,* 1978, *39*, 1411A. (University Microfilms No. 78-15987)

461. Fowler, S. A. Transition to public school. In K. E. Allen (Ed.), *Mainstreaming in early childhood education.* Albany, NY: Delmar, 1980.

462. Fox, M. J., Jr., & Stack, W. B. Education for all the Handicapped Children Act, hearing officer and the labor arbitrator. *Journal of Collective Negotiations in the Public Sector,* 1979, *8*(1), 67-76.

463. Fox, W. L. An introduction to a regular classroom approach to special education. In J. W. Schifani (Ed.), *Contemporary issues in mainstreaming handicapped citizens.* Dubuque, IA: Kendall/Hunt Pub. Co., 1976.

464. Franks, F. L., & Sanford, L. Using the light sensor to introduce laboratory science. *Science and Children,* 1978, *13*(6), 48-49.

465. Frederick, H. Integrating the moderately and severely handicapped preschool child into a normal day care setting. In M. J. Guralnick (Ed.), *Early intervention and the integration of handicapped and nonhandicapped children.* Baltimore, MD: University Park Press, 1978. (ERIC Document Reproduction Service No. ED 162 755)

466. Freeman, R. N. *Life in classrooms: Teacher interaction with successful and unsuccessful pupils.* Paper presented at the 58th Annual International Convention of the Council for Exceptional Children, Philadelphia, PA, April 1980. (ERIC Document Reproduction Service No. ED 187 044)

467. Frith, G. *Public Law 94-142, Education for All Handicapped Children Act: Some plain talk pursuant to the role of institutions of higher education.* Paper presented at the First World Congress on Future Special Education, Stirling, Scotland, June-July 1978. (ERIC Document Reproduction Service No. ED 157 337)

468. _____. *Variables affecting delivery of exceptional child services to rural areas and suggested educational approaches.* Paper presented at the 55th Annual International Convention of the Council for Exceptional Children, Atlanta, GA, April 1977. (ERIC Document Reproduction Service No. ED 139 217)

469. Frostig, M. Meeting individual needs of all children in the classroom setting. *Journal of Learning Disabilities,* 1980, *13,* 158-161.

470. Funding formula under Public Law 94-142. *Amicus,* 1977, *2*(3), 45-47.

471. Gainer, R. S., & Kukuk, E. Something to sing about. *Childhood Education,* 1979, *55,* 141-147.

472. Gair, S. B. Are the arts ready for special education? *Art Education,* 1978, *31*(7), 13-14.

473.   Gallagher, J. J. Phenomenal growth and new problems characterize special education. *Phi Delta Kappan*, 1974, *55*, 516-520. Also in J. W. Schifani (Ed.), *Contemporary issues in mainstreaming handicapped citizens*. Dubuque, IA: Kendall/Hunt Pub. Co., 1976.

474.   _____. The special education contract for mildly handicapped children. *Exceptional Children*, 1972, *38*, 527-535. Also in R. L. Jones, & D. L. Macmillan (Eds.), *Special education in transition*, Boston, MA: Allyn & Bacon, 1974.

475.   Galloway, C., & Chandler, P. The marriage of special and generic early education services. In M. J. Guralnick (Ed.), *Early intervention and the integration of handicapped and nonhandicapped children*. Baltimore, MD: University Park Press, 1978.

476.   Galloway, C. M. (Ed.). *Special education*. Columbus, OH: Ohio State University, College of Education, 1975.

477.   Galloway, J. R. *An evaluation: Regional program for exceptional children; a model for mainstreaming of exceptional children in school divisions of Culpeper, Madison, and Orange Counties, Virginia, school year 1973-74.* Richmond, VA: State Department of Education, 1974. (ERIC Document Reproduction Service No. ED 105 694)

478.   Gargantiel, C. W., Huang, J., Miller, J. K., & Munson, H. L. *Individualized educational planning*. Paper presented at the Alexander Graham Bell Association for the Deaf National Convention, Washington, D.C., 1978.

479.   Garka, R. C. *The effects of teacher expectations on the academic and intellectual performance of regular class and special education pupils.* Unpublished doctoral dissertation, Indiana University of Pennsylvania, 1974.

480.   Garry, V. V. Books about kids with special needs. *Instructor*, 1978, *88*(4), 113-114, 116.

481.   Gaskins, M. H. Horseback riding and the handicapped. *Science and Children*, 1976, *13*(6), 23.

482.   Gearhart, B. R., & Weishahn, M. W. *The handicapped child in the regular classroom*. St. Louis, MO: C. V. Mosby, 1976.

483.   Geddes, D. M. *Integrating persons with handicapping conditions into regular physical education and recreation programs*. Washington, D.C.: American Association for Health, Physical Education and Recreation, 1974. (ERIC Document Reproduction Service No. ED 104 092)

484.   _____, & Summerfield, L. *Integrating persons with handicap-ping conditions into regular physical education and recreation pro-grams.* Rev. ed. Washington, D.C.: American Association for Health, Physical Education and Recreation, 1977. (ERIC Docu-ment Reproduction Service No. ED 159 856)

485.   Gentry, B. (Ed.). *Preparation for tomorrow.* Lawrence, KS: Univer-sity of Kansas, Kansas Research Institute for the Early Childhood Education of the Handicapped, 1980.

486.   Gentry, D., & Parks, A. L. *Education of the severely/profoundly handicapped: What is the least restrictive alternative?* Austin, TX: Learning Concepts, 1977.

487.   Gentry, R. *Public Law 94-142: Ninety-nine (99) key terms pre-sented in a conceptual framework.* Paper presented at the 58th Annual International Convention of the Council for Exceptional Children, Philadelphia, PA, April 1980. (ERIC Document Repro-duction Service No. ED 187 055)

488.   George, B. V. A descriptive study of exemplary mainstreaming pro-grams: Their planning, implementation, and evaluation practices and procedures (Doctoral dissertation, Saint Louis University, 1978). *Dissertation Abstracts International,* 1978, *39,* 1473A. (University Microfilms No. 78-14565)

489.   Gerber, I. *The design, implementation, and evaluation of a special education program to meet the needs of handicapped students: Maxi II practicum.* Fort Lauderdale, FL: Nova University, National Education Department, Program for Educational Leaders, 1975.

490.   Gerber, P. J. Awareness of handicapping conditions and socio-metric status in an integrated pre-school setting. *Mental Retarda-tion,* 1977, *15,* 24-25.

491.   Gerke, R. E. The effects of mainstreaming on the self-concept and reading achievement of exceptional children at the elementary level (Doctoral dissertation, Lehigh University, 1975). *Dissertation Abstracts International,* 1975, *36,* 7337A. (University Microfilms No. 76-10366)

492.   Gerlach, K. P. *Preparing for mainstreaming in teacher education institutions.* Paper presented at the 55th Annual International Convention of the Council for Exceptional Children, Atlanta, GA, April 1977. (ERIC Document Reproduction Service No. ED 139 167)

493.   Gershman, J. *The evaluation of special education programs: Past attempts and present directions. No. 134.* Toronto, Ontario, Canada: Toronto Board of Education, Research Department, 1975. (ERIC Document Reproduction Service No. ED 119 415)

494.   _____, & Wright, E. N. *Student flow-through in special education. Research service paper, No. 127.* Toronto, Ontario, Canada: Toronto Board of Education, 1975. (ERIC Document Reproduction Service No. ED 115 034)

495.   *Get Set (Generic Education Training for Special Education Teachers). Description of teacher inservice education materials.* Washington, D.C.: National Education Association, Project on Utilization of Inservice Education, R & D Outcomes, 1976. (ERIC Document Reproduction Service No. ED 173 345)

496.   Ghodsian, M., & Calnan, M. Comparative longitudinal analysis of special education groups. *British Journal of Educational Psychology,* 1977, *47,* 162-174.

497.   Gibbins, S. Public Law 94-142: An impetus for consultation. *School Psychology Digest,* 1978, *7*(3), 18-25.

498.   Gibson, J., & Lazar, A. L. Orange Unified School District's special education career and vocational program. *Career Education Quarterly,* 1977, *2*(4), 21-28.

499.   Gickling, E. E., & Dickinson, D. J. *Delivery systems and instructional delivery: A necessary distinction when providing services for mainstreamed children.* Paper presented at the 55th Annual International Convention of the Council for Exceptional Children, Atlanta, GA, April 1977. (ERIC Document Reproduction Service No. ED 139 166)

500.   _____, & Theobald, J. T. Mainstreaming: Affect or effect. *Journal of Special Education,* 1975, *9,* 317-328.

501.   Giesen, R. A. Publishing for the handicapped learner. *Illinois Libraries,* 1977, *59,* 510-513.

502.   Gilbert, J. P. Mainstreaming in your classroom: What to expect. *Music Educators Journal,* 1977, *63*(6), 64-68.

503.   Gilhool, T. K. Changing public policies: Roots and forces. In M. C. Reynolds (Ed.), *Mainstreaming: Origins and implications.* Reston, VA: Council for Exceptional Children, 1976.

504.   _____. Education: An inalienable right. *Exceptional Children,* 1973, *39,* 597-610.

505.   Gill, D. H., & Sankovsky, R. *Cross-training vocational and special educators: Report of a workshop.* Statesboro, GA: Georgia Southern College, 1978. (ERIC Document Reproduction Service No. ED 168 271)

506.   Gillung, T. B., & Rucker, C. N. Labels and teacher expectations. *Exceptional Children,* 1977, *43,* 464-465.

507.   Gittens, W. Individualized educational programming. *British Journal of Special Education*, 1978, *2*, 3-7.

508.   Glass, R. M., & Meckler, R. S. Preparing elementary teachers to instruct mildly handicapped children in regular classrooms: A summer workshop. *Exceptional Children*, 1972, *39*, 152-156.

509.   Glazzard, P. Putting out the welcome mat. *Early Years*, 1977, 7(9), 41-43.

510.   Glickman, L. J. Research activities for handicapped children. *American Education*, 1975, *11*(8), 30-31.

511.   Glockner, M. Z. But how can I help a handicapped child? *Instructor*, 1973, *83*(1), 113-114, 116.

512.   _____. *Integrating handicapped children into regular classrooms.* Urbana, IL: University of Illinois, Urbana-Champaign, College of Education Curriculum Laboratory, 1973. (ERIC Document Reproduction Service No. ED 081 500)

513.   Glover, J. A., & Gary, A. L. *Mainstreaming exceptional children.* Pacific Grove, CA: Boxwood Press, 1976.

514.   Goldberg, I. I., & Lippman, L. Plato had a word for it. *Exceptional Children*, 1974, 40, 325-334.

515.   Goldberg, M. L., Passow, A. H., & Justman, J. *The effects of ability grouping.* New York, NY: Teachers College Press, Columbia University, 1966.

516.   Goldman, N. *Mainstreaming: Some hard questions.* Trenton, NJ: New Jersey Education Association, Division of Instruction, 1974.

517.   Goodman, L. V. A bill of rights for the handicapped. *American Education*, 1976, *12*(6), 6-8.

518.   Goodwin, L. A. *Mainstreaming—a negative approach.* Paper presented at the Annual Meeting of the American Alliance for Health, Physical Education and Recreation, Atlantic City, NJ, 1975. (ERIC Document Reproduction Service No. ED 106 289)

519.   Goor, J., Moore, M., & Demarest, E. *School districts participating in multiple federal programs. Winter 1978-79. FRSS Report No. 7.* Washington, D.C.: National Center for Education Statistics, 1980. (ERIC Document Reproduction Service No. ED 182 832)

520.   Goplerud, D., & Fleming, J. E. *Mainstreaming with learning sequences: Step-by-step scripts for teaching children with learning handicaps.* Belmont, CA: Fearon/Pitman, 1980.

521.   Gorelick, M. C. *Are preschools willing to integrate children with handicaps? Careers in integrated early childhood programs.* Northridge, CA: California State University, Northridge Preschool Laboratory, Home Economics Department, 1973. (ERIC Document Reproduction Service No. ED 098 736)

522. _____. *Developmental teacher competency checklist. Careers in integrated early childhood programs.* Northridge, CA: California State University, Northridge Preschool Laboratory, Home Economics Department, 1974. (ERIC Document Reproduction Service No. ED 097 794)

523. _____. *What's in a label? Careers in integrated early childhood programs.* Northridge, CA: California State University, Northridge Preschool Laboratory, Home Economics Department, 1973. (ERIC Document Reproduction Service No. ED 097 792)

524. _____, & Brown, P. A. *Preschools willing to integrate children with handicaps. Directory, 1974.* Northridge, CA: California State University, Northridge Preschool Laboratory, Home Economics Department, 1974. (ERIC Document Reproduction Service No. ED 090 745)

525. _____, Joseph, M. L., & Friedman, L. J. *Careers in integrated early childhood programs.* Northridge, CA: California State University, Northridge Preschool Laboratory, Home Economics Department, 1975. (ERIC Document Reproduction Service No. ED 112 628)

526. Gorham, K. A. Effect on parents. In N. Hobbs (Ed.), *Issues in the classification of children.* San Francisco, CA: Jossey-Bass, 1975.

527. Graeb, T., & Sage, D. Citizen advocacy and mainstream training—the interaction of university/community change processes. In R. A. Johnson, R. F. Weatherman, & A. M. Rehman (Eds.), *Special education leadership series, Vol. IV: Handicapped youth and the mainstream educator.* Minneapolis, MN: AudioVisual Extension Service, University of Minnesota, 1975.

528. Graham, C. From label to child. *Academic Therapy,* 1973, *8,* 277-285.

529. Graham, S., Burdg, N. B., Hudson F., & Carpenter, D. Educational personnel's perception of mainstreaming and resource room effectiveness. *Psychology in the Schools,* 1980, *17,* 128-134.

530. Graubard, P. S. Children with behavioral disabilities. In L. M. Dunn (Ed.), *Exceptional children in the schools: Special education in transition.* 2d. ed. New York, NY: Holt, Rinehart & Winston, 1973.

531. _____, & Rosenberg, H. *Classrooms that work: Prescriptions for change.* New York, NY: E. P. Dutton, n.d.

532. Green, J. H. Attitudes of special educators versus regular teachers toward education in Michigan (Doctoral dissertation, Michigan State University, 1967). *Dissertation Abstracts,* 1967, *28,* 4872A. (University Microfilms No. 68-07892)

533.   Green, M. *The individualized education program: A team approach.* Des Moines, IA: Drake University, Midwest Regional Resource Center, 1978. (ERIC Document Reproduction Service No. ED 169 712)

534.   Green, R. Integration—a philosophy of expectation. *Highlights,* 1973, *52,* 10-12.

535.   Greenbaum, J., Varas, M., & Markel, G. Using books about handicapped children. *Reading Teacher,* 1980, *33,* 416-419.

536.   Greenberg, L. *Test development procedures for including handicapped students in New Jersey's state assessment program.* Trenton, NJ: New Jersey State Department of Education, Division of Operations, Research and Evaluation, 1980. (ERIC Document Reproduction Service No. ED 187 767)

537.   Greene, M. A., & Retish, P. M. A comparative study of attitudes among students in special education and regular education. *Training School Bulletin,* 1973, *70*(1), 10-14.

538.   Greer, W. C. New era for special education. *American Education,* 1975, *11*(5), 24-27.

539.   Gregory, G. P. Using the newspaper in the mainstreamed classroom. *Social Education,* 1979, *43,* 140-143.

540.   Grenner, J. M. An in-service traning program for preparing regular classroom teachers to maintain mildly handicapped children in a regular classroom (Doctoral dissertation, University of Southern California, 1973). *Dissertation Abstracts International,* 1973, *34,* 5776A. (University Microfilms No. 74-05863)

541.   Grosenick, J. K. Academic, social and sociometric behaviors involved in the integration of primary aged males from a special education class into a regular public school class (Doctoral dissertation, University of Kansas, 1969). *Dissertation Abstracts International,* 1969, *30,* 2400A. (University Microfilms No. 69-21521)

542.   _____. Integration of exceptional children into regular classes: Research and procedure. *Focus on Exceptional Children,* 1971, *3*(5), 1-9. Also in R. L. Jones, & D. L. Macmillan (Eds.), *Special education in transition.* Boston, MA: Allyn & Bacon, 1974.

543.   _____, & Reynolds, M. C. (Eds.). *Teacher education: Renegotiating roles for mainstreaming.* Reston, VA: The Council for Exceptional Children, and Minneapolis, MN: University of Minnesota, National Support Systems Project 1978. (ERIC Document Reproduction Service No. ED 159 156)

544.   Gross, J. C. Making mainstreaming work. *Curriculum Review,* 1978, *17,* 254-257.

545.   _____, & Vance, V. *Mainstreaming educator training in a cooperative joint agreement and intermediate unit district.* Paper presented at the 4th Annual Invitational Special Education Leadership Conference, Minneapolis, MN, December 1974. Also in R. A. Johnson, R. F. Weatherman, & A. M. Rehman (Eds.), *Special education leadership series, Vol. IV: Handicapped youth and the mainstream educator.* Minneapolis, MN: AudioVisual Extension Service, University of Minnesota, 1975.

546.   Grosse, S. J. Mainstreaming the handicapped swimmer; rights and responsibilities. *Journal of Physical Eduation,* 1975, *73,* 53.

547.   Grotsky, J. N., Sabatino, D., & Ohrtman, W. (Eds.). *The concept of mainstreaming: A resource guide for regular classroom teachers.* Harrisburg, PA: Pennsylvania State Department of Education, 1976. (ERIC Document Reproduction Service No. ED 132 784)

548.   Guinagh, B. Social integration of handicapped children. *Phi Delta Kappan,* 1980, *62,* 27-29.

549.   Gunn, S. L. Mainstreaming is a two-way street. *Journal of Physical Education and Recreation,* 1976, *47,* 48-49.

550.   Guralnick, M. J. *Early intervention an the integration of handicapped and non handicapped children.* Baltimore, MD: University Park Press, 1978. (ERIC Document Reproduction Service No. ED 162 755)

551.   _____. Integrated preschools as educational and therapeutic environments—concepts, design, and analysis. In M. J. Guralnick (Ed.), *Early intervention and the integration of handicapped and nonhandicapped children.* Baltimore, MD: University Park Press, 1978.

552.   _____. *Integrating handicapped and non handicapped preschool children. Final report.* Columbus, OH: Ohio State University, Department of Communications, 1978. (ERIC Document Reproduction Service No. ED 162 472)

553.   _____. The value of integrating handicapped and non handicapped preschool children. *American Journal of Orthopsychiatry,* 1976, *46,* 236-245.

554.   Guskin, S. L. Simulation games on the "mainstreaming" of mildly handicapped children. *Viewpoints,* 1973, *49*(6), 85-95.

555.   Hackett, L. K. A journey for Timmy. *Bates College Alumnus Bulletin,* 1975, *7,* 2-6.

556.   Hadary, D., Cohen, S. H., Haushalter, R., Hadary, T. D., & Levine, R. Interaction and creation through laboratory science and art for special children. *Science and Children,* 1976, *13*(6), 31-33.

557. Hadley, R. G., & Stubbins, J. (Eds.). *Workshops for the handicapped, an annotated bibliography, number 4.* Los Angeles, CA: California State College, Rehabilitation Counseling Program, 1967. (ERIC Document Reproduction Service No. ED 021 359)

558. Hafner, D. A shift in emphasis in programming for handicapped children. *Exceptional Children,* 1972, *39,* 59-60.

559. Haisley, F. B., & Gilberts, R. D. Individual competencies needed to implement P.L. 94-142. *Journal of Teacher Education,* 1978, *29*(6), 30-33.

560. Hale, S., Prothro, E. H., & George, J. *Project S.E.R.T.—Special education for regular teachers.* Paper presented at the 54th Annual International Convention of the Council for Exceptional Children, Chicago, IL, April 1976. (ERIC Document Reproduction Service No. ED 122 479)

561. Hall, C. C., & Yarmal, A. Libraries and P.L. 94-142; awareness planning makes a difference. *Top of the News,* 1978, *35,* 67-73.

562. Hallenbeck, P. N. Teaching social studies to special children. *Journal of Learning Disabilities,* 1974, *7,* 18-21.

563. Halliday, C. *Integrating exceptional children into the regular classroom.* Paper presented at the First World Congress on Future Special Education, Stirling, Scotland, June-July 1978. (ERIC Document Reproduction Service No. ED 157 301)

564. Hammill, D. D. Evaluating children for instructional purposes. *Academic Therapy,* 1971, *6,* 341-353. Also in R. L. Jones, & D. L. Macmillan (Eds.), *Special education in transition.* Boston, MA: Allyn & Bacon, 1974.

565. _____. The resource-room model in special education. *The Journal of Special Education,* 1972, *6,* 349-354.

566. *Hand in hand: Parents and educators, planning special education for the child.* Raleigh, NC: State Department of Public Instruction, Division for Exceptional Children, and Washington, D.C.: Mid-East Regional Resource Center, George Washington University, 1979.

567. *Handicapped children in the classroom: Program no. 97.* Washington, D.C.: George Washington University, Institute for Educational Leadership, n.d. (ERIC Document Reproduction Service No. ED 149 554)

568. Hanley, D. E. *Guidance and the needs of the special child.* Boston: Houghton-Mifflin, 1975.

569. Hansen, P. A., & Hansen, S. B. *Mainstreaming: International perspectives.* Paper presented at the First World Congress on Future Special Education, Stirling, Scotland, June-July 1978). (ERIC Document Reproduction Service No. ED 157 275)

570. Hanson, R. M. Factors affecting elementary principals' decisions to maintain handicapped children in the regular class (Doctoral dissertation, Syracuse University, 1970). *Dissertation Abstracts International*, 1970, *31*, 5887A. (University Microfilms No. 71-11008)

571. Harasymiw, S. J., & Horne, M. D. Integration of handicapped children: Its effects on teacher attitudes. *Education*, 1975, *96*, 153-158.

572. _____, & Horne, M. D. Teacher attitudes toward handicapped children and regular class integration. *Journal of Special Education*, 1976, *10*, 393-400.

573. Haring, N. G. Improved learning conditions for handicapped children in regular classrooms. In J. S. Schifani (Ed.), *Contemporary issues in mainstreaming handicapped citizens*. Dubuque, IA: Kendall/Hunt Pub., 1976.

574. _____. A strategy for the training of resource teachers for handicapped children. In J. W. Schifani (Ed.), *Contemporary issues in mainstreaming handicapped citizens*. Dubuque, IA: Kendall/Hunt Pub., 1976.

575. _____. A study of the attitudes of classroom teachers toward exceptional children (Doctoral dissertation, Syracuse University, 1956), *Dissertation Abstracts*, 1957, *17*, 103-104. (University Microfilms No. 57-166)

576. _____, & Krug, D. A. Placement in regular programs: Procedures and results. *Exceptional Children*, 1975, *41*, 413-417.

577. _____, & Lovitt, T. C. *A program project for the investigation and application of procedures of analysis and modification of behavior of handicapped children. Final report.* Seattle, WA: University of Washington and the Child Development and Mentally Retarded Center, 1975. (ERIC Document Reproduction Service No. ED 131 631)

578. _____, & Stern, G. G., & Cruickshank, W. M. *Attitudes of educators toward exceptional children.* Syracuse, NY: Syracuse University Press, 1958.

579. Harrington, W. M., & Engerbretson, D. L. *The development of a competency based professional preparation program in physical education for work with handicapped children. Final report.* Pullman, WA: Washington State University, 1978. (ERIC Document Reproduction Service No. ED 161 871)

580. Harris, D. *A comparison of the achievements of low ability elementary pupils in two models of instruction.* Paper presented at the 54th Annual International Convention of the Council for Exceptional Children, April 1976. (ERIC Document Reproduction Service No. ED 126 641)

581. Harris, W. J., & Mahar, C. Problems in implementing resource pro-
      grams in rural schools. *Exceptional Children*, 1975, *42*, 95-99.

582. Harrison, J. & Phillips, D. Mainstreaming. *Journal of Career Edu-
      cation*, 1978, *5*, 44-52.

583. Harrison, S. B., & Johnson, M. *Establishing services for the severely
      handicapped in public schools*. Salt Lake City, UT: Southwest
      Regional Resource Center, 1976. (ERIC Document Reproduction
      Service No. ED 129 034)

584. Harste, J. C., & Atwell, M. A. *Mainstreaming the special child and
      the reading process. Handbook for an instructional packet*. Bloom-
      ington, IN: The Reading Program, University of Indiana at Bloom-
      ington, 1976.

585. Hartley, N. Channeling students into the mainstream. *VocEd*,
      1978, *53*(7), 39-42.

586. Hartman, W. T. *Policy effects of special education funding for-
      mulas. Program report No. 80-B1*. Stanford, CA: Stanford Univer-
      sity, Institute for Research on Educational Finance and Gover-
      nance, 1980. (ERIC Document Reproduction Service No. ED 188
      280)

587. Hartup, W. Peer interaction and the processes of socialization. In
      M. J. Guralnick (Ed.), *Early intervention and the integration of
      handicapped and nonhandicapped children*. Baltimore, MD: Uni-
      versity Park Press, 1978.

588. Harvey, J. Future trends in personnel preparation. *Exceptional
      Children*, 1976, *43*, 148-150.

589. _____. Legislative intent and progress. *Exceptional Children*,
      1978, *44*, 234-237.

590. Hasazi, S. E., Rice, P. D., & York, R. *Mainstreaming: Merging
      regular and special education*. Bloomington, IN: Phi Delta Kappa
      Educational Foundation, 1979.

591. _____, & York, R. Changing concepts of special education.
      Teacher, 1977, *95*(1), 99-100.

592. Hatch, E. J., Murphy, J., & Bognato, S. J. The comprehensive
      evaluation for handicapped children. *Elementary School Guidance
      and Counseling*, 1979, *13*, 171-187.

593. Haughton, D. D. *Mediating into the mainstream*. Paper presented
      at the First World Congress on Future Special Education, Stirling,
      Scotland, June-July 1978. (ERIC Document Reproduction Service
      No. ED 157 314)

594. _____. *Project PREM: Final report for Year I. (Preparing regular educators for mainstreaming).* Austin, TX: University of Texas, College of Education, 1976. (ERIC Document Reproduction Service No. ED 126 661)

595. _____, & Enos, D. F. *Project and PERT design manual for PREM. (Preparing regular educators for mainstreaming).* Austin, TX: University of Texas, College of Education, 1975. (ERIC Document Reproduction Service No. ED 117 788)

596. Have questions about mainstreaming? These groups are ready to help you find the answers. *Instructor,* 1978, *87*(6), 132-134.

597. Hawkinson, E. Mainstreaming at Wausau revisited: Some concerns and suggestions. *Bureau Memorandum,* 1973, *15*(1), 18-20.

598. Hayden, A. H., & Edgar, E. Developing individualized education programs for young handicapped children. *Teaching Exceptional Children,* 1978, *10,* 67-70.

599. Hayes, J., & Higgins, S. T. Issues regarding the IEP: Teachers on the front line. *Exceptional Children,* 1978, *44,* 267-273.

600. Healy, W. C. The Education for All Handicapped Children Act of 1975. *Language, Speech, and Hearing Services in Schools,* 1976, *7*(2), 67-73.

601. Heath, E. J. In-service training: Preparing to meet today's needs. *Academic Therapy,* 1974, *9,* 267-280.

602. Heffernan, M. Special education for everyone. *Changing Education,* 1974, *6*(1), 28-30.

603. Heinich, R. *Educating all handicapped children.* Englewood Cliffs, NJ: Educational Technology Pub., 1979.

604. Heller, H. W. Focus on in-service education. *Teacher Education and Special Education,* 1978, *2*(1), 3-6.

605. _____. The resource room: A mere change or real opportunity for the handicapped? *Journal of Special Education,* 1972, *6,* 369-375.

606. _____. Rural special education: A dilemma. *Theory into Practice,* 1975, *14,* 137-142.

607. *Helping teacher program.* Austin, TX: Austin Independent School District, 1976. (ERIC Document Reproduction Service No. ED 144 276)

608. Henderson, R. Mainstreaming: A fashionable idea. *The Washingtonian,* 1975, *10,* 2-5.

609. Henley, C. E. A model for a special education due process hearing. *Bureau Memorandum,* 1978, *20*(1), 2-11.

610.   Herda, E. A. *P.L. 94-142 and interrelated agendas: Research and evaluation.* Paper presented at the 57th Annual International Convention of the Council for Exceptional Children, Dallas, TX, April 1979. (ERIC Document Reproduction Service No. ED 171 085)

611.   Herlig, R. K. *Public Law 94-142. A topical conference.* Washington, D.C.: Council of Chief State School Officers, 1978. (ERIC Document Reproduction Service No. ED 159 859)

612.   Herlihy, J. G., & Herlihy, M. T. (Eds.). *Mainstreaming in the social studies. Bulletin 62.* Washington, D.C.: National Council for the Social Studies, 1980. (ERIC Document Reproduction Service No. ED 186 346)

613.   Heron, T. E. Maintaining the mainstreamed child in the regular classroom: The decision-making process. *Journal of Learning Disabilities,* 1978, *11,* 210-216.

614.   _____. Punishment: A review of the literature with implications for the teacher of mainstreamed children. *Journal of Special Education,* 1978, *12,* 243-252.

615.   Herr, S. Human tragedy in this society. *Mental Hygiene,* 1973, *57,* 26-27.

616.   Hesse, R. M. A procedure for determining needs for inservice training of classroom teachers in a mainstreaming approach to the education of the mildly handicapped (Doctoral dissertation, University of Oregon, 1977). *Dissertation Abstracts International,* 1977, *38,* 6055A. (University Microfilms No. 78-02527)

617.   Hewett, F. M. Handicapped children and the regular classroom. In J. W. Schifani (Ed.), *Contemporary issues in mainstreaming handicapped citizens.* Dubuque, IA: Kendall/Hunt Pub., 1976.

618.   _____, & Forness, S. R. *Education of exceptional learners.* Boston, MA: Allyn & Bacon, 1974.

619.   Higgins, F. D. *Mainstreaming: An overview and update:* Eugene, OR: University of Oregon, School of Study Council, 1976. (ERIC Document Reproduction Service No. ED 122 466)

620.   Higgins, S., & Barresi, J. The changing focus of public policy. *Exceptional Children,* 1979, *45,* 270-277.

621.   Hilliard, A. Mainstreaming: Assessment issues. In P. A. O'Donnell & R. H. Bradfield (Eds.), *Mainstreaming: Controversy and consensus.* San Rafael, CA: Academic Therapy, 1976.

622.   _____. Teacher education and mainstreaming in 1985. *Teacher Education and Special Education,* 1979, *2*(2), 11-13.

623.   Hirshoren, A., & Umansky, W. Certification for teachers of preschool handicapped children. *Exceptional Children,* 1977, *44,* 191-193.

624. Hobbs, N. (Ed.). *Issues in the classification of children* (2 vols.). San Francisco, CA: Jossey-Bass, 1975.

625. Hogan, M. F., & Bernstein, J. C. *Evaluating special education programs: Using PASS (Program analysis of service systems) to assess a district's mainstreaming project.* Paper presented at the 54th Annual International Meeting of the Council for Exceptional Children, Chicago, IL, April 1976. (ERIC Document Reproduction Service No. ED 122 520)

626. Holloway, A. H. (Ed.). Classroom forum: *Focus on Exceptional Children,* 1976, *8*(1), 11-12.

627. Homann, T. H., & Intriligator, B. A. Policy and practice: Varied dimensions of equity. *University Council for Educational Administration Review,* 1980, *21*(1), 9-11.

628. Hornburger, J. M., & Shapiro, P. P. The law and children's literature. *Teacher Educator,* 1977, *12*(4), 28-34.

629. Horne, M. D. Attitudes and mainstreaming: A literature review for school psychologists. *Psychology in the Schools,* 1979, *16*, 61-67.

630. How three laws are changing the picture. *Today's Education,* 1980, *69*(2), 49-52.

631. How your school buildings must change to comply with P.L. 94-142. *American School Board Journal,* 1977, *164*(11), 45-46, 54.

632. Howard, A. E. Viewpoint. Putting Humpty Dumpty together again? Mainstreaming in early childhood. Must I? Can I? Should I? *Young Children,* 1977, *33*(1), 14-15.

633. Howard, N. D. *Regular class placement of the exceptional child: An abstract bibliography.* Urbana, IL: Publications Office/IREC, College of Education, University of Illinois, 1974. (ERIC Document Reproduction Service No. ED 097 126)

634. Howe, C. *Speculations regarding mainstreaming and collective bargaining in education.* Paper presented at the 4th Annual Invitational Special Education Leadership Conference, Minneapolis, MN, December 1974. Also in R. A. Johnson, R. F. Weatherman, & A. M. Rehman (Eds.), *Special education leadership series, Vol. IV: Handicapped youth and the mainstream educator.* Minneapolis, MN: Audio Visual Extension Service, University of Minnesota, 1975.

635. Howe, C. E., Rodee, M. E., & Harrington, R. G. *Handbook for placement of handicapped children: From identification through initial placement with P.L. 94-142.* Des Moines, IA: Drake University, Midwest Regional Resource Center, 1977. (ERIC Document Reproduction Service No. ED 163 708)

636. Howe, J. T. How to discipline handicapped kids. *American School Board Journal,* 1980, *167*(2), 30.

637. Howsam, R. B. Mainstreaming higher education: A true collaboration. In P. H. Mann (Ed.), *Shared responsibility for handicapped students: Advocacy and programming.* Coral Gables, FL: University of Miami, Training and Technical Assistance Center, 1976. (ERIC Document Reproduction Service No. ED 132 136)

638. Hoyt, J. H. Feeling free. *American Education,* 1978, *14*(9), 24-28.

639. _____. Mainstreaming Mary Ann. *American Education,* 1978, *14*(9), 13-17.

640. _____. Something special in Portage; program for preschool handicapped children in Wisconsin. *American Education,* 1976, *12*(9), 19-23.

641. Huber, J., & Dearmin, E. *Regional state planning project program . . . Vol. II: Metric education, career education, exceptional children, education of the poor. Educational Governance Project. Seminar report.* Carson City, NV: Nevada State Department of Education, 1974. (ERIC Document Reproduction Service No. ED 141 935)

642. Hughes, J. H. *Mainstreaming the handicapped in preparatory occupational education programs in North Carolina. Final report.* Chapel Hill, NC: System Sciences Inc., 1978. (ERIC Document Reproduction Service No. ED 164 985)

643. _____. *Relationship of selected variables to attitudes of vocational education teachers toward mainstreaming handicapped students.* Unpublished doctoral dissertation, The University of North Carolina at Chapel Hill, 1978.

644. _____, & Rice, E. *Needs assessment procedure: Mainstreaming handicapped. Vol. I. Final technical report.* Chapel Hill, NC: System Sciences, Inc., 1978. (ERIC Document Reproduction Service No. ED 160 891)

645. _____, & Rice, E. *Needs assessment procedure: Mainstreaming handicapped. Vol. II. A manual for vocational education administrators. Final report.* Chapel Hill, NC: System Sciences, Inc., 1978. (ERIC Document Reproduction Service No. ED 160 892)

646. Hughes, S. L., Kauffman, J. M., & Wallace, G. What do labels really mean to classroom teachers? *Academic Therapy,* 1973, *8,* 285-289.

647. Hull, M. C. *Vocational education for the handicapped: A review. Information Series No. 119.* Columbus, OH: Ohio State University, ERIC Clearinghouse on Career Education, 1977. (ERIC Document Reproduction Service No. ED 149 188)

648. Humes, C. W. Implications of P.L. 94-142 for training and supervision. *Counselor Education and Supervision*, 1978, *18*, 126-129.

649. _____. School counselors and P.L. 94-142. *School Counselor*, 1978, *25*, 192-195.

650. Humphrey, G. *The AFT (American Federation of Teachers) position on mainstreaming*. Paper presented at the 4th Annual Invitational Special Education Leadership Conference, Minneapolis, MN, December 1974. Also in R. A. Johnson, R. F. Weatherman, & A. M. Rehman (Eds.), *Special education leadership series, Vol. IV: Handicapped youth and the mainstream educator*. Minneapolis, MN: AudioVisual Extension Service, University of Minnesota, 1975.

651. Humpston, W. D. Together or apart?—the education of handicapped children in comprehensive schools. *Remedial Education*, 1976, *11*(1), 9-12.

652. Hurley, O. L., O'Donnell, P. A., & Bradfield, R. H. Mainstreaming—controversy and consensus. *American Journal of Mental Deficiency*, 1978, *82*, 418-419.

653. Hurwitz, J. *Development of instructional strategies in reading in the mainstreamed elementary school classroom*. Fort Lauderdale, FL: Nova University, 1978. (ERIC Document Reproduction Service No. ED 172 499)

654. Ideas explored to teach handicapped chemistry. *Chemical and Engineering News*, 1980, *58*(19), 24.

655. The IEP and personnel preparation. *American Education*, 1977, *13*(8), 6-8.

656. *IEP: Individualized educational program: What is it/how does it work?* Silver Springs, MD: Montgomery County Association for Retarded Citizens, 1978. (ERIC Document Reproduction Service No. ED 154 559)

657. Imhoff, C. B. *An evaluation: Regional program for exceptional children*. Madison, VA: Author, 1973.

658. *IMPACT 9 of the Title VI programs in the State of Oregon, Sept. 1, 1974-Aug. 31, 1975*. Salem, OR: Oregon State Board of Education, and Monmouth, OR: The Oregon State System of Higher Education, 1975. (ERIC Document Reproduction Service No. ED 131 637)

659. Implementing the IEP concept. *American Education*, 1977, *13*(7), 6-8.

660. *Improving library services for handicapped children: Proceedings of the Institute. Buffalo, NY, February 1-4, 1971*. Albany, NY: New York State Education Dept., Division for Handicapped Children, 1971. (ERIC Document Reproduction Services No. ED 057 523)

661. The individual educational plan: Questions and answers. *Exceptional Parent,* 1978, *8*(4), L7-L10.

662. *Individualized educational program (A multimedia inservice training program). Description of teacher inservice education materials.* Washington, D.C.: National Education Association, Project on Utilization of Inservice Education R & D Outcomes, 1978. (ERIC Document Reproduction Service No. ED 171 688)

663. *Individualized educational programming (IEP): A child study team process (Mainstreaming Training Series). Description of teacher inservice education materials.* Washington, D.C.: National Education Association, Project on Utilization of Inservice Education R & D Outcomes, 1979. (ERIC Document Reproduction Service No. ED 173 346)

664. Ingram, S. H. An assessment of regular classroom teachers' attitudes toward exceptional children subsequent to training in mainstreaming (Doctoral dissertation, University of Michigan, 1976). *Dissertation Abstracts International,* 1976, *37*, 1307A. (University Microfilms No. 76-19163)

665. *Innovative non-categorical and interrelated projects in the education of the handicapped.* Proceedings of the Special Study Institute, Washington, D.C., 1971. (ERIC Document Reproduction Service No. ED 060 609)

666. *Integration of children with special needs (Overview of a series of ten programs). Description of teacher inservice education materials.* Washington, D.C.: National Education Association, Project on Utilization of Inservice Education R & D Outcomes, 1977. (ERIC Document Reproduction Service No. ED 173 285)

667. *Into the mainstream: Bridging the gap between disadvantaged youth and other youth in metropolitan Washington area. Final report.* Washington, D.C.: National Conference of Christians and Jews, 1972. (ERIC Document Reproduction Service No. ED 063 440)

668. Into the mainstream; Education for all handicapped children act. *Time,* November 15, 1976, p. 90.

669. *An introduction to individualized education program plans in Pennsylvania: Guidelines for school age IEP development.* King of Prussia, PA: Eastern Pennsylvania Regional Resources Center for Special Education and the National Learning Resource Center of Pennsylvania, and Harrisburg, PA: Pennsylvania State Department of Education, Bureau of Special and Compensatory Education, 1977. (ERIC Document Reproduction Service No. ED 148 095)

670.   *An introduction to individualized education program plans in Pennsylvania: Guidelines for school age IEP development. Revised.* King of Prussia, PA: Eastern Pennsylvania Regional Resource Center for Special Education and the National Learning Resource Center of Pennsylvania, and Harrisburg, PA: Pennsylvania State Department of Education, Bureau of Special and Compensatory Education, 1978. (ERIC Document Reproduction Service No. ED 165 361)

671.   *An introduction to mainstreaming (a four-part series). Description of teacher inservice education materials.* Washington, D.C.: National Education Association, Project on Utilization of Inservice Education R & D Outcomes, 1978. (ERIC Document Reproduction Service No. ED 168 992)

672.   Irvin, T. Implementation of Public Law 94-142. *Exceptional Children*, 1976, *43*, 135-137.

673.   Isaacson, S. *Personnel training to facilitate mainstreaming: Design of instruction for classroom teachers serving handicapped children.* Paper presented at the 55th Annual International Convention of the Council for Exceptional Children, Atlanta, GA, April 1977. (ERIC Document Reproduction Service No. ED 139 211)

674.   Ispa, J., & Matz, R. Integrating handicapped preschool children within a cognitively oriented program. In M. J. Guralnick (Ed.), *Early intervention and the integration of handicapped and non-handicapped children.* Baltimore, MD: University Park Press, 1978.

675.   Ives, R. *Complementary teacher project.* Tallahassee, FL: Florida State University, College of Education, 1972. (ERIC Document Reproduction Service No. ED 060 609)

676.   Jackson, H. J. A survey of the attitudes of administrators, regular and special education teachers regarding changes in educational methodology in special education (Doctoral dissertation, University of Houston, 1974). *Dissertation Abstracts International*, 1974, *35*, 2084A. (University Microfilms No. 74-21388)

677.   Jackson, P., Noon, B., Silberman, A., Dunn, R., & Sylwester, B. Getting ready—looking into education's crystal ball. *Instructor*, 1977, *87*(1), 38-41.

678.   Jacobs, F. H., & Walker, D. K. Pediatricians and education for all handicapped children act of 1975 (Public Law 94-142). *Pediatrics*, 1978, *61*(1), 135-137.

679.   Jacobs, T. G. *A parent's guide to hearings under Public Law 94-142: The Education for All Handicapped Children Act.* Unpublished manuscript, 1978. (ERIC Document Reproduction Service No. ED 163 745)

680. Jansen, M., Ahm, J., Jensen, P. E., & Leerskou, A. Is special education necessary? Can this program possibly be reduced? *Journal of Learning Disabilities*, 1970, *3*, 434-439.

681. Jansma, P. Get ready for mainstreaming! *Journal of Physical Education and Recreation*, 1977, *48*(7), 15-16.

682. Jelinek, J. A., & Flamboe, T. C. *The Wyoming Infant Stimulation Program—Go WISP, Young Baby, Go WISP*. Paper presented at the 57th Annual International Convention of the Council for Exceptional Children, Dallas, TX, April 1979. (ERIC Document Reproduction Service No. ED 171 090)

683. Jenkins, J. R., & Mayhall, W. F. Describing resource teacher programs. *Exceptional Children*, 1973, *40*, 35-36.

684. _____, & Mayhall, W. F. Development and evaluation of a resource teacher program. *Exceptional Children*, 1976, *43*, 21-29.

685. Jensen, R. N. *Microteaching in training teachers of handicapped learners*. Paper presented at the Special Study Institute, Washington, D.C., 1971. (ERIC Document Reproduction Service No. ED 060 609)

686. _____, & Schaefer, C. J. Making inservice for special needs work for vo-ed teachers. *School Shop*, 1978, *38*(1), 35-36.

687. Johnson, G. F., & Reilly, R. *Interpretive study: Mainstreaming vocational education for the handicapped in California secondary schools. Final report*. Los Angeles, CA: California State Department of Education, 1976. (ERIC Document Reproduction Service No. ED 133 491)

688. Johnson, J. E. *Preferences and opinions of regular education teachers on the placement of educationally handicapped students in regular school programs*. Unpublished dissertation, University of Southern California, 1976.

689. Johnson, R. A., Gross, J. C., & Weatherman, R. F. (Eds.). *Special education leadership series. Vol. I: Decategorization and performance based systems. Vol. II: Special education in court*. Minneapolis, MN: University of Minnesota, Leadership Training Institute/Special Education, 1973. (ERIC Document Reproduction Service No. ED 115 000)

690. _____, Gross, J., & Weatherman, R. F. (Eds.). *Special education leadership series. Vol. III: The right to an education mandate: Implications for special education*. Minneapolis, MN: AudioVisual Library Services, University of Minnesota, 1974. (ERIC Document Reproduction Service No. ED 115 001)

691.   _____, Weatherman, R. F., & Rehman, A. M. (Eds.). *Special education leadership series. Vol. IV: Handicapped youth and the mainstream educator.* Minneapolis, MN: AudioVisual Extension Service, University of Minnesota, 1975.

692.   Johnson, S. B., & Radius, M. *Teacher In-Service.* Castro Valley, CA: Castro Valley Unified School District, 1974. (ERIC Document Reproduction Service No. ED 109 856)

693.   Johnson, W. First things first. *Early Years,* 1977, 7(9), 48-49, 82, 84.

694.   Johnston, W. *A study to determine teacher attitude toward teaching special children with regular children.* N.p., 1972. (ERIC Document Reproduction Service No. ED 065 950)

695.   Jones, H. B. Very special special education—a cooperative effort. *Today's Education,* 1973, 62(3), 53-54.

696.   Jones, J. Federal aid to states. *Exceptional Children,* 1976, 43, 138-139.

697.   Jones, P. R., & Wilkerson, W. R. Preparing special education administrators. *Theory into Practice,* 1975, 14, 105-109.

698.   Jones, R. L. Student views of special placement and their own special classes: A clarification. *Exceptional Children,* 1974, 41, 22-29.

699.   _____ (Ed.). *New Directions in special education.* Boston, MA: Allyn & Bacon, 1970.

700.   _____, Gottlieb, J., Guskin, S., & Yoshida, R. K. Evaluating mainstreaming programs: Models, caveats, considerations and guidelines. *Exceptional Children,* 1978, 44, 588-601.

701.   _____, & Macmillan, D. C. (Eds.). *Special education in transition.* Boston, MA: Allyn & Bacon, 1974.

702.   _____, & Wilderson, F. B. (Eds.). *Mainstreaming and the minority child.* Reston, VA: The Council for Exceptional Children, 1976.

703.   Jonsson, T. *Training methods for special education teachers of the future.* Paper presented at the First World Congress on Future Special Education, Stirling, Scotland, June-July 1978. (ERIC Document Reproduction Service No. ED 157 303)

704.   Jordan, J. *All together now.* Reston, VA: The Council for Exceptional Children, 1976.

705.   Jordan, J. B. Invisible college on mainstreaming addresses critical factors in implementing programs. *Exceptional Children,* 1974, 41, 31-33.

706.   ———. On the educability of intelligence and related issues—A conversation with Burton Blatt. *Education and the Training of the Mentally Retarded,* 1973, *8,* 219-222.

707.   ——— (Ed.). The challenge of renegotiating relations between regular and special education—A conversation with Maynard C. Reynolds. *Education and the Training of the Mentally Retarded,* 1978, *13,* 303-308.

708.   ——— (Ed.). *Teacher, please don't close the door; the exceptional child in the mainstream.* Reston, VA: The Council for Exceptional Children, 1976. (ERIC Document Reproduction Service No. ED 116 410)

709.   ———, & Dailey, R. F. (Eds.). *Not all little wagons are red—the exceptional child's early years.* Reston, VA: The Council for Exceptional Children, 1976. (ERIC Document Reproduction Service No. ED 074 676)

710.   ———, & Robbins, L. S. (Eds.). *Let's try doing something else kind of thing: Behavioral principles and the exceptional child.* Reston, VA: The Council for Exceptional Children, 1972. (ERIC Document Reproduction Service No. ED 060 581)

711.   Jordan, J. E., & Proctor, D. I. Relationships between knowledge of exceptional children, kind and amount of experience with them, and teacher attitudes toward their classroom integration. *Journal of Special Education,* 1969, *3,* 433-439.

712.   Jordan, P. H. Serenity, courage, wisdom and mainsteaming. *Journal for Special Educators of the Mentally Retarded,* 1977, *13,* 208-212.

713.   Jordon, T. E. Problems, needs, and issues in early childhood special education. St. Louis, MO: University of Missouri, 1971. (ERIC Document Reproduction Service No. ED 094 857)

714.   Justice, W. P. Serendipity—integrated summer preschool program. *Deficience Mentale/Mental Retardation,* 1974, *24*(3), 4-9.

715.   Kameen, M. C., & Parker, L. G. The counselor's role in developing the individualized educational program. *Elementary School Guidance and Counseling,* 1979, *13,* 189-196.

716.   Kaplan, L. (Ed.). Special education Public Law 94-142. What's happening? *Journal of Teacher Education,* 1978, *29*(6), 74-75.

717.   Kaplan, S. M. A. Mainstreaming: An evaluation of the integrated preschool (Doctoral dissertation, University of Virginia, 1977). *Dissertation Abstracts International,* 1977, *39,* 758A. (University Microfilms No. 78-12152)

718.   Karagianis, L. D., & Nesbit, W. C. Special education: A changing perspective for educational administrators. *Canadian Administrator,* 1980, *19*(4), 1-6.

719.   Karnes, M. B. Implications of research with disadvantaged children for early intervention with the handicapped. In J. B. Jordan, & R. F. Dailey (Eds.), *Not all little wagons are red—the exceptional child's early years.* Reston, VA: The Council for Exceptional Children, 1976. (ERIC Document Reproduction Service No. ED 074 676)

720.   _____. Mainstreaming parents of the handicapped. *Teacher,* 1977, *95*(2), 90-91.

721.   _____, & Lee, R. C. *Mainstreaming in the preschool.* Urbana, IL: ERIC Clearinghouse on Early Childhood Education, 1977. (ERIC Document Reproduction Service No. ED 152 419)

722.   _____, Teska, J. A., & Hodgins, A. S. The successful implementation of a highly specific preschool instructional program by paraprofessional teachers. *The Journal of Special Education,* 1970, *4,* 69-80.

723.   Katz, G., & Bushnell, S. Meeting special needs through environmental education. *Teaching Exceptional Children,* 1979, *11,* 110-113.

724.   Kaufman, J. F., Gottlieb, J., Agard, J. A., & Kukic, M. B. *Project PRIME, mainstreaming toward an explication of the construct.* Washington, D.C.: Office of Education, Bureau for the Handicapped, Intramural Research Program, 1975.

725.   Kaufman, M., & Faulman, J. Mainstreaming and instructional media and materials. In F. B. Withrow, & C. J. Nygren (Eds.), *Language, materials, and curriculum management for the handicapped learner.* Columbus, OH: C. E. Merrill, 1976.

726.   Kaufman, M. J., Semmel, M. I., & Agard, J. A. Project PRIME—an overview (programmed reentry into mainstream education). *Education and Training of the Mentally Retarded,* 1974, *9,* 107-112.

727.   Kavanagh, E. A classroom teacher looks at mainstreaming. *Elementary School Journal,* 1977, 77, 318-322.

728.   Kawahara, H. A state perspective on special education. *Educational Perspectives,* 1974, *13*(3), 4-8.

729.   Kazdin, A. E. Toward a client administered token reinforcement program. In J. W. Schifani (Ed.), *Contemporary issues in mainstreaming handicapped citizens.* Dubuque, IA: Kendall/Hunt Pub., 1976.

730. Kean, M. H. *The role of the educational evaluator in malpractice litigation; strategems for change.* Paper presented at the 63rd Annual Meeting of the American Educational Research Association, San Francisco, CA, April 1979. (ERIC Document Reproduction Service No. ED 173 444)

731. Keller, H. R. Issues in the use of observational assessment. *School Psychology Review,* 1980, 9(1), 21-30.

732. Kelley, E. A. Implementing the IGE model: Impact on teachers. *Phi Delta Kappan,* 1974, *55,* 570.

733. Kendall, D. Towards integration. *Special Education in Canada,* 1971, *46,* 19-25, 28-34.

734. Kendall, D. J. A proposed specialized education center for boys who have not been able to adjust to the regular school program (Doctoral dissertation, University of Kansas, 1970). *Dissertation Abstracts International,* 1970, *31,* 5710A. (University Microfilms No. 71-13397)

735. Kendall, W. S. Public Law 94-142: Implications for the classroom teacher. *Peabody Journal of Education,* 1978, *55,* 226-230.

736. Kennedy, E. M. P.L. 94-142 poses "lofty challenge." Guest editorial. *Journal of Teacher Education,* 1978, *29*(6), 7.

737. Kent, C. N. Mainstreaming in the shop class. *Industrial Education,* 1977, *66,* 24-26.

738. Keogh, B. Psychological evaluation of exceptional children: Old hangups and new directions. *Journal of School Psychology,* 1972, *10,* 141-145. Also in R. L. Jones, & D. L. Macmillan (Eds.), *Special education in transition.* Boston, MA: Allyn & Bacon, 1974.

739. _____. What research tells us about mainstreaming. In P. A. O'Donnell & R. H. Bradfield (Eds.), *Mainstreaming: Controversy and consensus.* San Rafael, CA: Academic Therapy Pub., 1976.

740. _____, & Levitt, M. L. Special education in the mainstream: A confrontation of limitations. *Focus on Exceptional Children,* 1976, *8*(1), 1-11.

741. _____, Levitt, M. L., & Hall, R. J. *Follow-up study of transition pupils in regular education programs.* Los Angeles, CA: University of California at Los Angeles, 1975.

742. Kidd, J. Parents and Public Law 94-142. *Volta Review,* 1977, *79,* 275-280.

743. Kingsley, R. F. Prevailing attitudes toward exceptional children. *Education,* 1967, *87,* 426-430.

744. Kiop, D. L., & Yudof, M. G. *Educational policy and the law.* Berkeley, CA: McCutchen Pub. Corp., 1974.

745. Kirby, D. F. Renovate, rejuvenate, and release: A plan to abolish the special class. *Pointer,* 1973, *17*(3), 170-175.

746. Kirk, S. *Labelling, categorizing and mainstreaming.* Paper presented at the International Conference of Special Education, Kent, England, 1975.

747. Kirk, S. A. *Educating exceptional children.* 2d. ed. Boston, MA: Houghton-Mifflin, 1972.

748. _____, & Gallagher, J. J. *Educating exceptional children.* 3d. ed. Boston, MA: Houghton-Mifflin, 1979.

749. _____, & Lord, F. E. (Eds.). *Exceptional children: Educational resources and perspectives.* Boston, MA: Houghton-Mifflin, 1974.

750. Kirp, D. L. The great sorting machine. *Phi Delta Kappan,* 1974, *55*, 521-525.

751. _____. Schools as sorters: The constitutional and policy implications of student classification. Childhood and Government Project Reprint Series No. 1. *University of Pennsylvania Law Review,* 1973, *121*(4).

752. _____. The "special" child goes to court. *Trends in Education Series.* Columbus, OH: University Council for Educational Administration, 1976. (ERIC Document Reproduction Service No. ED 132 718)

753. _____. Student classification, public policy, and the courts. *Harvard Educational Review,* 1974, *44*, 7-52.

754. _____, Kuriloff, P. J., & Buss, W. G. Legal mandates and organizational change. In N. Hobbs (Ed.), *Issues in the classification of children* (2 vols.). San Francisco, CA: Jossey-Bass, 1975.

755. _____, & Yudof, M.G. *Educational policy and the law.* Berkeley, CA: McCutchan Press, 1974.

756. Klein, J. *Teaching the special child in the regular classroom.* Urbana, IL: ERIC Clearinghouse on Early Childhood Education, Office of Child Development, 1977. (ERIC Document Reproduction Service No. ED 136 902)

757. Klein, J. W. Mainstreaming the preschooler. *Young Children,* 1975, *30*, 317-326.

758. _____, & Randolph, L. A. Placing handicapped children in Head Start programs. *Children Today,* 1974, *3*(6), 7-10.

759. Klein, N. K. Least restrictive alternative: An educational analysis. *Education and Training of the Mentally Retarded,* 1978, *13*, 102-114.

760. _____. Special education: Implementation of new rules. *Theory into Practice*, 1978, *17*, 348-360.

761. Klein, S. D., & Schleifer, M. J. (Eds.). Parental participation: What will it be? *Exceptional Parent*, 1977, 7(2), 52-53.

762. Klinger, R. L. A shift of emphasis in Texas education. *Journal of School Psychology*, 1972, *10*, 153-156.

763. Klopf, G. J. *The principal and staff development in the school (with a special focus on the role of the principal in mainstreaming)*. New York, NY: Bank Street College of Education, 1979. (ERIC Document Reproduction Service No. ED 168 730)

764. Knowles, C. J. *Concerns of teachers about implementing individualized instruction in the physical education setting*. Austin, TX: University of Texas at Austin, Research and Development Center for Teacher Education, 1980. (ERIC Document Reproduction Service No. ED 189 071). Also in *Research Quarterly*, 1981, *52*, 48-57.

765. Kokaska, C. California trainers of special educators view the implications of mainstreaming. In P. H. Mann, *Shared responsibility for handicapped students. Advocacy and programming*. Coral Gables, FL: University of Miami, Training and Technical Assistance Center, 1976. (ERIC Document Reproduction Service No. ED 132 136)

766. Korn, M. The integration of handicapped children with non-handicapped children in a municipal day care center. *Deficience Mentale/Mental Retardation*, 1974, *24*(3), 26-30.

767. Kovacevich, D. A. A comparative study of the morale of regular and special education teachers (Doctoral dissertation, Kent State University, 1974). *Dissertation Abstracts International*, 1974, *35*, 7157A. (University Microfilms No. 75-07458)

768. Kowal, S. A. *Education of the handicapped litigation brought under P.L. 94-142 and Section 504*. Washington, D.C.: George Washington University, Institute for Educational Leadership, 1978. (ERIC Document Reproduction Service No. ED 162 470)

769. Kraft, A. Down with (most) special education classes! *Academic Therapy*, 1972, *8*, 207-216.

770. Krauch, V. Fitting the handicapped for jobs. *American Education*, 1972, *8*(5), 28-32.

771. Krein, G. J., Jr. Environmental forces in a mainstreamed elementary classroom (Doctoral dissertation, The University of North Carolina at Chapel Hill, 1977). *Dissertation Abstracts International*, 1977, *39*, 222A. (University Microfilms No. 78-10472)

772. Kreinberg, N., & Chow, S. H. L. *Configuration of change: The integration of mildly handicapped children into the regular classroom.* San Francisco, CA: Far West Laboratory for Educational Research and Development, 1973. (ERIC Document Reproduction Service No. ED 089 513)

773. Kroth, R. L., & Scholl, G. T. *Getting schools involved with parents.* Reston, VA: The Council for Exceptional Children, 1978. (ERIC Document Reproduction Service No. ED 155 831)

774. Krug, D. A., & McMinn, D. Classroom integration of exceptional children. *Educating Children: Early and Middle Years,* 1975, *20*(1), 7-9.

775. Kuhn, J. M. *Public Law 94-142: Language arts teacher's concerns; professional rights.* Paper presented at the Annual Meeting of the Illinois Association of Teachers in English, Chicago, IL, October 1978. (ERIC Document Reproduction Service No. ED 170 768)

776. Kuik, D. G. *The effects of in-service training on the development of integrative plans for exceptional children.* Ann Arbor, MI: University Microfilms, 1976.

777. Kupisch, A. G. Indiana elementary teachers' preferences of inservice training models on mainstreaming (Doctoral dissertation, Indiana University, 1975). *Dissertation Abstracts International,* 1975, *36,* 6017A. (University Microfilms No. 76-06281)

778. Lamb, A. C. Tutoring the handicapped. *National Elementary Principal,* 1976, *56*(1), 43-46.

779. Lance, W. D. Learning resource systems for special education. *Theory into Practice,* 1975, *14,* 90-97.

780. _____. Technology and media for exceptional learners: Looking ahead. *Exceptional Children,* 1977, *44,* 92-97.

781. Landers, B. *Early childhood-handicapped resource guide.* Elkader, IA: Keystone Area Education, 1980. (ERIC Document Reproduction Service No. ED 188 382)

782. Lansdowne, S. C. *The handicap primer: An introduction to working with young handicapped children.* Austin, TX: Austin Independent School District, 1978. (ERIC Document Reproduction Service No. ED 155 844)

783. Lapides, J. *Exceptional children in Head Start: Characteristics of preschool handicapped children.* College Park, MD: University of Maryland, Head Start Regional Resource and Training Center, 1973. (ERIC Document Reproduction Service No. ED 089 844)

784. Larsen, S. C. The influence of teacher expectations on the school performance of handicapped children. *Focus on Exceptional Children,* 1975, *6*(8), 1-14.

785. _____, & Poplin, M. S. *Methods for educating the handicapped: An individualized education program approach.* Boston, MA: Allyn & Bacon, 1980.

786. Larson, H. J., Barner, S., Safarik, J., & Shaw, M. *The effects of least restrictive alternatives on relevant education role groups.* Pleasant Hill, CA: Contra Costa County Department of Education, 1978. (ERIC Document Reproduction Service No. ED 162 454)

787. Larson, J. In the mainstream. *Instructor,* 1978, *87*(10), 99-100.

788. Latest in dealing with handicapped pupils. *U.S. News & World Report,* February 27, 1978, pp. 49-50.

789. Lawsuit on the right of handicapped children. *New Outlook for the Blind,* 1974, *68*(1), 33.

790. Laycock, V. K., & Schwartzberg, I. M. *Mainstreaming through peer assisted learning.* N.p., 1976. (ERIC Document Reproduction Service No. ED 143 150)

791. Learner, S. *P.L. 94-142; related federal legislation for handicapped children and implications for coordination.* Washington, D.C.: National Education Association, 1978. (ERIC Document Reproduction Service No. ED 168 251)

792. *Learning analysis: A PACE project.* Steamboat Springs, CO: Child Study Center, 1969. (ERIC Document Reproduction Service No. ED 033 093)

793. Lehrer, B. E., & Daiker, J. F. Computer based information management for professionals serving handicapped learners. *Exceptional Children,* 1978, *44,* 578-585.

794. Lehrer, R.A. Facilitating generalization of improved pupil behavior from resource rooms to regular classrooms (Doctoral dissertation, Temple University, 1976). *Dissertation Abstracts International,* 1976, *37,* 2079A. (University Microfilms No. 76-22052)

795. Leishman, K. Welcoming special students; mainstreaming. *McCalls,* April 1978, p. 60.

796. Lenkowsky, R. S. The effects of categorical labels on judgements of the academic competency and social acceptability of handicapped children by teachers and parents of regular grade pupils (Doctoral dissertation, Columbia University, 1973). *Dissertation Abstracts International,* 1973, *34,* 6486A. (University Microfilms No. 74-09643)

797.   Leonetti, P. A. The compatibility of selected California elementary principals' attitudes toward and knowledge of appropriate placement of exceptional children with the master plan mainstreaming philosophy (Doctoral dissertation, University of Southern California, 1977). *Dissertation Abstracts International,* 1977, *38,* 203A.

798.   Lepire, A. J. The effects of mainstreaming versus special class on the locus-of-control of educationally handicapped children (Doctoral dissertation, University of California at Berkeley with San Francisco State University, 1976). *Dissertation Abstracts International,* 1977, *38,* 730A. (University Microfilms No. 77-15928)

799.   Lessen, E. I., & Rose, T. L. State definitions of preschool handicapped populations. *Exceptional Children,* 1980, *46,* 467-469.

800.   Levenson, D. Whatever happened to early childhood education? *Instructor,* 1977, *87*(3), 66-71, 134-138.

801.   Levey, R. M. Why are handicapped children a headache for some school superintendents? *PTA Magazine,* 1974, *68*(10), 2-3.

802.   Levitt, E., & Cohen, S. Attitudes of children toward their handicapped peers. *Childhood Education, 1976, 52,* 171-173.

803.   _____, & Cohen, S. *Parents as teachers: A rationale for involving parents in the education of young handicapped children.* New York, NY: City University of New York, Hunter College, Special Education Development Center, 1974. (ERIC Document Reproduction Service No. ED 099 141)

804.   Lewandowski, D. Chicago. Effects of federal legislation of physical education programs in three big cities. *Journal of Physical Education and Recreation,* 1980, *51*(1), 38-42.

805.   Lewis, A. J. Increasing educational services to handicapped children in regular schools. In J. W. Schifani (Ed.), *Contemporary issues in mainstreaming handicapped citizens.* Dubuque, IA: Kendall/Hunt Pub., 1976.

806.   Lewis, E. G. The case for "special" children. *Young Children,* 1973, *28,* 368-374.

807.   Lewis, W. W. From Project Re-ED to ecological planning. *Phi Delta Kappan,* 1974, *55,* 538-540.

808.   Lichtenberger, W. Education and instruction of the handicapped inside and outside of the "gesamtschule." *Psychologie in Erziehung and Unterricht,* 1973, *20,* 130-135.

809.   Lichtenstein, E. Suspension, expulsion, and the special education student. *Phi Delta Kappan,* 1980, *61,* 459-461.

810.   Lillian, G. L. Simulation training for regular administrators to in-
        crease knowledge and alter attitudes about exceptional children
        (Doctoral dissertation, University of Kansas, 1971). *Dissertation
        Abstracts International,* 1971, *32,* 5505A. (University Microfilms
        No. 72-11710)

811.   Lilly, M. S. Forum: A training based model for special education.
        Exceptional Children, 1971, *37,* 745-749.

812.   _____. Forum: Special education: A teapot in a tempest. *Excep-
        tional Children,* 1970, *37,* 43-49.

813.   _____. Special education: A cooperative effort. *Theory into Prac-
        tice,* 1975, *14,* 82-89. Also in *Education Digest,* 1975, *41*(3),
        11-15.

814.   _____. Special education in transition: A competency base for
        classroom teachers. In R. A. Johnson, R. F. Weatherman, & A. M.
        Rehman (Eds.), *Special education leadership series, Vol. IV: Hand-
        icapped youth and the mainstream educator.* Minneapolis, MN:
        AudioVisual Extension Service, University of Minnesota, 1975.

815.   Linder, T. Diverting the stream. *Educating Children: Early and
        Middle Years,* 1975, *20*(1), 17-21.

816.   Lindsey, J. D., & Watts, E. M. Cross-age (exceptionality) peer
        tutoring programs: Have you tried one? *Clearinghouse,* 1979, *52,*
        366-368.

817.   Linton, T. E., & Juul, K. D. Mainstreaming: Time for reassess-
        ment. *Educational Leadership,* 1980, *37,* 433-437.

818.   Lippman, L., & Goldberg, I. I. *The right to education: Anatomy of
        the Pennsylvania case and its implications for exceptional children.*
        New York, NY: Teachers College Press, Columbia University,
        1973.

819.   Litzenberger, J. P. *Increasing elementary students' assignment
        completion: A data based method for mainstreaming.* N.p., 1978.
        (ERIC Document Reproduction Service No. ED 165 390)

820.   Lockard, G. Mainstreaming—one child's experience; Rachel L.
        Carson School, Queens, New York. *Phi Delta Kappan, 1978, 59,*
        527-528.

821.   Lombana, J. H. Fostering positive attitudes toward handicapped
        students: A guidance challenge. *School Counselor,* 1980, *27,*
        176-182.

822.   Lord, F. E. Categories and mainstreaming in special education: Per-
        spectives and critique. In S. A. Kirk, & F. E. Lord (Eds.), *Excep-
        tional children: Educational resources and perspectives.* Boston,
        MA: Houghton-Mifflin, 1974.

823.   Loring, J. (Ed.). *Integration of handicapped children in society.* Boston, MA: Routledge & K. Paul, 1975.

824.   Losen, S. M., & Diament, B. Parent involvement in school planning. *Exceptional Parent,* 1978, *8*(4), 19-20, 22.

825.   Lott, L. A., Jr. *Strategies and techniques for mainstreaming: A resource room handbook.* Monroe, MI: Monroe County Intermediate School District, 1975. (ERIC Document Reproduction Service No. ED 117 890)

826.   Louviere, V. Handicapped youngsters prove to be an asset; St. Regis Paper Co. project at the Coleytown Developmental Center. *Nations Business,* December 1976, p. 62.

827.   Love, H. D. *Educating exceptional children in a changing society.* Springfield, IL: C. C. Thomas, 1974.

828.   _____. *Educating exceptional children in regular classrooms.* Springfield, IL: C. C. Thomas, 1972.

829.   Lovitt, T. Precision teaching. *Early Years,* 1977, *7*(9), 44-45, 64.

830.   _____. *Writing and implementing an IEP: A step-by-step plan.* Belmont, CA: Fearon-Pitman, 1979.

831.   Lowell, E. L. Comments on CSUN program. *American Annals of the Deaf,* 1976, *121,* 309-311.

832.   Lowenbraun, S., & Affleck, J. Q. (Eds.). *Teaching mildly handicapped children in regular classes.* Columbus, OH: Charles Merrill, 1976.

833.   Luby, R. R. Detroit. Effects of federal legislation on physical education programs in three big cities. *Journal of Physical Education and Recreation,* 1980, *51*(1), 34-36.

834.   Lutz, C. H., Leiss, R. H., & Proger, B. B. *Preschool services project. July 1, 1977 to June 30, 1978. Final report.* Blue Bell, PA: Montgomery County Intermediate Unit 23, 1978. (ERIC Document Reproduction Service No. ED 168 273)

835.   Lynch-Richards, E. V. A model for inservice teacher training in the Caribbean: Curriculum development for teaching the educationally handicapped in the regular classroom (Doctoral dissertation, University of Massachusetts, 1976). *Dissertation Abstracts International,* 1976, *37,* 2796A. (University Microfilms No. 76-14706)

836.   Lyons, C. M. Public Law 94-142: Politics and professionalism. *Journal for Special Educators of the Mentally Retarded,* 1978, *14,* 123-130.

837.   McAleer, I. M. The parent, teacher, and child as conference partners. *Teaching Exceptional Children,* 1978, *10,* 103-105.

838. McArthur, L. Learning to be self-sufficient. *Volta Review,* 1967, *69,* 259-261.

839. McCarthy, J. M. *A legacy of service: A commitment to excellence. Exceptional child education: A dumping ground for all educational failures?* Paper presented at the 25th Annual Convention of the Florida Federation of the Council for Exceptional Children, Jacksonville, FL, February 1972. (ERIC Document Reproduction Service No. ED 077 172)

840. McCarthy, M. M., & Thomas, S. B. The right to an education: New trends emerging from special education litigation. *NOLPE School Law Journal,* 1977, *7,* 76-87.

841. McCarthy, R. M., & Stodden, R. A. Mainstreaming secondary students: A peer tutoring model. *Teaching Exceptional Children,* 1979, *11,* 162-163.

842. McCauley, R. W., Morris, P. S., & Cooper, J. K. The placement of handicapped children by Canadian public school personnel. *Education and Training of the Mentally Retarded,* 1978, *13,* 367-379.

843. McClung, M. Do handicapped children have a legal right to a minimally adequate education? *Journal of Law and Education,* 1974, *3,* 153-173.

844. McCormack, J. E. *Developing individualized educational plans for the severely handicapped: A systems approach.* Gloucester, MA: Seaside Education Association, 1977.

845. McDonnell, T. E. A comparison of a resource room, a remedial reading group and a regular classroom. (Doctoral dissertation, Saint Louis University, 1975). *Dissertation Abstracts International,* 37, 2114A. (University Microfilms No. 76-22569)

846. McDuffie, T. E. Jr. Predicting success in ISCS Level II. *Journal of Research in Science Teaching,* 1979, *16,* 39-44.

847. McGarigal, J. The NEA position on mainstreaming. In R. A. Johnson, R. F. Weatherman, & A. M. Rehman (Eds.), *Special Education leadership series. Vol. IV: Handicapped youth and the mainstream educator.* Minneapolis, MN: Audio Visual Extension Service, University of Minnesota, 1975.

848. McGrew, J. B. Establishing a public school program for the severely handicapped: A case study. In E. Sontag (Ed.), *Educational programming for the severely and profoundly handicapped.* Boothwyn, PA: The Council for Exceptional Children, Division on Mental Retardation, 1977.

849. MacGugan, K. *An analysis of the implications of Section 504 of the 1973 Rehabilitation Act related to Leeward Community College.* Unpublished manuscript, 1978. (ERIC Document Reproduction Service No. ED 164 032)

850. McHenry, D. F., & Cansdale, R. W. *Curriculum ideas for the elementary educationally handicapped student: Mainstreaming of exceptional children, 1974-75 school year. Working copy.* Las Vegas, NV: Clark County School District, 1975. (ERIC Document Reproduction Service No. ED 111 121)

851. McIntosh, D. K., Minifie, E. L., Rotter, J. C., Salmond, T., & Turner, K. P.L. 94-142 and the elementary school counselor: An interview. *Elementary School Guidance and Counseling,* 1979, *13,* 152-163.

852. McIntyre, M. Science is for all children. *Science and Children,* 1976, *13*(6), 50-51.

853. McKenna, J. New vistas in special education. *UNESCO Courier,* 1974, *27,* 15-17, 33.

854. McKenzie, H. S. *Special education and consulting teachers.* Paper presented at the 3rd Banff International Conference on Behavior Modification, University of Calgary, Calgary, Alberta, Canada, April 1971. (ERIC Document Reproduction Service No. ED 102 102)

855. _____. Special education in Vermont: The consulting teacher approach. In P. A. O'Donnell, & R. H. Bradfield (Eds.), *Mainstreaming: Controversy and consensus.* San Rafael, CA: Academic Therapy, 1976.

856. _____, Egner, A. N., Knight, M. F., Perelman, P. F., Schneider, B. M., & Garvin, J. S. Training consulting teachers to assist elementary teachers in the management and education of handicapped children. *Exceptional Children,* 1970, 37, 137-143. Also in R. L. Jones, & D. C. Macmillan (Eds.), *Special education in transition.* Boston, MA: Allyn & Bacon, 1974.

857. McKinney, L. A., & Seay, D. M. *Development of individualized education programs (IEPs) for the handicapped in vocational education.* Washington, D.C.: Department of Health, Education and Welfare, Office of Education, Bureau of Occupational and Adult Education, 1979.

858. McLeod, J. The role and training of remedial teachers. *Australian Journal of Remedial Education,* 1975, 7(3), 4-6.

859. McLoughlin, J. A., & Kershman, S. M. Mainstreaming in early childhood; strategies and resources. *Young Children,* 1979, *34,* 54-66.

860. McLure, W. P., Burnham, R. A., & Henderson, R. A. *Special education: Needs-costs-methods of financing. A report of a study.* Urbana, IL: University of Illinois, Urbana-Champaign, Bureau of Education and Research, 1975. (ERIC Document Reproduction Service No. ED 106 985)

861. MacMillan, D. L. Research on mainstreaming: Promise and reality. In P. H. Mann (Ed.), *Shared responsibility for handicapped students. Advocacy and programming.* Coral Gables, FL: University of Miami Training and Technical Assistance Center, 1976. (ERIC Document Reproduction Service No. ED 132 136)

862. _____, & Semmel, M. I. Evaluation of mainstreaming programs. *Focus on Exceptional Children,* 1977, *9,* 1-14.

863. McNab, W. L. The sexual needs of the handicapped. *Journal of School Health,* 1978, *48,* 301-306.

864. _____. *TEACH: Teacher education and children with handicaps. Vol. 1, No. 2.* Washington, D.C.: American Association of Colleges for Teacher Education, 1979. (ERIC Document Reproduction Service No.ED 170 298)

865. McNally, A. R. One mainstreaming program that works. *Teacher,* 1975, *93*(4), 39.

866. Macy, D. J. *Evaluating an individualized mainstream special education program in a large urban school district.* Paper presented at the 54th Annual International Convention of the Council for Exceptional Children, Chicago, April 1976. (ERIC Document Reproduction Service No. ED 138 032)

867. Mahan, G. H. Special provisions for handicapped students in college. *Exceptional Children,* 1974, *41,* 51-53.

868. Maher, C. A. Evaluation of special service delivery systems: An organizational domain-referenced approach. *Psychology in the Schools,* 1980, *17,* 60-68.

869. _____. A system approach for delivering supplemental instruction to handicapped children. *Educational Technology,* 1978, *18*(12), 25-29.

870. _____, & Barbrack, C. R. Aggregation of criterion referenced data for special service program outcome evaluation: Practical and technical considerations. *Journal of the International Association of Pupil Personnel Workers,* 1980, *24,* 224-235.

871. *Mainstreaming: Helping teachers meet the challenge.* Washington, D.C.: National Advisory Council on Education Professions Development, 1976. (ERIC Document Reproduction Service No. ED 127 271)

872. *Mainstreaming in IPS.* Indianapolis, IN: Indianapolis Public Schools, 1975. (ERIC Document Reproduction Service No. ED 116 368)

873. Mainstreaming—is it right for Jean? *Exceptional Parent,* 1976, *6*(1), 22-26.

874.   *Mainstreaming: 1977 topical bibliography.* Reston, VA: Council for Exceptional Children, Information Services and Publications, 1977. (ERIC Document Reproduction Services No. ED 146 739)

875.   *Mainstreaming. Part I.* Pittsburgh, PA: Pittsburgh Area Preschool Association, 1978. (ERIC Document Reproduction Service No. ED 153 381)

876.   *Mainstreaming. Part II.* Pittsburgh, PA: Pittsburgh Area Preschool Association, 1978. (ERIC Document Reproduction Service No. ED 153 382)

877.   *Mainstreaming: Program descriptions in areas of exceptionality. A selective bibliography. Exceptional Child Bibliography Series No. 623).* Reston, VA: Council for Exceptional Children, Information Services and Publications, 1976. (ERIC Document Reproduction Services No. ED 129 004)

878.   Mainstreaming special education. *Insights into Open Education,* 1976, *8*(5). (ERIC Document Reproduction Service No. ED 156 629)

879.   Mainstreaming; symposium. *Exceptional Parent,* 1977, *7*(4), 6-45; also in *Exceptional Parent,* 1977, *7*(5), 6-44.

880.   Mainstreaming the handicapped. *Human Behavior,* 1978, *7*(5), 37-38.

881.   Mainstreaming: What's it all about? (Special feature). *Today's Education,* 1976, *65*(2), 18-29.

882.   Major, I. How do we accept the handicapped? *Elementary School Journal,* 1961, *61,* 328-330.

883.   Makuch, G. J. Year-round special education and related services: A state director's perspective. *Exceptional Children,* 1981, *47,* 272-274.

884.   Mandell, C. J. Factors related to the regular teacher's attitudes toward mainstreaming mildly educational handicapped children into the regular classroom (Doctoral dissertation, The American University, 1976). *Dissertation Abstracts International,* 1977, *37,* 7076A. (University Microfilms No. 77-10916)

885.   _____, & Strain, P. S. Analysis of factors related to attitudes of regular classroom teachers toward mainstreaming mildly handicapped children. *Contemporary Educational Psychology,* 1978, *3*(2), 154-162.

886.   Mangieri, J. N., & Readence, J. E. Mainstreaming: Implications for the teaching of reading. *Reading Improvement,* 1977, *14,* 165-167.

887. Mann, L. (Ed.). Part XI: Integration with normal children, effect on normal children in regular classrooms, resource rooms versus special classes, mainstreaming: Some issues. In *The human side of exceptionality*. Philadelphia, PA: JSE Press, 1974.

888. _____, & Proger, B. B. (Eds.). *Research and applied theory in special education: Conversations with the experts*. Blue Bell, PA: Montgomery County Intermediate Unit 23, 1976. (ERIC Document Reproduction Service No. ED 144 268)

889. _____, & Sabatino, D. A. (Eds.). *The third review of special education*. New York: Grune & Stratton, 1976.

890. Mann, P. H. *Shared responsibility for handicapped students. Advocacy and programming*. Coral Gables, FL: University of Miami, Training and Technical Assistance Center, 1976. (ERIC Document Reproduction Service No. ED 132 136)

891. _____. Training teachers to work with the handicapped. *National Elementary Principal*, 1978, *58*, 14-20.

892. _____ (Ed.). *Mainstream special education: Issues and perspectives in urban centers*. Proceedings of the University of Miami Conference on Special Education in the Great Cities, Washington, D.C. 1974. (ERIC Document Reproduction Service No. ED 093 141)

893. Manzitti, E. T., Boratynski, F., & Rader, B. T. *An evaluation of mainstreaming in vocational education programs in the State of Michigan*. Lansing, MI: Michigan State University, College of Education, 1976. (ERIC Document Reproduction Service No. ED 132 767)

894. Marcy, C., Gemignani, M., Grace, M., Egner, A., & Lates, B. J. *Implementing an individualized data based model of education to keep a nine year old boy in his regular public school classroom*. Bristol, VT: Addison Northeast Supervisory Union, 1973. (ERIC Document Reproduction Service No. ED 104 040)

895. Margolese, A. The relationship of hyperacusis to hyperkinesis among regular classroom pupils as compared to educationally handicapped pupils (Doctoral dissertation, University of Southern California, 1971). *Dissertation Abstracts, 32*, 1945A. (University Microfilms No. 71-21476)

896. Markell, C. *Exceptional students in regular classes. Interviews with 43 North Dakota elementary teachers*. Minot, SD: Minot State College, Division of Education and Psychology, 1976. (ERIC Document Reproduction Service No. ED 117 912)

897. Marrs, L. W. The relationship of critical thinking ability and dogmatism to changing regular class teachers' attitudes toward exceptional children (Doctoral dissertation, The University of Texas at Austin, 1971). *Dissertation Abstracts International, 33*, 6380A. (University Microfilms 72-15800)

898. Martin, A. W. The vocational status of former special class and regular class students from lower socio/economic backgrounds. (Doctoral dissertation, Boston University, 1967). *Dissertation Abstracts International*, 1967, 29, 4330A. (University Microfilms No. 69-07819)

899. Martin, D. L. Are our public schools really ignoring the very children who need the schools most? *American School Board Journal*, 1975, *162*, 52-54.

900. Martin, E. W. Education of the Handicapped Act and teacher education. *Journal of Teacher Education*, 1978, *29*(6), 8.

901. _____. An end to dichotomous constructs: A reconceptualization of teacher education. *Journal of Teacher Education*, 1974, *25*(3), 217-220.

902. _____. Helping the handicapped: Gold for all parents. *Parents Magazine*, July 1973, p. 10.

903. _____. Individualism and behaviorism as future trends in educating handicapped children. *Exceptional Children*, 1972, *38*, 517-525.

904. _____. Mainstream educator training and the Federal government. In R. A. Johnson, R. F. Weatherman, & A. M. Rehman (Eds.), *Special education leadership series. Vol. IV: Handicapped youth and the mainstream educator*. Minneapolis, MN: Audio Visual Extension Service, University of Minnesota, 1975.

905. _____. A national commitment to the rights of the individual—1776 to 1976. *Exceptional Children*, 1976, *43*, 132-135.

906. _____. New outlook for education of handicapped children. *American Education*, 1970, *6*(3), 7-10.

907. _____. Some thoughts on mainstreaming. *Exceptional Children*, 1974, *41*, 150-153. Also in *The High School Journal*, 1976, *59*, 271-274.

908. Martin, M. *Mainstreaming bibliography*. Norristown, PA: Montgomery County Intermediate Unit Special Education Center, 1976.

909. Martinez, M. P. *A comparison of attitudes toward and knowledge of mainstreaming as a function of educational level and type of educator*. Unpublished doctoral dissertation, George Peabody College of Teachers, 1978.

910. Martinson, M. Mainstream educator training and regional center. In R. A. Johnson, R. F. Weatherman, & A. M. Rehman (Eds.), *Special education leadership series. Vol. IV: Handicapped youth and the mainstream educator.* Minneapolis, MN: Audio Visual Extension Service, University of Minnesota, 1975.

911. Maryland State Department of Education/Baltimore Office of Education. *A design for a continuum of special education services. Interim report.* Baltimore, MD: Author, 1971. (ERIC Document Reproduction Service No. ED 072 604)

912. Massachusetts Department of Education and Worcester Public Schools. *Mainstreaming: Integration of children with special needs into a regular classroom environment.* Bedford, MA: Institute for Educational Services, 1974.

913. _____. *Training programs for the teaching of children with special needs.* Boston, MA: Author, 1974.

914. Massachusetts Teachers' Association. *Open door in '74: Chapter 766.* Boston, MA: Author, 1974.

915. Massey, S., & Henderson, R. (Eds.). *The range of variability: Inservice design in special education.* Portsmouth, NH: New England Teacher Corp Network, 1977. (ERIC Document Reproduction Service No. ED 168 234)

916. Massie, D. Update on education of the handicapped. *Today's Education,* 1978, 67(3), 60-62, 73.

917. Maurer, A. Whatever happened to witches? *Journal of School Psychology,* 1972, *10,* 107-110.

918. May, B. J., & Furst, E. J. *Evaluation and revision of an inventory for measuring attitudes toward mainstreaming.* Fayetteville, AK: University of Arkansas, College of Education, 1977. (ERIC Document Reproduction Service No. ED 160 642)

919. May, B. P. P.L. 94-142 and vocational education: Parallel, picture, and prophecy. *Journal of Career Education,* 1978, *5,* 53-62.

920. *Media gets the message: An inservice package on P.L. 94-142 for special educators and media personnel.* Springfield, IL: Illinois State Office of Education, 1978. (ERIC Document Reproduction Service No. ED 158 731)

921. Meers, G. D. Roles for teachers of the handicapped. *School Shop,* 1978, *37*(10), 15, 17.

922. Meisels, S. J. First steps in mainstreaming; some questions and answers. *Young Children,* 1977, *33*(1), 4-13.

923.   _____. Open education and the integration of children with special needs. In M. J. Guralnick (Ed.), *Early intervention and the integration of handicapped and nonhandicapped children.* Baltimore, MD: University Park Press, 1978.

924.   _____. *Project LINC: Learning in integrated classrooms. Final program performance report and third annual interim report. July 1, 1975-June 30, 1978.* Medford, MA: Tufts University, n.d. (ERIC Document Reproduction Service No. ED 169 686)

925.   Meisgeier, C. The Houston plan: A program that works. In P. A. O'Donnell, & R. H. Bradfield (Eds.), *Mainstreaming: Controversy and consensus.* San Rafael, CA: Academic Therapy, 1976.

926.   _____. The training needs of regular education. In P. H. Mann (Ed.), *Mainstreaming special education.* Reston, VA: The Council for Exceptional Children, 1974.

927.   Melcher, J. W. Some questions from a school administrator. *Exceptional Children,* 1972, *38,* 547-551.

928.   Meltzer, D. R. Mainstreaming: As the parent sees it. *Volta Review,* 1978, *80,* 109-111.

929.   Menheusen, B. R., & Gromme, R. O. Science for handicapped children—why? *Science and Children,* 1976, *13*(6), 35-37.

930.   Menocal, A. The IQ test and classification: An inherently harmful situation. In P. A. O'Donnell, & R. H. Bradfield (Eds.), *Mainstreaming: Controversy and consensus.* San Rafael, CA: Academic Therapy, 1976.

931.   Merchant, D. (Ed.). *TEACH: Teacher education and children with handicaps, Vol. 1, No. 1.* Washington, D.C.: American Association of Colleges for Teacher Education, 1979. (ERIC Document Reproduction Service No. ED 170 297)

932.   Merlin, S. B., & Rogers, S. F. The role of the reading specialists in developing IEP's (individual education programs). *Reading Horizons,* 1980, *20,* 118-122.

933.   Merz, C. Mainstreaming as a natural experience. *Education Leadership,* 1980, *37,* 438-440.

934.   Merz, W. R., & Raske, D. E. *Least restrictive educational environment/pupil match.* Sacramento, CA: State Department of Education, 1978. (ERIC Document Reproduction Service No. ED 163 667)

935.   Metsker, C. *Hints and activities for mainstreaming.* New York, NY: Instructor, 1979.

936.   Meyen, E. L. Mainstreaming colleges of education. *Teacher Education and Special Education,* 1979, *2*(2), 5-8.

937.   _____, Vergason, G. A., & Whelan, R. J. (Eds.). *Alternatives for teaching exceptional children.* Denver, CO: Love Pub. Co., 1975.

938.   _____, Vergason, G. A., & Whelan, R. J. (Eds.). *Strategies for teaching exceptional children.* Denver, CO: Love Pub. Co., 1972.

939.   Michigan State Board of Education. *Program descriptions for special education.* Lansing, MI: Author, 1966. (ERIC Document Reproduction Service No. ED 012 977)

940.   Michigan State Department of Education. *Models for resource rooms.* Lansing, MI: Author, 1973. (ERIC Document Reproduction Service No. ED 094 500)

941.   Middleton, E. J., Morsink, C., & Cohen, S. Program graduates' perception of need for training in mainstreaming. *Exceptional Children,* 1979, *45,* 257-261.

942.   Milazzo, T. C. *Special class placement or how to destory in the name of help.* Paper presented at the 48th Annual Convention of the Council for Exceptional Children, Chicago, April 1970. (ERIC Document Reproduction Service No. ED 039 383)

943.   Milbauer, B. Mainstreaming puzzle. *Teacher,* 1977, *94*(9), 44-46.

944.   Milburn, J. F. Special education and regular class teacher attitudes regarding social behaviors of children: Steps toward the development of a social skills curriculum (Doctoral dissertation, The Ohio State University, 1974). *Dissertation Abstracts International, 35,* 5174A. (University Microfilms No. 75-03144)

945.   Miley, B. An integrated resource model. *Pointer,* 1973, *18,* 149-151.

946.   Millar, C. J., & Osborne, G. S. Friendships in an unstreamed school. *Scottish Educational Review,* 1978, *10,* 47-49.

947.   Miller, J. G., & Schoenfelder, D. S. A rational look at special class placement. *Journal of Special Education,* 1969, *3,* 397, 399.

948.   Miller, M. D. *Research designs and results. Demonstration center for language handicapped children.* Houston, TX: Education Service Center, Region 4, 1973. (ERIC Document Reproduction Service No. ED 096 792)

949.   Miller-Jacobs, S. *Mainstreaming special needs children into open settings.* Unpublished manuscript, 1975. (ERIC Document Reproduction Service No. ED 117 898)

950.   Mills, P. J. Use the handicapped law to help educate nonhandicapped kids, too. *American School Board Journal,* 1979, *166*(5), 29.

951. Milofsky, C. D. Schooling the kids no one wants; mainstreaming in Massachusetts. *New York Times Magazine,* January 2, 1977, pp. 24-25, 28, 33.

952. _____. Why special education isn't special. *Harvard Education Review,* 1974, *44,* 437-458.

953. Milwaukee Public Schools/Division of Curriculum and Instruction. *Second interim report of the broadly-based community study of exceptional children.* Mikwaukee, WI: Author, 1972. (ERIC Document Reproduction Service No. ED 071 222)

954. Minor, J. *Can school systems respond—perspectives from line administrators.* Paper presented at the 4th Annual Invitational Special Education Leadership Conference, Minneapolis, MN, 1974. Also in R. A. Johnson, R. F. Weatherman, & A. M. Rehman (Ed.), *Special education leadership series. Vol. IV: Handicapped youth and the mainstream educator.* Minneapolis, MN: Audio Visual Extension Service, University of Minnesota, 1975.

955. Mitchell, M. M. Teacher attitudes. *The High School Journal,* 1976, *59,* 302-312.

956. Molloy, L. The changing mandate for special education. In one out of ten: School planning for the handicapped. *Education Digest,* 1975, *40*(7), 6-9.

957. _____. The handicapped child in everyday classroom. Teachers and designers are discovering that facilities for the handicapped added to the classroom enrich the lives and learning of all children. *Phi Delta Kappan,* 1975, *56,* 337-340.

958. _____. Law and the handicapped. *Science and Children,* 1976, *13*(6), 7-10.

959. Monaco, T. M. Mainstreaming, who? *Science and Children,* 1976, *13*(6), 11.

960. _____. *Student research report—mainstreaming.* Houston, TX: University of Houston, College of Education, n.d.

961. _____, & Chiappeta, E. L. Identifying competencies for mainstream teachers through the perceptions of state directors of special instruction. *Education,* 1978, *99,* 59-63.

962. Monroe County Intermediate School District. *Strategies and techniques for mainstreaming: A resource room handbook.* Monroe, MI: Author, 1975.

963. Monroe, G. E. Introducing provisions for perceptually handicapped learners to regular public school curricula (Doctoral Dissertation, Michigan State University, 1966). *Dissertation Abstracts International, 27,* 2405A. (University Microfilms No. 66-14153)

964. Mopsick, S., & Agard, J. A. *Handbook for parents of handicapped children.* Cambridge, MA: Abt Books, 1978.

965. Moran, M. R. *Assessment of the exceptional learner in the regular classroom.* Denver, CO: Love Pub. Co., 1978.

966. Morgan, G. Integration v. segregation in Ontario. *Special Education: Forward Trends,* 1977, *4,* 18-21.

967. Morris, J. T. Mainstreaming/integration in the province of Ontario (Doctoral dissertation, University of Oregon, 1977). *Dissertation Abstracts International, 39,* 183A. (University Microfilms No. 78-10209)

968. Morris, P., & McCauley, R. W. *Placement of handicapped children by Canadian mainstream administrators and teachers: A Rucker-Gable survey.* Paper presented at the 55th Annual International Convention of the Council for Exceptional Children, Atlanta, GA, April 1977. (ERIC Document Reproduction Service No. ED 139 139)

969. Morrison, N., Spera, F. G., Menne, M., Backes, J. M., McCorkle, M. B., & Welcher, R. S. Six principals talk about P.L. 94-142. *National Elementary Principal,* 1978, *58*(1), 21-24.

970. Morse, W. C. The helping teacher/crisis teacher concept. *Focus on Exceptional Children,* 1976, *8*(4), 1-11.

971. _____. Special pupils in regular classes: Problems of accommodation. In M. C. Reynolds, & M. D. Davis (Eds.), *Exceptional children in regular classrooms.* Minneapolis, MN: University of Minnesota, Department of Audio Visual Extension, 1971.

972. Mosley, W. J., & Sitko, M. C. *A model program for training teachers of the mildly handicapped. Teacher Education Forum, V. 4, No. 4.* Bloomington, IN: Indiana University, Bloomington, School of Education, 1976. (ERIC Document Reproduction Service No. ED 128 299)

973. _____, & Spicker, H. H. Mainstreaming for the educationally deprived. *Theory into Practice,* 1975, *14,* 73-81.

974. Mowery, C. W., & Replogle, A. A new language barrier to hurdle. *Early Years,* 1977, *7*(9), 50, 66-67.

975. Moynahan, T. Vocational education and the handicapped. *Today's Education,* 1980, *69*(2), 47-48.

976. Mueller, M. Research and education of the handicapped. *Exceptional Children,* 1976, *43,* 151-153.

977. Mulholland, A. M., & Hourihan, J. P. Parents and due process in education of the handicapped: A case history. *Volta Review,* 1977, *79,* 303-313.

978.   Muller, P. Are pupils in special education schools dull? *Praxis der Kinderpsychiatrie,* 1972, *21*(3), 86-89.

979.   Munson, H. L., Miller, J. K., Gargantiel, C. W., & Huang, J. *Pupil selection and program development problems in mainstreaming the handicapped child.* Paper presented at the Annual Meeting of the American Educational Research Association, Toronto, Ontario, Canada, March 1978. (ERIC Document Reproduction Service No. ED 154 552)

980.   Murphy, P. *A special way for the special child in the regular classroom.* San Rafael, CA: Academic Therapy Pub., 1976.

981.   Myers, L. K. H. An evaluation of selected Illinois public school administrators' attitudes toward and knowledges of mainstreaming handicapped children (Doctoral dissertation, Southern Illinois University, 1975). *Dissertation Abstracts International,* 1975, *36,* 7992A. (University Microfilms No. 76-13277)

982.   Myers, R. Something special. *Journal of Teacher Education,* 1978, *29*(6), 9.

983.   National Advisory Committee on the Handicapped. Education of the handicapped today. *American Education,* 1976, *12*(5), 6-8.

984.   _____. *First class citizenship for handicapped people: 1974 report of the National Advisory Committee on the Handicapped.* Washington, D.C.: Government Printing Office, 1974. (ERIC Document Reproduction Service No. ED 102 768)

985.   _____. IEP and nonacademic services. *American Education,* 1977, *13*(9), 23-25.

986.   _____. *The individualized education program: Key to an appropriate education for the handicapped child. (1977 annual report).* Washington, D.C.: Department of Health, Education and Welfare, 1977. (ERIC Document Reproduction Service No. ED 149 516)

987.   _____. *The unfinished revolution: Education for the handicapped. (1976 annual report).* Washington, D.C.: Department of Health, Education and Welfare, 1976. (ERIC Document Reproduction Service No. ED 127 738)

988.   National Advisory Council on Education Professions Development. *Mainstreaming; helping teachers meet the challenge.* Washington, D.C.: Author, 1976. (ERIC Document Reproduction Service No. ED 127 271)

989.   National Association of State Directors of Special Education. *An analysis of P.L. 94-142.* Washington, D.C.: Author, 1976.

990. National Education Association. Mainstreaming handicapped students with regular students: Are teachers prepared? *Briefing Memo: Instruction and Professional Development,* August 1975, p. 8.

991. _____. *Mainstreaming the handicapped into the regular classroom: Are teachers prepared? Briefing Memo No. 1.* Washington, D.C.: Author, 1975.

992. _____. *Project 1975: Educational neglect. On-site and research reports.* Paper presented at the Conference on Educational Neglect, Washington, D.C., February 1975. (ERIC Document Reproduction Service No. ED 101 925)

993. National Information Center for the Handicapped. *It's okay to be different: Memo on mainstreaming.* Washington, D.C.: Closer Look, n.d.

994. National School Public Relations Association. *Educating children with special needs: Current trends in school policies and programs.* Arlington, VA: Authors, 1974.

995. _____. *Preschool breakthrough: What works in early childhood education.* Washington, D.C.: Author, 1970.

996. Nazzaro, J. N. Innovation in teacher training: A conversation with Melvyn I. Semmel. *Education and Training of the Mentally Retarded,* 1976, *11,* 353-360.

997. _____. *Second dimension: Special education administrators view the field.* Reston, VA: The Council for Exceptional Children, 1973. (ERIC Document Reproduction Service No. ED 073 585)

998. NEA resolution 77-33: Education for all handicapped children. *Today's Education,* 1977, *66*(3), 25.

999. NEA resolution 77-33: Education for all handicapped children. *Today's Education,* 1977, *66*(4), 57.

1000. NEA resolution 78-37: Education for all handicapped children. *Today's Education,* 1978, *67*(3), 62.

1001. NEA warns of hazards in "mainstreaming." *Report on Education Research,* 1975, *7*(22), 7.

1002. Neale, M. D. Social alignment and educability. *Deficience Mentale/Mental Retardation,* 1973, *23*(1), 6-10.

1003. Neff, H. B., & Pilch, J. *Teaching handicapped children easily; a manual for the average classroom teacher without specialized training.* Springfield, IL: Thomas Co., 1976.

1004.   Neisworth, J. T., & Madle, R. A. Normalized day care: A philosophy and approach to integrating exceptional and normal children. *Child Care Quarterly,* 1975, *4,* 163-171.

1005.   Nelson, C. C., & Schmidt, L. J. Forum: The question of the efficacy of special classes. *Exceptional Children,* 1971, *37,* 381-384.

1006.   Nesbitt, J. A. *Educating the handicapped child for leisure fulfillment. Institute Report, National Institute on Community Recreation for the Handicapped.* Rev. ed. Iowa City, IA: Iowa University, 1978. (ERIC Document Reproduction Service No. ED 154 593)

1007.   Neumann, E. M. & Harris, A. C. *Comparisons of attitudes toward mainstreaming preschool and kindergarten children with special needs.* Sacramento, CA: California State Department of Education, 1977. (ERIC Document Reproduction Service No. ED 148 092)

1008.   Nevin, A. Special education administration competencies required of the general education administrator. *Exceptional Children,* 1979, *45,* 363-365.

1009.   New aid for handicapped children. *U.S. News & World Report,* December 15, 1975, p. 73.

1010.   New day for the handicapped; mainstreaming. *Time,* September 19, 1977, p. 109.

1011.   *The new education law: What does it mean?* Washington, D.C.: Closer Look, 1977.

1012.   New England Special Education Instructional Materials Center. Boston University. *Descriptions of innovative training programs directed toward: 1. Integration of children with special needs in regular classrooms; 2. Serving severely handicapped children.* Boston, MA: Author, 1973. (ERIC Document Reproduction Service No. ED 081 146)

1013.   New law to provide all disabled children an educational opportunity. *Accent on Living,* 1976, *21*(2), 84-87.

1014.   Newberger, D. A. Situational socialization: An effective interaction component of the mainstreaming reintegration construct (Doctoral dissertation, University of Houston, 1976). *Dissertation Abstracts International,* 1977, *37,* 5041A. (University Microfilms No. 77-01521)

1015.   Newcomer, P. L. Special education services for the mildly handicapped: Beyond a diagnostic and remedial model. *Journal of Special education,* 1977, *11,* 153-165; discussion followup, 1977, *11,* 167-200.

1016. Newman, G., & Wilkins, L. T. Sources of deviance in the schooling process. *International Review of Education*, 1974, *20*, 306-319.

1017. Newsline: New help for the handicapped. *Psychology Today*, 1975, *8*(11), 35-36.

1018. Newsnotes: Minimum competency testing and the handicapped child. *Phi Delta Kappan*, 1978, *59*, 646-647.

1019. Niederer. M. Media/information/services for exceptional students. *Illinois Libraries*, 1977, *59*, entire issue.

1020. NJEA policy statement on mainstreaming. *NJEA Review*, 1977, *50*(9), 19.

1021. Noble, V. N., & Kampwirth, T. J. PL 94-142 and counselor activities. *Elementary School Guidance and Counseling*, 1979, *13*, 164-169.

1022. _____, & Kampwirth, T. J. *Pupil personnel services and P.L. 94-142.* Unpublished manuscript, 1977. (ERIC Document Reproduction Service No. ED 159 512)

1023. Noli, P. M. *Implications of class size research.* Paper presented at the 112th Annual Meeting of the American Association of School Administrators, Anaheim, CA, February 1980. (ERIC Document Reproduction Service No. ED 184 237)

1024. Nordquist, V. A behavioral approach to the analysis of peer interactions. In M. J. Guralnick (Ed.), *Early intervention and the integration of handicapped and nonhandicapped children.* Baltimore, MD: University Park Press, 1978.

1025. de Noronha, M., & de Noronha, Z. E. F. *Family involvement makes education more economic.* Paper presented at the 1st World Congress on Future Special Education, Stirling, Scotland, June-July 1978. (ERIC Document Reproduction Service No. ED 158 481)

1026. de Noronha, Z. E. F. *Mothers involved in mainstreaming.* Paper presented at the 1st World Congress on Future Special Education, Stirling, Scotland, June-July 1978. (ERIC Document Reproduction Service No. ED 158 463)

1027. Novak, B. J., Wicas, E. A., & Elias, G. S. School counselor and retarded youth—opportunity or threat? *Personnel and Guidance Journal*, 1977, *56*, 131, 133.

1028. Nugent, T. J. More than ramps and braille. *American Education*, 1978, *14*(7), 11-18.

1029. Nuschy, M. J. Points of view of Texas superintendents and special education supervisors with respect to mainstreaming (Doctoral dissertation, East Texas State University, 1976). *Dissertation Abstracts International*, 1977, *37*, 4287A. (University Microfilms No. 77-00491)

1030. Nystrom, R. K. Standardized achievement measurement with the educationally handicapped—normalization or further segregation? (Doctoral dissertation, University of Southern California, 1976). *Dissertation Abstracts International,* 1977, *37,* 2082A.

1031. Ober, S., & Heller, J. Typing for the handicapped: Methods and materials. *Business Education World,* 1978, *59*(1), 3-5.

1032. Ochoa, A. S., & Shuster, S. K. *Social studies in the mainstreamed classroom, K-6.* Boulder, CO: ERIC Clearinghouse for Social Studies/Social Science Education and Social Science Education Consortium, Inc., 1980. (ERIC Document Reproduction Service No. ED 184 911)

1033. O'Connor, K. B. *The why and how of supportive help for the student in the mainstream.* Paper presented at the Alexander Graham Bell Association Convention, St. Louis, MO, June, 1978.

1034. O'Donnell, P. A., & Bradfield, R. H. (Eds.). *Mainstreaming: Controversy and consensus.* San Rafael, CA: Academic Therapy, 1976.

1035. O'Donnell, T. An advocate's view: The role of the surrogate parent. *Amicus,* 1977, *2*(4), 28-30.

1036. _____. Sources of law: Right to an equal educational opportunity. *Amicus,* 1977, *2*(3), 22-26.

1037. _____. Unmet legislative needs. *Volta Review,* 1977, *79,* 335-342.

1038. O'Leary, S. G., & Schneider, M. R. Special class placement for conduct problem children. *Exceptional Children,* 1977, *44,* 24-30.

1039. Olson, L., & Weckler, E. *Mainstreaming USA: 1977 update. Project impact.* Paper presented at the 55th Annual International Convention of The Council for Exceptional Children, Atlanta, GA, April 1977. (ERIC Document Reproduciton Service No. ED 139 218)

1040. Orelove, F. P. Administering education for the severely handicapped after P.L. 94-142. *Phi Delta Kappan,* 1978, *59,* 699-702.

1041. Osguthorpe, R. T. The school psychologist as a tutorial systems supervisor. *Psychology in the Schools,* 1979, *16,* 88-92.

1042. Ottina, J. R. *The federal commitment to education for the handicapped.* Commissioner's address at the 52nd Annual Convention of the Council for Exceptional Children, New York, NY, April 1974. (ERIC Document Reproduction Service No. ED 093 112)

1043. Overline, H. M. *Mainstreaming—making it happen.* Sacramento, CA: California State Department of Education, 1977. (ERIC Document Reproduction Service No. ED 149 514)

1044. Ovnik, M. A. Contract teaching. *Science and Children*, 1976, *13*(6), 44-45.

1045. Padover, A. Some words are not healthy for children and other living things. *Academic Therapy*, 1973, *8*, 437-445.

1046. Palacino, V., Jr. A comparative study of the effectiveness of simulation in changing regular classroom teachers attitudes toward the integration of exceptional children into the regular classroom (Doctoral dissertation, Michigan State University, 1973). *Dissertation Abstracts International, 34*, 3218A. (University Microfilms No. 73-29757)

1047. Palmer, D. J. Regular classroom teachers' attributions and instructional prescriptions for handicapped and non-handicapped pupils. *Journal of Special Education*, 1979, *13*, 325-337.

1048. Pappanikou, A. J., Kochanek, T. T., & Reich, M. L. Continuity and unity in special education. *Phi Delta Kappan*, 1974, *55*, 546-548.

1049. Parish, T. S., Baker, S. K., Arheart, K. L., & Adamchak, P. G. Normal and exceptional children's attitudes toward themselves and one another. *Journal of Psychology*, 1980, *104*, 249-253.

1050. _____, & Copeland, T. F. Teachers' and students' attitudes in mainstreamed classrooms. *Psychological Reports*, 1978, *43*(1), 54.

1051. _____, Ohlsen, R. L., & Parish, J. G. A look at mainstreaming in light of children's attitudes toward the handicapped. *Perceptual and Motor Skills*, 1978, *46*, 1019-21.

1052. Park, C. C. Elly and the right to education. *Phi Delta Kappan*, 1974, *55*, 535-537.

1053. Parker, C. A. (Ed.). *Psychological consultation: Helping teachers meet special needs.* Minneapolis, MN: University of Minnesota, Leadership Training Institute for Special Education, 1975. (ERIC Document Reproduction Service No. ED 107 092)

1054. Parker, G. O. You put whom in my typing class? *Journal of Business Education*, 1977, *53*(3), 113-115.

1055. Parker, L. G., & Mohr, L. L. *Secondary handicapped students? I thought they were all cured!* Paper presented at the 1st World Congress on Future Special Education, Stirling, Scotland, June-July 1978. (ERIC Document Reproduction Service No. ED 158 474)

1056. _____, & Stodden, R. A. Attitudes toward the handicapped. *Journal for Special Education of the Mentally Retarded*, 1977, *14*, 24-28, 34.

1057.   Parks, A. L., & Rousseau, M. K. *The public law supporting main-streaming: A guide for teachers and parents.* Austin, TX: Learning Concepts, 1977.

1058.   Parlato, S., Jr. Read any good films lately? *Audiovisual Instruction,* 1977, *22*(7), 30-31.

1059.   Partridge, D. L. *The least restrictive alternative: A proposed curriculum model.* Paper presented at the 1st World Congress on Future Special Education, Stirling, Scotland, June-July 1978. (ERIC Document Reproduction Service No. ED 157 352)

1060.   Pate, J. Viewpoint. *Early Years,* 1977, 7(9), 10, 12, 14, 34.

1061.   Patrick, W. L. New responsibility: Tending to needs of the handicapped. *Journalism Educator,* 1978, *33*(1), 18-19.

1062.   Paul, J. L., Turnbull, A. P., & Cruikshank, W. M. *Mainstreaming: A practical guide.* Syracuse, NY: Syracuse University Press, 1977. (ERIC Document Reproduction Service No. ED 157 606)

1063.   Payne, R., & Murray, C. J. Principals' attitudes toward integration of the handicapped. *Exceptional Children,* 1974, *41*, 123-125.

1064.   Pecheone, R. L., & Gable, R. K. *The identification of inservice training needs and their relationship to teacher demographic characteristics, attitude toward, and knowledge of mildly handicapped children. Research report series.* Paper presented at the Annual Meeting of the American Educational Research Association, Toronto, Canada, March 1978. (ERIC Document Reproduction Service No. ED 156 628)

1065.   Pedrini, B. C., & Pedrini, D. T. *Special education: A position paper.* Omaha, NE: University of Nebraska at Omaha, 1973. (ERIC Document Reproduction Service No. ED 085 927)

1066.   *PEECH OUTREACH (A program for early education of children with handicaps) 1977-78 final report.* Wichita Falls, TX: Education Service Center, Region 9, 1978. (ERIC Document Reproduction Service No. ED 161 204)

1067.   Pellant, W. R. Comparison of individualization of instruction between special education classes and regular education classes in Idaho (Doctoral dissertation, University of Idaho, 1972). *Dissertation Abstracts International,* 1972, *33*, 2201A. (University Microfilms No. 72-30513)

1068.   *People . . . just like you. About handicaps and handicapped people (an activity guide).* Washington, D.C.: President's Committee on Employment of the Handicapped, Committee on Youth Development, 1978. (ERIC Document Reproduction Service No. ED 150 809)

1069.   Pepper, F. Teaching the American Indian Child in mainstream set-
        tings. In R. L. Jones, & F. B. Wilderson (Eds.), *Mainstreaming and
        the minority child.* Reston, VA: The Council for Exceptional Chil-
        dren, 1976.

1070.   Perelman, P. F. *Observations on integration and mainstreaming in
        three different cultures.* Paper presented at the First World Con-
        gress on Future Special Education, Stirling, Scotland, June-July
        1978. (ERIC Document Reproduction Service No. ED 157 292)

1071.   _____, Nevin, A., & Knight, M. F. *The consulting teacher pro-
        gram: Ten years later.* Burlington, VT: University of Vermont, Col-
        lege of Education, 1978. (ERIC Document Reproduction Service
        No. ED 164 460)

1072.   Perier, O. The integrated school. *Scandinavian Audiology,* 1972,
        2, 69-75.

1073.   Perlman, M., & Dubrovin, V. The exceptional child in the regular
        classroom. *Curriculum Review,* 1978, *17,* 258-259.

1074.   Peters, R. S. A study of the attitudes of elementary teachers toward
        exceptional children in the mainstream (Doctoral dissertation, Uni-
        versity of Maryland, 1977). *Dissertation Abstracts International,*
        1977, *38,* 5396A. (University Microfilms No. 78-00396)

1075.   Peterson, C., Peterson, J., & Scriven, G. Peer imitation by
        nonhandicapped preschoolers. *Exceptional Children,* 1977, *43,*
        223-224.

1076.   Peterson, N. L., & Haralick, J. G. Integration of handicapped and
        nonhandicapped preschoolers: An analysis of play behavior and
        social interaction. *Education and Training of the Mentally Retarded,*
        1977, *12,* 235-245.

1077.   Peterson, R. L. *Mainstreaming: A working bibliography.* 2d. ed.
        Minneapolis, MN: University of Minnesota, Leadership Training
        Institute/Special Education, 1976. (ERIC Document Reproduction
        Service No. ED 127 745)

1078.   _____. *Mainstreaming training systems, materials, and resources:
        A working list.* 3d ed. Minneapolis, MN: University of Minnesota,
        Leadership Training Institute/Special Education, 1976. (ERIC
        Document Reproduction Service No. ED 127 746)

1079.   Petriwskyj, A. Integrating handicapped pre-school children.
        Australian Journal of Early Childhood, 1977, *2*(3), 20-21.

1080.   Pettit, N., & Robinson, R. D. The impact of mainstreaming on
        pre-service reading education. *Reading Horizons,* 1977, *17,*
        198-200.

1081.   Phelps, L. A., & Halloran, W. D. Legislation and special needs
         teacher education: The Education for All Handicapped Children
         Act of 1975 (P.L. 94-142) and the Rehabilitation Act of 1973 (P.L.
         93-516). *Journal of Industrial Teacher Education,* 1977, *14*(4),
         23-27.

1082.   Phelps, W. R. *Responses of teachers and non-teachers regarding
         placement of exceptional children. Final report.* Charleston, WV:
         West Virginia State Board of Vocational Education, Division of
         Vocational Rehabilitation, 1974. (ERIC Document Reproduction
         Service No. ED 102 743)

1083.   Physical education for handicapped children. *American Education,*
         1974, *10*(5), 30.

1084.   Pieper, E. J. Preparing children for a handicapped classmate.
         Instructor, 1974, *84*(1), 128-129.

1085.   _____. Toward real integration. *Exceptional Parent,* 1974, *4*(4),
         5-6.

1086.   Pierson, D. E. The Brookline Early Education Project: Model for a
         new education priority. *Childhood Education,* 1974, *50,* 132-134.

1087.   Pipes, L. (Ed.). *Teachers talk: P.L. 94-142 reaches the classoom. A
         look at early reactions to the Education for All Handicapped Chil-
         dren Act.* Washington, D.C.: ERIC Clearinghouse on Teacher
         Education and the National Education Association, 1978. (ERIC
         Document Reproduction Service No. ED 150 121)

1088.   Pisano, M. Public Law 94-142: Reading, writing and rehabilita-
         tion. *SA, The Magazine for San Antonio,* 1978, *2*(4), 35-42.

1089.   Planakis, A., & Harris, S. S. *Commentary on mainstreaming.* New
         York, NY: United Federation of Teachers, 1975.

1090.   Platt, N., & Cook, N. Celebrating the similarities: An experience
         in mainstreaming preschoolers. *Pointer,* 1976, *20*(3), 10-16.

1091.   Plummer, B. A. *Integration of preschool severely handicapped
         children.* Fairfield, CA: Solano County School System, 1977.
         (ERIC Document Reproduction Service No. ED 148 091)

1092.   Podell, S. M. The effectiveness of developmental training. *Opto-
         metric Weekly,* 1976, *67*(40), 1074-1076.

1093.   Pokorni, J. *CDT—the comprehensive development teams: Meeting
         the needs of mainstreamed handicapped younger children.* Paper
         presented at the 55th Annual International Convention of The
         Council for Exceptional Children, Atlanta, GA, April 1977. (ERIC
         Document Reproduction Service No. ED 139 158)

1094. *Policies and procedures manual for special education in Oklahoma.* Oklahoma City, OK: Oklahoma State Department of Education, 1980. (ERIC Document Reproduction Service No. ED 181 692)

1095. Policies for the development of written individualized education programs. *Volta Review*, 1977, *79*, 347-348. Also in *Exceptional Children*, 1977, *43*, 554-555.

1096. Pollock, N., & Taylor, M. *Formulating intervention strategies to maintain the mildly handicapped student in the regular classroom.* Paper presented at the 55th Annual International Convention of The Council for Exceptional Children, Atlanta, GA, April 1977. (ERIC Document Reproduction Service No. ED 139 155)

1097. Porter, R. B. If not special class, what? *The Training School Bulletin*, 1968, *65*(3), 87-88.

1098. _____. The significance of similarities between education and special education. *Contemporary Education*, 1971, *42*, 109-114.

1099. Post, T. R., Humphreys, A. H., & Pearson, M. Laboratory-based mathematics and science for the handicapped child. *Science and Children*, 1976, *13*(6), 41-43.

1100. Potter, W. H., & Tolley, W. R. *Development and implementation of an interagency program for emotionally handicapped children. Practicum report.* Fort Lauderdale, FL: Nova University, 1977. (ERIC Document Reproduction Service No. ED 169 689)

1101. Powell, J. V. Mainstreaming becomes a reality through continuous progress programs. *Education*, 1980, *100*, 382-385.

1102. _____. Mainstreaming eight types of exceptionalities. *Education*, 1978, *99*, 55-58.

1103. Powell, T. H. Educating all disabled children: A practical guide to P.L. 94-142. *Exceptional Parent*, 1978, *8*(4), L3-L6.

1104. Powers, L. Science and art in mainstream education: Toward the normalization of the handicapped child. *Amicus*, 1977, *2*(4), 37-41.

1105. Prehm, H. J. *Personnel training to facilitate mainstreaming.* Paper presented at the 55th Annual International Convention, Atlanta, GA, April 1977. (ERIC Document Reproduction Service No. ED 139 209)

1106. _____, & Goldschmidt, S. Mainstreaming handicapped children and related legal implications. *Oregon School Study Council Bulletin*, 1974/75, *8*(4&5).

1107. *The preparation of regular classroom teachers to work with students with special learning problems: A preservice training project.* Greeley, CO: University of Northern Colorado, 1976.

1108.   *A prevention-intervention model for student's learning and behavior problems. Final report, July 1974-July 1975.* Nashville, TN: Davidson County Metropolitan Public Schools, Tennessee State Department of Mental Health, and Child and Youth Development Institute, 1975. (ERIC Document Reproduction Service No. ED 131 634)

1109.   Price, M., Weiner, R. B., & D'Ippolito, M. *Project partners in education: Final report.* Blue Bell, PA: Montgomery County Intermediate Unit 23, 1978. (ERIC Document Reproduction Service No. ED 168 274)

1110.   Priddy, D. Advocacy: An emerging role for special educators. *Educational Perspectives,* 1974, *13*(3), 27-29.

1111.   Priest, L. Integrating the disabled into aquatics programs. *Journal of Physical Education and Recreation,* 1979, *50*(2), 57, 59.

1112.   *A primer on due process: Education decisions for handicapped children.* Reston, VA: The Council for Exceptional Children, 1975.

1113.   *Principal's guide to mainstreaming.* Waterford, CT: Croft-NEI Publications, 1975.

1114.   Priorities of the U.S. Office of Education; a conversation with Ernest L. Boyer on exceptional child education. *Exceptional Children,* 1978, *44,* 570-574.

1115.   *A procedural manual for the Cooperstown model: A project to serve preschool children with special needs.* Cooperstown, NY: Opportunities for Otsego, Inc., 1976.

1116.   *Proceedings: National Training Workshop on Head Start services to handicapped children. St. Louis, MO, May 22-24, 1973.* Washington, D.C.: Office of Child Development, 1973. (ERIC Document Reproduction Service No. ED 100 084)

1117.   Proctor, D. I. An investigation of the relationships between knowledge of exceptional children, kind and amount of experience, and attitudes toward their classroom integration (Doctoral Dissertation, Michigan State University, 1967). *Dissertation Abstracts,* 1967, *28,* 1721A. (University Microfilms No. 67-14538)

1118.   Proger, B. B. *IEP handbook: A teacher manual for the implementation of Public Law 94-142. (Project Aid: Assistance for the IEP Development.)* Blue Bell, PA: Montgomery County Intermediate Unit 23, 1978. (ERIC Document Reproduction Service No. ED 150 807)

1119.   _____. *A manual for local education agency (LEA) representatives. (Project Aid: Assistance for the IEP Development.)* Blue Bell, PA: Montgomery County Intermediate Unit 23, 1978. (ERIC Document Reproduction Service No. ED 150 808)

1120. *Project CAREER/Handicapped. Final report.* Boston, MA: Massachusetts State Department of Education, Division of Occupational Education, n.d. (ERIC Document Reproduction Service No. ED 121 932)

1121. *Project mainstream: San Mateo Union High School District.* San Mateo, CA: San Mateo Union High School District, 1979. (ERIC Document Reproduction Service No. ED 170 519)

1122. *Project team: Teacher encouragement to activate mainstreaming. I. Administrative and resource personnel kit.* Fullerton, CA: Fullerton Union High School District, 1977. (ERIC Document Reproduction Service No. ED 149 494)

1123. *Project team: Teacher encouragement to activate mainstreaming. II. Teacher handbook.* Fullerton, CA: Fullerton Union High School District, 1977. (ERIC Document Reproduction Service No. ED 149 495)

1124. *Project team: Teacher encouragement to activate mainstreaming. Final report.* Fullerton, CA: Fullerton Union High School District, 1977. (ERIC Document Reproduction Service No. ED 149 496)

1125. Prouty, R. W. *Diagnostic-prescriptive teacher project.* Paper presented at the Special Study Institute, Washington, D.C., October 1971. (ERIC Document Reproduction Service No. ED 060 609)

1126. _____, & F. M. McGarry. The diagnostic/prescriptive teacher. In J. W. Schifani (Ed.), *Contemporary issues in mainstreaming handicapped citizens.* Dubuque, IA: Kendall/Hunt Pub., 1976.

1127. Provincialism has many dimensions. *Pennsylvania School Journal,* 1975, *124,* 15-17.

1128. Przewlocki, L. E. *Boston College's integrated curriculum. Preserving the past, responding to the present, anticipating the future.* Unpublished manuscript, 1977. (ERIC Document Reproduction Service No. ED 155 130)

1129. P.L. 94-142 and teachers. *Today's Education,* 1977, 66(4) 57.

1130. *Public Law 94-142, 94th Congress, S.6, Nov. 29, 1975: An act to amend the Education of the Handicapped Act to provide educational assistance to all handicapped children, and for other purposes.* Washington, D.C.: Government Printing Office 1975. (ERIC Document Reproduction Service No. ED 116 425)

1131. *P.L. 94-142, "Not just a law—a darn good idea." A resource packet for use in the conference: Advancing the handicapped and school administration.* Des Moines, IA: Drake University and Midwest Regional Resource Center, 1977. (ERIC Document Reproduction Service No. ED 161 188)

1132. *P.L. 94-142: Related federal legislation for handicapped children and implications for coordination.* Washington, D.C.: National Education Association, 1978.

1133. *P.L. 94-142—The Education for All Handicapped Children Act.* Reston, VA: The Council for Exceptional Children, 1976.

1134. *The public law supporting mainstreaming (Mainstreaming Training Series). Description of teacher inservice education materials.* Washington, D.C.: NEA Projection Utilization of Inservice Education R & D Outcomes, 1979. (ERIC Document Reproduction Service No. ED 173 347)

1135. Public policy and the education of exceptional children. Reston, VA: The Council for Exceptional Children, 1976.

1136. Pugmire, J., & Farrer, K. *A program to assist educational personnel to teach students of wide variability in regular classrooms. Director's annual progress report (July 1, 1970 to June 30, 1971).* Logan, UT: Utah State University, 1971. (ERIC Document Reproduction Service No. ED 054 069)

1137. Punzo, R. A., Jr., & Caetano, A. P. *A full service model for implementing P.L. 94-142: A team planning approach.* Paper presented at the Annual Meeting of the National Association of Elementary School Principals, Miami Beach, FL, April 1980. (ERIC Document Reproduction Service No. ED 185 700)

1138. Putnam, R. W. Books can introduce your class to the mainstreamed child. *Learning,* 1978, 7(2), 118-120.

1139. *Puzzled about 766? Evaluation and planning.* Boston, MA: Massachusetts Teachers Association, 1974.

1140. *Puzzled about 766? Identification and assessment.* Boston, MA: Massachusetts Teachers Association, 1974.

1141. *Puzzled about 766? Mainstreaming.* Boston, MA: Massachusetts Teachers Association, 1974.

1142. Quick, C. *Procedures and processes in the identification, referral, assessment and programming of infants and preschool handicapped children.* Paper presented at the Alexander Graham Bell Association for the Deaf Convention, St. Louis, MO, June 1978.

1143. Rabin, J. Placement in special classes: The defendant's viewpoint, the Larry P. case. In P. A. O'Donnell, & R. H. Bradfield (Eds.), *Mainstreaming: Controversy and consensus.* San Rafael, CA: Academic Therapy, 1976.

1144. Rafael, B. Early education for multihandicapped children. *Children Today,* 1973, 2(1), 22-26.

1145. Rafferty, B. F. *Special education for the children of our cities—Philadelphia.* Paper presented at the 57th Annual International Convention of the Council for Exceptional Children, Dallas, TX, April 1979. (ERIC Document Reproduction Service No. ED 171 029)

1146. Rainear, A. D. *Resource room approach to mainstreaming: Supplemental manual of representative materials.* Pitman, NJ: Educational Improvement Center, n.d. (ERIC Document Reproduction Service No. ED 111 125)

1147. _____, & McCool, J. *Resource room approach to mainstreaming: Learning center: Integrated alternative to special education.* Pitman, NJ: Educational Improvement Center, and Blue Anchor, NJ: Winslow Township Public Schools, 1974. (ERIC Document Reproduction Service No. ED 111 124)

1148. Ramirez, B., & Smith, B. J. Law review: Federal mandates for the handicapped: Implications for American Indian children. *Exceptional Children,* 1978, *44,* 521-528.

1149. Randolph, L. OCD's policy issuance to local Head Start: Identify, recruit, and serve handicapped children. *Exceptional Children,* 1973, *40,* 46-47.

1150. Raph, J. *Early childhood education interdepartmental project.* Paper presented at the Special Study Institute, Washington, D.C., October 1971. (ERIC Document Reproduction Service No. ED 060 609)

1151. Rausher, S. A. Mainstreaming: A return to yesteryear? *Childhood Education,* 1976, *53*(2), 89-93.

1152. Rauth, M. *The Education for All Handicapped Children Act (P.L. 94-142); preserving both children's and teachers' rights.* Washington, D.C.: American Federation of Teachers, 1978. (ERIC Document Reproduction Service No. ED 162 979)

1153. _____. *A guide to understanding the Education for All Handicapped Children Act (P.L. 94-142).* Washington, D.C.: American Federation of Teachers, 1978. (ERIC Document Reproduction Service No. ED 162 980)

1154. _____. Mainstreaming: A river to nowhere or a promising current? *American Teacher,* 1976, *60*(8), 1-4.

1155. _____. *Mainstreaming: A river to nowhere or a promising current? A special report to the AFT task force on educational issues.* Washington, D.C: American Federation of Teachers, 1978. (ERIC Document Reproduction Services No. ED 162 976)

1156.   *Reaching the preschool handicapped child.* New York, NY: New
York State Department of Education, Division for Handicapped
Children, 1972. (ERIC Document Reproduction Service No. ED
069 086)

1157.   Rebore, R. W. Faculty leadership in implementing Public Law
94-142. *Education,* 1980, *100,* 295-297.

1158.   _____. Public Law 94-142 and the building principal. *National
Association for Secondary School Principals Bulletin,* 1979, *63,*
26-30.

1159.   Redden, M. R. An investigation of mainstreaming competencies of
regular elementary teachers (Doctoral dissertation, University of
Kentucky, 1976). *Dissertation Abstracts International,* 1976, *37,*
3322A. (University Microfilms No. 76-28120)

1160.   _____, & Blackhurst, A. E. Mainstreaming competency specifica-
tions for elementary teachers. *Exceptional Children,* 1978, *44,*
615-617.

1161.   _____, & Malcolm, S. M. A move toward the mainstream.
Science and Children, 1976, *13*(6), 14.

1162.   Reger, R. How can we influence teacher-training programs? *The
Journal of Special Education,* 1974, *9,* 7-13.

1163.   _____. Resource rooms: Change agents or guardians of the status
quo? *Journal of Special Education,* 1972, *6,* 355-359.

1164.   _____. What does "mainstreaming" mean? *Journal of Learning
Disabilities,* 1974, *7,* 513-515.

1165.   _____, & Koppmann, M. Out of the classroom: The child
oriented resource room program. *Exceptional Children,* 1971, *37,*
460-462.

1166.   *Regional mainstreaming conference, Kansas City, Missouri,
December 12-13, 1976.* Minneapolis, MN: Leadership Training Institute, 1976.

1167.   *Regular class placement/special classes; a selective bibliography.*
Reston, VA: The Council for Exceptional Children, 1972. (ERIC
Document Reproduction Service No. ED 065 967)

1168.   *Regular class placement/special classes; exceptional child biblio-
graphy series.* Reston, VA: The Council for Exceptional Children,
Handicapped and Gifted Children, 1971. (ERIC Document
Reproduction Service No. ED 052 567)

1169.   Reilly, T. E. Differences in programming and placement decisions
for mildly handicapped children made by special and regular education teachers (Doctoral dissertation, University of Southern California, 1974). *Dissertation Abstracts International,* 1974, *35,*
2813A. (University Microfilms No. 74-21502)

1170. *Related vocational instruction for the handicapped. Workshop summary.* Unpublished manuscript, 1978. (ERIC Document Reproduction Service No. ED 162 482)

1171. Renter, C., Renter, G., Werth, J., & Shanks, B. *The Assessment Placement and Monitoring Index: A non-categorical severity scale for handicapped students.* Paper presented at the 57th Annual International Convention of the Council for Exceptional Children, Dallas, TX, April 1979. (ERIC Document Reproduction Service No. ED 171 088)

1172. Resource center for special education. *Intellect,* 1972, *101*(2344), 78-79.

1173. *Resource training package on special education/mainstreaming.* Fort Lauderdale, FL: Nova University, 1975.

1174. *A review of research: Implications for the Head Start handicapped effort.* Syracuse, NY: Syracuse University, Division of Special Education and Rehabilitation, 1974. (ERIC Document Reproduction Service No. ED 108 442)

1175. Reynolds, M. C. *An Analysis of the Bureau of Education for the Handicapped (BEH) Deans' Project.* Paper presented at the 30th Annual Meeting of the American Association of Colleges for Teacher Education, Chicago, IL, February 1978. (ERIC Document Reproduction Service No. ED 157 865)

1176. _____. Basic issues in restructuring teacher education. *Journal of Teacher Education,* 1978, *29*(6), 25-29.

1177. _____. Career education and mainstreaming. *Journal of Career Education,* 1978, *5*, 4-15.

1178. _____. *Criteria in the public education of the severely handicapped.* Minneapolis, MN: University of Minnesota, 1973. (ERIC Document Reproduction Service No. ED 093 123)

1179. _____. *Current practices and programs in training the mainstream educator.* Paper presented at the 4th Annual Invitational Special Education Leadership Conference, Minneapolis, MN, December 1974.

1180. _____. *Educating exceptional children in regular classes.* An unpublished address presented at the Leadership Training Institute Conference, Chicago, IL, October 1974.

1181. _____. A framework for considering some issues in special education. *Exceptional Children,* 1962, *28*, 367-370.

1182. _____. Mainstreaming: Historical perspectives. In P. A. O'Donnell, & R. H. Bradfield (Eds.), *Mainstreaming: Controversy and consensus.* San Rafael, CA: Academic Therapy Pub., 1976.

1183.   _____. *Mainstreaming: Origins and implications.* Reston, VA: The Council for Exceptional Children, 1976. (ERIC Document Reproduction Service No. ED 123 837)

1184.   _____. More process than is due. *Theory into Practice,* 1975, *14,* 61-68.

1185.   _____. Policy statement: Call for response. *Exceptional Children,* 1971, *37,* 421-433.

1186.   _____. The surge in special education. *Today's Education,* 1967, *56*(8), 46-48.

1187.   _____ (Ed.). *Psychology and the process of schooling in the next decade: Alternative conceptions.* Minneapolis, MN: University of Minnesota, Department of Audio Visual Extension, 1971. (ERIC Document Reproduction Service No. ED 071 208)

1188.   _____ (Ed.). *Social environment of the schools. What research and experience say to the teacher of exceptional children.* Reston, VA: The Council for Exceptional Children, ERIC Clearinghouse on Handicapped and Gifted Children, 1980. (ERIC Document Reproduction Service No. ED 188 357)

1189.   _____ (Ed.). *Special education in school system decentralization. Report of a conference.* Minneapolis, MN: Leadership Training Institute/Special Education, University of Minnesota, 1975. (ERIC Document Reproduction Service No. ED 112 590)

1190.   _____ (Ed.). *Technical assistance systems in special education.* Minneapolis, MN: Leadership Training Institute/Special Education, University of Minnesota, 1976.

1191.   _____, & Balow, B. Categories and variables in special education. *Exceptional Children,* 1972, *38,* 357-366. Also in H. D. Love (Ed.), *Exceptional children in regular classrooms.* Minneapolis, MN: University of Minnesota, 1970. Also in R. L. Jones, & D. L. MacMillan (Eds.), *Special education in transition.* Boston, MA: Allyn & Bacon, 1974.

1192.   _____, & Birch, J. W. *Education for exceptional children in all America's schools.* Reston, VA: The Council for Exceptional Children, 1977.

1193.   _____, & Birch, J. W. *Mainstream education: Focus on individualization.* Columbus, OH: University Council for Educational Administration, 1977. (ERIC Document Reproduction Service No. ED 135 116)

1194.   _____, & Birch, J. W. *Teaching exceptional children in all America's schools; a first course for teachers and principals.* Reston, VA: The Council for Exceptional Children, 1977. (ERIC Document Reproduction Service No. ED 145 626)

1195. _____, & Rosen, S. W. Special education: Past, present and future. *Educational Forum,* 1976, *40,* 551-562.

1196. _____, & Davis, M. D. (Eds.). *Exceptional children in regular classrooms.* Minneapolis, MN: University of Minnesota, Department of Audio Visual Extention, 1971. (ERIC Document Reproduction Service No. ED 056 432)

1197. Rezmierski, L. R. *Northville Public Schools/Institution Special Education Program: Comprehensive administrative planning.* Paper presented at the 1st World Congress on Future Special Education, Stirling, Scotland, June-July, 1978. (ERIC Document Reproduction Service No. ED 158 512)

1198. Rhodes, H. C. *The Alberta Special Education Study. Organizing special education for moderately handicapped pupils in Alberta schools: A study of selected administrative arrangements and support services. Complete report.* Edmonton, Alberta, Canada: Alberta Department of Education, Planning and Research Branch, 1977. (ERIC Document Reproduction Service No. ED 148 081)

1199. Richardson, S. A., Ronald, L. L., & Kleck, R. E. The social status of handicapped and non-handicapped boys in a camp setting. *Journal of Special Education,* 1974, *8,* 143-152.

1200. Riggar, W. J. *Mainstreaming the mildly handicapped: A handbook for teachers.* Blackwood, NJ: Kaleidoscope Press, Inc., 1978.

1201. Riggen, T. F. An investigation of the covariance of dogmatism and inservice training on the attitudes of principals and classroom teachers concerning the mainstreaming of mildly handicapped children (Doctoral dissertation, Syracuse University, 1975). *Dissertation Abstracts International,* 1977, *38,* 6454A. (University Microfilms No. 77-24856)

1202. Riley, D. P., Nash, H. D., & Hunt, J. I. *National incentives in special education: A history of legislative and court action.* Washington, D.C.: National Association of State Directors of Special Education, 1978. (ERIC Document Reproduction Service No. ED 166 901)

1203. Rinaldi, R. T. Deinstitutionalization and beyond. *Bailiwick,* 1976, *6*(2), 8-9.

1204. Rittenhouse, R. K. *The Bartley-Daly Act: Regulations for the implementation of Chapter 766 of the acts of 1972: The Comprehensive Special Education Law of the Commonwealth of Massachusetts; an analysis within the context of Public Law 94-142.* Normal, IL: University of Illinois, 1980. (ERIC Document Reproduction Service No. ED 182 956)

1205.   Rivera-Viera, D. *Descriptive presentation of a model integrating classroom in accordance with Chapter 766 and 71A.* Unpublished manuscript, 1975. (ERIC Document Reproduction Service No. ED 166 927)

1206.   Roberts, B. Making it into the mainstream. *Teacher,* 1975, *93*(4), 37-39.

1207.   Robinson, R. E. Teachers' attitudes toward and knowledges of mainstreaming handicapped children (Doctoral dissertation, Illinois University at Carbondale, 1977). *Dissertation Abstracts International,* 1977, *38,* 5836A. (University Microfilms No. 78-04305)

1208.   Rocha, R. M., & Gregory, G. P. The resource room: Delivery systems for mainstreaming in elementary social studies. *Social Education,* 1979, *43,* 63-64.

1209.   _____, & Sanford, H. G. Mainstreaming: Democracy in action. *Social Education,* 1979, *43,* 59-62.

1210.   Rockoff, E. Classroom utilization of ancillary personnel: Delivery systems for mainstreaming in elementary social studies. *Social Education,* 1979, *43,* 67-68.

1211.   Roddy, E. A. *"Teacher," the forgotten component of the IEP.* Paper presented at the 57th Annual International Convention of The Council for Exceptional Children, Dallas, TX, April 1979. (ERIC Document Reproduction Service No. ED 171 027)

1212.   Rodham, H. Children under the law. *Harvard Educational Review,* 1973, *43,* 487-514.

1213.   Rodman, A. J. *Getting on track.* San Rafael, CA: Academic Therapy Pub., 1973.

1214.   Rogow, S., & David, C. Special education: Perspectives, trends, and issues. *Phi Delta Kappan,* 1974, *55,* 514-515.

1215.   *The role of the public school administrator related to special education programs.* Proceedings of the Special Study Institute, Westchester County, NY, November 1969. (ERIC Document Reproduction Service No. ED 042 290)

1216.   Rosen, R. *A parent's guide to the individualized education program (IEP) as required by P.L. 94-142 (Education for All Handicapped Children Act).* Washington, D.C.: Gallaudet College, 1978. (ERIC Document Reproduction Service No. ED 166 914)

1217.   Rosenberg, H. Modifying teacher's behavior. *Special Education: Forward Trends,* 1976, *3*(2), 8-9.

1218.   Rosenthal, R. S. Differences in teacher behavior in mainstreamed vs. nonmainstreamed schools (Doctoral dissertation, Yeshiva University, 1977). *Dissertation Abstracts International,* 1977, *38,* 5366A. (University Microfilms No. 77-32522)

1219.   Rosner, B., & Kay, P. M. Will the promise of C/PBTE be fulfilled? In J. W. Schifani (Ed.), *Contemporary issues in mainstreaming handicapped citizens*. Dubuque, IA: Kendall/Hunt Pub., 1976.

1220.   Ross, E. C. *UCPA affiliates report implementation experiences with P.L. 94-142: The Education for All Handicapped Children Act*. Washington, D.C.: United Cerebral Palsy Association, 1978. (ERIC Document Reproduction Service No. ED 165 429)

1221.   Ross, M. Mainstreaming—some social considerations. *Volta Review*, 1978, *80*, 21-30.

1222.   Ross, S. L., DeYoung, H., & Cohen, J. Confrontation: Special education placement and the law. *Exceptional Children*, 1971, *38*, 5-12.

1223.   Roubinek, D. L. Individualized mainstreaming: Another option for principals? *National Elementary Principal*, 1977, *56*, 43-46.

1224.   _____. Will mainstreaming fit? *Educational Leadership*, 1978, *35*, 410-412.

1225.   _____, & Cheek, C. W. Instructional implications of least-restrictive environments for children. *Humanist Educator*, 1978, *17*(2), 54-63.

1226.   Rowland, G. T., & Patterson, E. G. Curiosity—an educational key to change. In J. W. Schifani (Ed.), *Contemporary issues in mainstreaming handicapped citizens*. Dubuque, IA: Kendall/Hunt Pub., 1976.

1227.   Rowley, J. A. *First you get their attention*. Austin: Texas Education Agency, 1978. (ERIC Document Reproduction Service No. ED 155 843)

1228.   Rubin, R. *Identification of handicapped children and the classroom teacher*. Paper presented at the 4th Annual Invitational Special Education Leadership Conference, Minneapolis, MN, December 1974. Also in R. A. Johnson, R. F. Weatherman, & A. M. Rehman (Eds.), *Special education leadership series. Vol. IV: Handicapped youth and the mainstream educator*. Minneapolis, MN: Audio Visual Extension Service, University of Minnesota, 1975.

1229.   _____, & Balow, B. Factors in special class placement. *Exceptional Children*, 1973, *39*, 525-532.

1230.   Rumble, R. R. The "Education for All Handicapped Act": Teacher attitudes and the school administrator. *Illinois Schools Journal*, 1980, *59*(4), 18-24.

1231.   _____. *Mainstreaming the handicapped in vocational education. Literature review. (A research project in vocational education in the Portland Public Schools.)* Portland, OR: Portland Public Schools, 1978. (ERIC Document Reproduction Service No. ED 162 475)

EMORY & HENRY LIBRARY

1232.   _____. *A survey of the attitudes of secondary teachers toward the mainstreaming of handicapped learners. (A research project in vocational education in the Portland Public Schools.)* Portland, OR: Portland Public Schools, 1978. (ERIC Document Reproduction Service No. ED 162 477)

1233.   _____. *A survey of the attitudes of secondary vocational cluster teachers toward the mainstreaming of handicapped learners. (A research project in vocational education in the Portland Public Schools.)* Portland, OR: Portland Public Schools, 1978. (ERIC Document Reproduction Service No. ED 162 478)

1234.   _____. *A synthesis of information obtained from a literature review and field research activities regarding the mainstreaming of handicapped learners in vocational education.* Portland, OR: Portland Public Schools, 1978. (ERIC Document Reproduction Service No. ED 162 476)

1235.   _____. Vocational education for the handicapped. *Clearinghouse,* 1978, *52,* 132-135.

1236.   Rusalen, H., & Cohen, J. S. Guidance of the exceptional student. In W. M. Cruickshank, & G. O. Johnson (Eds.), *Education of exceptional children & youth.* Englewood Cliffs, NJ: Prentice-Hall, 1975.

1237.   _____, & Rusalem, H. Implementing innovative special education ideas. *Exceptional Children,* 1971, *37,* 384-386.

1238.   Russell, G. H., & Bulter, D. M. The five-county vocational skills training program, 1970-1972. *New Outlook for the Blind,* 1973, *67,* 7.

1239.   Russo, J. R. Mainstreaming handicapped students: Are your facilities suitable? *American School and University,* 1974, *47*(2), 25-32. Also in *Education Digest,* 1975, *40,* 18-21.

1240.   Ryor, J. Editorial: Integrating the handicapped. *Today's Education,* 1977, *66*(3), 24-25.

1241.   _____. Editorial: Mainstreaming. *Today's Education,* 1976, *65*(2), 5.

1242.   Sabatino, D. A. Resource rooms: The renaissance in special education. *Journal of Special Education,* 1972, *6,* 335-347.

1243.   _____. Revolution: Viva resource rooms. *Journal of Special Education,* 1972, *6,* 389-395.

1244.   Saettler, H. Current priorities in personnel preparation. *Exceptional Children,* 1976, *43,* 147-148.

1245.   Safford, P. L. Mental health counseling dimensions of special education programs. *Journal of School Health,* 1978, *48,* 541-543, 546-547.

1246. Sage, D. D., & Guarino, R. Unintended consequences: A law which purports to aid handicapped children. *Phi Delta Kappan,* 1974, *55,* 533-535.

1247. St. John, W. D., Child, C., & Kelly, S. B. Paul-Justin, two case studies. *Instructor,* 1976, *85*(6), 114-117.

1248. Sampson, O. Children in a world apart. *Special Education,* 1971, *60*(2), 6-9.

1249. Sanders, J. E. *Multiple inputs for special education/mainstreaming: Working papers series.* Chelmsford, MA: Merrimack Educational Center, 1975.

1250. _____. *Training complex model for appraising and programming. Summary report.* Chelmsford, MA: Merrimack Educational Center, 1977. (ERIC Document Reproduction Service No. ED 157 866)

1251. Sanford, A., Semrau, B., & Wilson, D. *The Chapel Hill model for training Head Start personnel in mainstreaming handicapped children.* Chapel Hill, NC: Chapel Hill Training-Outreach Project, 1974. (ERIC Document Reproduction Service No. ED 136 539)

1252. Sanford, H. G. Prescriptive teaching: Delivery systems for mainstreaming in elementary social studies. *Social Education,* 1979, *43,* 64-67.

1253. Sapon-Shevin, M. Another look at mainstreaming: Exceptionality, normality and the nature of difference. *Phi Delta Kappan,* 1978, *60,* 119-121.

1254. Sarandoulias, L. Getting handicapped students into the mainstream. *American Vocational Journal,* 1975, *50,* 22-25.

1255. Sarason, S. B. The special child in school—report in a paper. *Bulletin of the Orton Society,* 1972, *22,* 117-122.

1256. _____, & Doris, J. Dilemmas, opposition, opportunities. *Exceptional Parent,* 1977, *7*(4), 21-24.

1257. Sargent, L. W. State certification requirements. *Journal of Teacher Education,* 1978, *29*(6), 47.

1258. Sattler, J. L. An evaluative case study of educational services for mildly handicapped students in the mainstream (Doctoral dissertation, University of Illinois at Urbana-Champaign, 1977). *Dissertation Abstracts International,* 1977, *38,* 6060A. (University Microfilms No. 78-04142)

1259. _____, & Notari, C. *Results of a questionnaire on integration of nonsensory handicapped children.* Urbana, IL: University of Illinois at Urbana-Champaign, 1973. (ERIC Document Reproduction Service No. ED 081 149)

1260. Sauer, R. B. *Handicapped children and day care. Revised and updated second edition.* New York, NY: Bank Street College of Education, 1975. (ERIC Document Reproduction Service No. ED 119 808)

1261. Savage, D. G. *Educating all the handicapped: What the law says and what the schools are doing.* Arlington, VA: National School Public Relations Association, 1977. (ERIC Document Reproduction Service No. ED 143 186)

1262. _____. How—starting the Fall—the new "handicapped law" will jolt nearly every school board in the U.S. *American School Board Journal,* 1977, *164*(8), 53-55.

1263. Schallhorn, D. History of total communication in Oshkosh. *Bureau Memorandum,* 1977, *18*(3), 9-13.

1264. Schifani, J. W. (Ed.). *Contemporary issues in mainstreaming handicapped citizens.* Dubuque, IA: Kendall/Hunt Pub., 1976.

1265. _____, Anderson, R. M., & Odle, S. J. *Implementing learning in the least restrictive environment.* Baltimore, MD: University Park Press, 1980.

1266. Schildkraut, M. L. New school rights for handicapped kids. *Good Housekeeping,* June 1978, p. 254.

1267. Schipper, W., & Boston, B. O. *Writing individualized assessment reports in special education: A resource manual.* Washington, D.C.: National Association of State Directors of Special Education, 1978. (ERIC Document Reproduction Service No. ED 166 902)

1268. Schlechty, P. C., & Turnbull, A. P. Bureaucracy or professionalism: Implications of P.L. 94-142. *Journal of Teacher Education,* 1978, *29*(6), 34-38.

1269. Schleifer, M. J. (Ed.). Mainstreaming: "We did a terrible thing in sending Ed to camp." *Exceptional Parent,* 1977, 7(3), 21-26.

1270. _____. The school year has been a total disaster? *Exceptional Parent,* 1977, 7(4), 25-29.

1271. Schmatz, R. R. A comparison of achievement and attitudes of sixth-grade students in regular and combination grades (Doctoral dissertation, Michigan State University, 1965). *Dissertation Abstracts,* 1965, *26*, 9. (University Microfilms No. 65-08403)

1272. Schmidt, M. R., & Sprandel, H. Z. Concluding remarks and sources of additional assistance: Organizations, agencies, and literature. *New Directions for Student Services,* 1980, *1*(10), 71-77.

1273. Schmid, R. E., Moneypenny, J., & Johnston, R. *Contemporary issues in special education.* New York: McGraw-Hill, 1977.

1274. Schoenfelder, D. S., Staff development in special education for regular classroom teachers (Doctoral dissertation, Lehigh University, 1971). *Dissertation Abstracts International,* 1971, *32,*2539A. (University Microfilms No. 71-27741)

1275. Schofer, R. C. Cooperative manpower planning. A status study. *Teacher Education and Special Education,* 1978, *2*(1), 7-11.

1276. Schoka, R. R. *A comparative followup study of the mainstreamed graduate at Ocean County Vocational-Technical School.* Unpublished manuscript, 1980. (ERIC Document Reproduction Service No. ED 182 538)

1277. Schorr, J. H. A model for intrasystemic linkage for the implementation of mainstreaming (Doctoral dissertation, Boston University School of Education, 1976). *Dissertation Abstracts International,* 1976, *37,* 1494A. (University Microfilms No. 76-21254)

1278. Schrag, J. A. *Individualized educational programming. (IEP): A child study team process.* Austin, TX: Learning Concepts, 1977.

1279. Schultz, J. B., Kohlmann, E., & Davisson, J. *Assessment of learning centers as a teaching/learning strategy in mainstreamed classes.* Paper presented at the 62nd Annual Meeting of the American Educational Research Association, Toronto, Ontario, Canada, March 1978. (ERIC Document Reproduction Service No. ED 170 327).

1280. _____, & Rougvie, B. S. *Group learning centers. Illustrated for home economics. A strategy for use in classes mainstreaming disabled students.* Ames, IA: Iowa State University of Science and Technology, Department of Home Economics Education, 1977. (ERIC Document Reproduction Service No. ED 156 846)

1281. Schwartz, B., & Ezrachi, O. *Pilot study of the efficacy of mainstreaming—integrating handicapped children. Final report.* New York, NY: New York University Medical Center, 1978. (ERIC Document Reproduction Service No. ED 165 387)

1282. Schwartz, L. A clinical teacher model for interrelated areas of special education. *Exceptional Children,* 1971, *37,* 565-571. Also in J. W. Schifani (Ed.), *Contemporary issues in mainstreaming handicapped citizens.* Dubuque, IA: Kendall/Hunt Pub., 1976.

1283. _____. An integrated teacher education program for special education—a new approach. *Exceptional Children,* 1967, *33,* 411-416.

1284. _____, Oseroff, A., Drucker, H., & Schwartz, R. *Innovative noncategorical interrelated projects in the education of the handicapped. Proceedings of the Special Study Institute, Washington, D.C., 1971.* (ERIC Document Reproduction Service No. ED 060 609)

1285. Schwartz, S. E. *Evaluation and placement.* Gainesville, FL: University of Florida, College of Education, 1977. (ERIC Document Reproduction Service No. ED 153 046)

1286. _____. *Mainstreaming handicapped students into the regular classroom.* Gainesville, FL: University of Florida, College of Education, 1977. (ERIC Document Reproduction Service No. ED 153 044)

1287. _____. Special education joins the mainstream. *Florida Vocational Journal,* 1978, *3*(9), 23-26.

1288. _____. *A system of management.* Gainesville, FL: University of Florida, College of Education, 1977. (ERIC Document Reproduction Service No. ED 153 045)

1289. Science for the handicapped. Part 1: Definition and description. Part 2: Science programs. Part 3: Activities. *Science and Children,* 1976, *13*(6), 7-51.

1290. Sclater, J. Supporting mainstreaming in special education with the IRR approach: Immediate reinforcement and remediation. *Journal for Special Educators,* 1980, *16*, 113-116.

1291. Scriven, M. Some issues in the logic and ethics of mainstreaming. Proceedings of the Deans' Projects Conference, July 1975. *Minnesota Education,* 1976, *2*, 61-68. Also in M. C. Reynolds (Ed.). *Mainstreaming: Origins and implications.* Reston, VA: Council for Exceptional Children, 1976.

1292. *A selected annotated bibliography on P.L. 94-142: Practical programs for the classroom. Bibliographies on educational topics No. 13.* Washington, D.C.: ERIC Clearinghouse on Teacher Education, 1980. (ERIC Document Reproduction Service No. ED 181 025)

1293. Semb, G., & Green, D. R. (Eds.). *Behavior analysis and education.* Lawrence, KS: University of Kansas, Support and Development Center for Follow Through, Department of Human Development, 1972.

1294. Semmel, M. I., & Adler, M. *The role of the Center for Innovation in Teaching the Handicapped in Project PRIME (Programmed Reentry into Mainstream Education).* Bloomington, IN: Indiana University, Bloomington. Center for Innovation in Teaching the Handicapped, 1971. (ERIC Document Reproduction Service No. ED 111 135)

1295. _____, & Heinmiller, J. L. (Eds.). *Viewpoint: A special report. The Education for All Handicapped Children Act (P.L. 94-142). Issues and implications.* Bloomington, IN: Indiana University, Bloomington. Center for Innovation in Teaching the Handicapped, 1977.

1296. Seymour, L. Recent legislation: It affects you! *Academic Therapy,* 1977, *13,* 53-56.

1297. Shaffer, J. D., & Bell, J. E. *Parents and educators: Partners in individualized educational program planning for handicapped students. An in-service training package.* Des Moines, IA: Drake University, Midwest Regional Resource Center, 1978. (ERIC Document Reproduction Service No. ED 163 706)

1298. Shane, E., & Shane, M. An exceptional child in the normal classroom: A psychoanalytic-developmental approach to teacher education. *California Journal of Teacher Education,* 1974, *2*(2), 86-101.

1299. Shanker, B. C. Mainstreaming and its underlying issues (Doctoral dissertation, Saint Louis University, 1974). *Dissertation Abstracts International,* 1974, *36,* 3572A. (University Microfilms No. 75-26320)

1300. Shannon, R. D. *The effects of integrating young severely handicapped children into regular preschool Headstart and child development programs. Year II.* Merced, CA: Merced County Schools, 1978. (ERIC Document Reproduction Service No. ED 163 714)

1301. Sharp, B. L. Unresolved issues for teacher education. *Journal of Teacher Education,* 1978, *29*(6), 39-41.

1302. Shaw, S. F. *A comprehensive inservice training program to enable school districts to move toward full compliance with P.L. 94-142.* Paper presented at the 56th Annual International Convention, Council for Exceptional Children, Kansas City, MO, May 1978. (ERIC Document Reproduction Service No. ED 153 395)

1303. _____, & Shaw, W. K. The in-service experience plan; or changing the bath without losing the baby. *Journal of Special Education,* 1972, *6,* 121-126.

1304. Shearer, E. Special needs. *Times Education Supplement (London),* December 17, 1976, no. 3211, p. 26.

1305. Shears, L. N., & Jensema, C. J. Social acceptability of anomalous persons. *Exceptional Children,* 1969, *36,* 91-96.

1306. Sheehy, E. Special child in the regular classroom. *Clearinghouse,* 1975, *49,* 14-16.

1307. Shepherd, G. The education of educably mentally retarded students in secondary schools: A review of the literature. *Curriculum Bulletin,* 1967, *23,* 280.

1308. Sherrill, C. *Creative arts for the severely handicapped.* Austin, TX: Texas Education Agency, 1977.

1309. _____. *Mainstreaming in physical education: A positive approach.* Denton, TX: Texas Woman's University, 1975. (ERIC Document Reproduction Service No. ED 107 615)

1310. Shiman, D., Nevin, A., Leean, C., & Myers, B. *Conference proceedings of the 1977 University of Vermont Summer Institute on a free appropriate public education for all.* Minneapolis, MN: University of Minnesota, Leadership Training Institute/Special Education and University of Vermont, Burlington, 1978. (ERIC Document Reproduction Service No. ED 165 354)

1311. Shiman, D. A. When mainstreaming comes in, are the poor left out? *Learning,* 1978, 7(2), 120-121.

1312. Sholl, G. T., & Milazzo, T. C. The Federal program and the preparation of professional personnel in the education of handicapped children and youth. *Exceptional Children,* 1965, 32, 157-165.

1313. Schorn, F. R. A study of an inservice practicum's effects on teachers' attitudes about mainstreaming. (Doctoral dissertation, University of Massachusetts, 1976). *Dissertation Abstracts International,* 1976, 37, 5762A. (University Microfilms No. 77-06402)

1314. Shotel, J. R., Iano, R. P., & McGettigan, J. F. Teacher attitudes associated with the integration of handicapped children. *Exceptional Children,* 1972, 38, 677-683.

1315. Shrag, J. A. Individualized educational programming (IEP): A child study team process. In T. N. Fairchild (Ed.), *The mainstreaming series.* Austin, TX: Learning Concepts, 1977.

1316. Shriver, E. K. Physical education: Shortest road to success for the handicapped. *Science and Children,* 1976, 13(6), 24-26.

1317. Shrybman, J., & Matsoukas, G. The principal and the special education hearing. *National Elementary Principal,* 1978, 58, 30-33.

1318. Shulman, B. The regulations for P.L. 94-142: A superintendent's view. *Exceptional Parent,* 1977, 7(5), 8-11.

1319. Shulman, V. L. An open systems model mainstreaming exceptional and bilingual elementary education children conceptualized along a Piagetian developmental continuum (Doctoral dissertation, Fordham University, 1978). *Dissertation Abstracts International,* 1978, 39, 1328A. (University Microfilms No. 78-16579)

1320. Shumway, H.S. The highway of the future. *Rehabilitation Teacher,* 1974, 6(11), 3-8.

1321. Shworles, T. R. The community college system: A resource for rehabilitation. *American Rehabilitation,* 1976, 1(3), 8-12.

1322. Siegel, E. *Special education in the regular classroom.* New York: John Day, 1969.

1323. Sigety, B., & Levine, E. *The educational plan game: Activity leader's guide.* Rev. ed. Miami, FL: Florida Learning Resources System/South, n.d. (ERIC Document Reproduction Service No. ED 150 813)

1324.   _____, & Levine, E. *The educational plan game: Participant's copy.* Rev. ed. Miami, FL: Florida Learning Resources System/South, n.d. (ERIC Document Reproduction Service No. ED 150 812)

1325.   Simches, R. F. The inside outsiders. *Exceptional Children,* 1970, *37,* 5-15.

1326.   Simons, J. M., & Dwyer, B. Education of the handicapped. In M. F. Williams (Ed.), *Government in the classroom: Dollars and power in education.* New York: American Academy of Political Science, 1979.

1327.   Simpson, R. L., Parrish, N. E., & Cook, J. J. Modification of attitudes of regular class children towards the handicapped for the purpose of achieving integration. *Contemporary Educational Psychology,* 1976, *1*(1), 46-51.

1328.   Singh, S. P. *An integrated psycho-educational program. Technical report.* Unpublished paper, 1977. (ERIC Document Reproduction Service No. ED 154 599)

1329.   *Single skills training courses—E.S.E.A., Title IV-C. Final evaluation report.* Washington, D.C.: District of Columbia Public Schools, 1980. (ERIC Document Reproduction Service No. ED 188 354)

1330.   Singleton, K. W. Creating positive attitudes and expectancies of regular classroom teachers toward mainstreaming educationally handicapped children: A comparison of two inservice methods (Doctoral dissertation, University of Southern California). *Dissertation Abstracts International,* 1977, *38,* 186A.

1331.   Sivasailam, C. A path analytic model of causal relations between dynamic learner variables and school goals applied to the problem of mainstreaming (Doctoral dissertation, Indiana University, 1978). *Dissertation Abstracts International,* 1978, *39,* 820A. (University Microfilms No. 78-12986)

1332.   Skindrud, K. In-service preparation for mainstreaming. A continuum of strategies for instructional planning (IEP) teams. *Teacher Education and Special Education,* 1978, *2*(1), 41-52.

1333.   _____. *In-service training for mainstreaming under P.L. 94-142.* Paper presented at the Association for Advancement of Behavior Therapy, Atlanta, GA, December 1977.

1334.   Slack, G. Child find; identification of handicapped children who are not in school; Dade and Monroe Counties, Fla. *American Education,* 1976, *12*(10), 29-33.

1335.   Sletved, H. *Pedagogical background and evaluation for an admin-istrative and functional combination of all Danish special education facilities.* Washington, D.C.: Department of Health, Education and Welfare, 1972. (ERIC Document Reproduction Service No. ED 071 223)

1336.   Smergut, P. Making P.L. 92-142 work in the intermediate school. *National Association for Secondary School Principals Bulletin,* 1980, *64,* 106-109.

1337.   Smith, A. P. *Mainstreaming: Idea and actuality.* Albany, NY: The New York State Education Department, Division for Handicapped Children, 1973. (ERIC Document Reproduction Service No. ED 111 157)

1338.   Smith, J. O., & Arkans, J. R. Now more than ever; a case for the special class. *Exceptional Children,* 1974, *40,* 497-502.

1339.   Smith, P. B., & Bently, G. I. *Teacher training program: Main-streaming mildly handicapped students into the regular classroom.* Austin, TX: Education Service Center, 1975.

1340.   Smith, R. E., George, J. E., & Glover, L. E. *Meeting inservice teacher education needs through special projects: Changing curri-culum for exceptional children and special education for regular teachers.* Paper presented at the 54th Annual International Meet-ing of the Council for Exceptional Children, Chicago, IL, April 1976. (ERIC Document Reproduction Service No. ED 122 480)

1341.   Smith, S. L. When learning is a problem. *American Education,* 1978, *14*(9), 18-23.

1342.   Smith, W. G. Competencies for teachers of educationally handi-capped and normal children as viewed by special and regular classroom teachers and administrators (Doctoral dissertation, University of California, Los Angeles, 1969). *Dissertation Abstracts International,* 1969, *30,* 3257A. (University Microfilms No. 70-02261)

1343.   Smith, W. L. Ending the isolation of the handicapped. *American Education,* 1971, 7(9), 29-31.

1344.   Snapp, M. Resource classrooms or resource personnel? *Journal of Special Education,* 1972, *6,* 383-387.

1345.   Snider, R. C. Can we go back to the basic in the mainstream with career education for the handicapped? *Journal of Career Education,* 1978, *5*(1), 16-23.

1346.   Snow, R. E. Consequences for instruction: The state of the art of individualizing. In M. C. Reynolds (Ed.), *Mainstreaming: Origins and implications.* Reston, VA: The Council for Exceptional Chil-dren, 1976. (ERIC Document Reproduction Service No. ED 123 837)

1347. Snyder, L. K., Apolloni, T., & Cooke, T. P. Integrated settings at the early childhood level: The role of nonretarded peers. *Exceptional Children*, 1977, *43*, 262-266.

1348. Solomon, E. L. New York City's prototype school for educating the handicapped. *Phi Delta Kappan*, 1977, *59*, 7-10.

1349. Solomon, S. R. *Mainstreaming as an approach to special education services: Organization and training.* Unpublished paper, n.d. (ERIC Document Reproduction Service No. ED 140 519)

1350. Soloway, M. M. The development and evaluation of a special education inservice training program for regular classroom teachers (Doctoral dissertation, University of California, Los Angeles, 1974). *Dissertation Abstracts International*, 1974, *36*, 4425A. (University Microfilms No. 75-05693)

1351. *Solution oriented seminars (3 products in a series on behavior and learning problems). Description of teacher inservice education materials.* Washington, D.C.: National Education Association Project on Utilization of Inservice Education Research and Development Outcomes, 1977. (ERIC Document Reproduction Service No. ED 169 023)

1352. Sommers, P. A. *Medical implications for the education of exceptional children for implementing P.L. 94-142.* Paper presented at the 57th Annual International Convention of the Council for Exceptional Children, Dallas, TX, April 1979. (ERIC Document Reproduction Service No. ED 170 997)

1353. Sosnowsky, W. P., & Coleman, T. W. Special education in the collective bargaining process. In R. L. Jones, & D. L. MacMillan (Eds.), *Special education in transition.* Boston, MA: Allyn & Bacon, 1974.

1354. _____, Simpkins, E., & LaPlante, F. M. *Teachers' unions on mainstreaming.* Unpublished paper, 1976. (ERIC Document Reproduction Service No. ED 126 651)

1355. Souweine, J. D. W., Mazel, C., & Crimmins, S. A. *A teacher's guide to mainstreaming young children.* Washington, D.C.: National Association for the Education of Young Children, n.d.

1356. Sowers, G. H. *Observations of a primary school principal after four years of experience with mainstreaming.* Paper presented at the Annual Meeting of the American Educational Research Association, Toronto, Ontario, Canada, March 1978. (ERIC Document Reproduction Service No. ED 153 342).

1357. Spear, D. Head Start: A positive approach to serving handicapped children. *Reading Improvement*, 1980, *17*, 149-152.

1358.   *Special class placement—a continuing debate.* Papers presented at the 48th Annual International Convention of the Council for Exceptional Children, Chicago, IL, April 1970. (ERIC Document Reproduction Service No. ED 039 383)

1359.   *Special education early childhood project in Fort Worth Independent School District, Title VI, ESEA. Final report.* Fort Worth, TX: Fort Worth Independent School District, 1971. (ERIC Document Reproduction Service No. ED 052 550)

1360.   Special education needs of American Indian children. *Amicus,* 1976, *2*(1), 33-36.

1361.   *The special education resource room and teacher training program.* Philadelphia, PA: Temple University/College of Education, 1973. (ERIC Document Reproduction Service No. ED 086 645)

1362.   Special education yesterday, today and tomorrow: An interview with Frances Connor, Samuel Kirk, and Burton Blatt. *Exceptional Parent,* 1977, *7*(4), 9-14.

1363.   Spencer, D. Cautious responses to integrating handicapped. *Times Educational Supplement (London),* May 14, 1976, no. 3180, p. 7.

1364.   Spencer, J. & Lohman, J. Mainstreaming the handicapped in home economics. *Forecast for Home Economics,* 1977, *23*(2), 66.

1365.   Spicker, H. H., Anastasiow, N. J., & Hodges, W. L. (Eds.). *Children with special needs: Early development and education.* Minneapolis, MN: Leadership Training Institute, University of Minnesota, 1976.

1366.   Spiess, J. A. Literature and hidden handicaps. *Language Arts,* 1976, *53,* 435-437.

1367.   Spogen, D. Take the label off the handicapped child. *Education Digest,* 1972, *38*(1), 44-46.

1368.   Sproles, H. A., Panther, E. E., & Lanier, J. E. P.L. 94-142 and its impact on the counselor's role. *Personnel and Guidance Journal,* 1978, *57,* 210-212.

1369.   Stadtmueller, J. H. Federal programs—impact: P.L. 94-142. Update. *Bureau Memorandum,* 1977, *18*(3), 23-26.

1370.   _____. Highlights from P.L. 94-142. *Bureau Memorandum,* 1977, *18*(2), 16-18.

1371.   _____. A new Federal era in the education of children with exceptional needs. *Bureau Memorandum,* 1976, *17*(4), 4-6.

1372.   Stannard, F. Mainstreaming: Some basis for caution. In P. A. O'Donnell & R. H. Bradfield (Eds.), *Mainstreaming: Controversy and consensus.* San Rafael, CA: Academic Therapy Pub., 1976.

1373.   Stashower, G. Mainstreaming in the work world; vocational pro-
        grams in Westport, Connecticut. *American Education,* 1976,
        12(5), 9-13.

1374.   *State of the art literature review on the mainstreaming of handi-
        capped children and youth.* Silver Springs, MD: Applied Manage-
        ment Sciences, 1976. (ERIC Document Reproduction Service No.
        ED 168 240)

1375.   *A statement on policy recommendations on the handicapped effort
        in Head Start.* Syracuse, NY: Syracuse University, Division of Spe-
        cial Education and Rehabilitation, 1974. (ERIC Document Repro-
        duction Service No. ED 108 444)

1376.   Stearns, M. S., & Cooperstein, R. A. Equity in educating the hand-
        icapped. *Educational Leadership,* 1981, *38,* 324-325.

1377.   Stedman, D. J. Education's missing link. *Theory into Practice,*
        1975, *14,* 143-145.

1378.   Steigman, M. J. Paradox in special education? A critique of John-
        son's paper. *Exceptional Children,* 1964, *31,* 67-68.

1379.   Stein, J. Sense and nonsense about mainstreaming. *Journal of Phy-
        sical Education and Recreation,* 1976, *47,* 43.

1380.   Stenholm, B. The teaching of children with educational difficulties
        and handicaps in Sweden. *Journal for Special Educators of the
        Mentally Retarded,* 1975, *12,* 18-24, 83-85.

1381.   Stephens, T. M. *A comprehensive bibliography on mainstreaming.*
        Columbus, OH: Ohio State University, College of Education,
        Faculty for Exceptional Children, 1976.

1382.   _____. *Implementing behavioral approaches in elementary and
        secondary schools.* Columbus, OH: Charles E. Merrill, 1975.

1383.   _____, & Braun, B. L. Measures of regular classroom teachers'
        attitudes toward handicapped children. *Exceptional Children,*
        1980, *46,* 292-294.

1384.   Stephens, T. W. *An evaluation study of the efficacy of pupil educa-
        tional plans as developed by school assessment teams in the Sequoia
        Union High School District.* Redwood, CA: Sequoia Union High
        School District, 1977. (ERIC Document Reproduction Service No.
        ED 149 499)

1385.   Stephens, W. E. Mainstreaming: Some natural limitations. *Mental
        Retardation,* 1975, *13*(3), 40-41.

1386.   Stern, V. W. Role models for the handicapped. *National Elemen-
        tary Principal,* 1978, *58,* 43-45.

1387. Stewart, D. L. *The effect of collective negotiations on mainstreaming Michigan's special education students into regular education.* Unpublished doctoral dissertation, Michigan State University, 1978.

1388. Stewart, F. J. A vocal-motor program for teaching nonverbal children. In J. W. Schifani (Ed.), *Contemporary issues in mainstreaming handicapped citizens.* Dubuque, IA: Kendall/Hunt Pub., 1976.

1389. Stills, A. B. Student perceptions of and attitudes toward the special general education project and regular general education program at Indiana State University (Doctoral dissertation, Indiana State University, 1975). *Dissertation Abstracts International,* 1975, *36,* 4273A. (University Microfilms No. 75-29862)

1390. Stockglausner, J. *Successful mainstreaming in a large public school setting—Montgomery County, Maryland.* Paper presented at the Alexander Graham Bell National Convention, St. Louis, MO, June, 1978.

1391. Stoweli, I. J., & Terry, C. Mainstreaming—present shock. *Illinois Libraries,* 1977, *59,* 475-477.

1392. Stowell, M. A. *Handicapped learner participation in vocational education: A report on student, parent and teacher interviews.* Portland, OR: Portland Public Schools, 1978. (ERIC Document Reproduction Service No. ED 162 479)

1393. Strain, P. S., Cooke, T. P., & Apolloni, T. *Teaching exceptional children:* Assessing and modifying social behavior. New York, NY: Academic Press, 1976.

1394. _____, & Kerr, M. M. (Eds.). *Mainstreaming of children in schools: Research and programmatic issues.* New York, NY: Academic Press, 1981.

1395. Strang, L., Smith, M. D., & Rogers, C. M. Social comparison, multiple reference groups, and the self-concepts of academically handicapped children before and after mainstreaming. *Journal of Educational Psychology,* 1978, *70,* 487-497.

1396. Stroud, J. G. Selecting materials which promote understanding and acceptance of handicapped students. *English Journal,* 1981, 70(1), 49-52.

1397. Stuart, M., & Gilbert, J. Mainstreaming: Needs assessment through a videotape visual scale. *Journal of Research in Music Education,* 1977, *25,* 283-289.

1398. Sullivan, J. D. *Mainstreaming: Infopac No. 9.* Washington, D.C.: National Education Association, 1975.

1399. Sund, M. A. N. A comparison of attitudes of general education teachers in schools with different special education delivery systems toward the educable mentally handicapped (Doctoral dissertation, University of Michigan, 1975). *Dissertation Abstracts International*, 1975, *36*, 1441A. (University Microfilms No. 75-20459)

1400. Sundberg, N. I. UNESCO and special education for the handicapped. *UNESCO Courier*, 1974, *27*, 31-32.

1401. Sunderlin, S. (Ed.). *Most enabling environment: Education is for all children.* Washington, D.C.: Association for Childhood Education International, 1977.

1402. Swenson, S. H. Effects of peer tutoring in regular elementary classrooms on sociometric status, self-concept and arithmetic achievement of slow learning tutors and learners in a special education resource program (Doctoral dissertation, Indiana University, 1975). *Dissertation Abstracts International*, 1975, *36*, 6003A. (University Microfilms No. 76-06351)

1403. Sylwester, R. Looking into education's crystal ball. *Instructor*, 1977, *87*, 39.

1404. Tallent, N. *Report writing in special education.* Englewood Cliffs, NY: Prentice-Hall, 1980.

1405. Tarrier, R. B. *Mainstreamed handicapped students in occupational education: Exemplary administrative practices.* New York, NY: City University of New York, Institute for Research and Development in Occupational Education, 1978. (ERIC Document Reproduction Service No. ED 154 163)

1406. Taylor, F. D., Artuso, A. A., Soloway, M. M., Hewett, F. M., Quay, H. C., & Stillwell, R. J. A learning center plan for special education. *Focus on Exceptional Children*, 1972, 4(3), 1-7. Also in R. L. Jones & D. C. Macmillan (Eds.), *Special education in transition.* Boston MA: Allyn & Bacon, 1974.

1407. _____, & Soloway, M. M. *The Madison school plan: A functional model for merging the regular and special classrooms.* Unpublished paper, n.d. (ERIC Document Reproduction Service No. ED 074 678)

1408. Taylor, F. M. *Motivating reluctant learners: A manual for successful learning.* Denver, CO: Love Pub., 1974.

1409. The teacher and mainstreaming: "I'm ashamed to admit how angry I can feel." *Exceptional Parent*, 1978, 8(5), S3-S6.

1410. *Teacher centers as an approach to staff development in special education.* Papers presented at the Rhode Island Teacher Center Conference, Newport, RI, June 1977. (ERIC Document Reproduction Service No. ED 142 536)

1411. *Teacher education for mainstreaming: A casebook on school-college collaboration.* Minneapolis, MN: University of Minnesota, Leadership Training Institute/Special Education, 1978.

1412. Teachers' experiences in Massachusetts. *Today's Education,* 1976, *65*(2), 23-27.

1413. *A teacher's reference guide to P.L. 94-142, Infopac No. 11.* Washington, D.C.: National Education Association, Division of Instruction and Professional Development, 1978. (ERIC Document Reproduction Service No. ED 156 663)

1414. The teacher's rights in P.L. 94-142: A conversation with attorney Reed Martin. *Journal of Learning Disabilities,* 1978, *11*, 331-341.

1415. Teaching the handicapped in regular classrooms. *Ohio Schools,* 1975, *53*(4), 20-22.

1416. Thiagarajan, S., Semmel, D. S., & Semmel, M. I. *Instructional development for training teachers of exceptional children: A sourcebook.* Minneapolis, MN: Leadership Training Institute/ Special Education, University of Minnesota, 1974.

1417. Thurman, R. L. Mainstreaming: A concept general educators should embrace. *Educational Forum,* 1980, *44,* 285-293.

1418. Thurman, S. K., & Lewis, M. Children's response to differences: Some possible implications for mainstreaming. *Exceptional Children,* 1979, *45,* 468-470.

1419. Tilker, H., & Schell, R. Concurrent validity of the Porteus Maze Test: A comparative study of regular and educationally handicapped high school students. *Educational and Psychological Measurement,* 1967, *27,* 447-455.

1420. Tindall, L. W., & Gugerty, J. J. *Least restrictive alternative for handicapped students.* Washington, D.C.: Department of Health, Education and Welfare, Office of Education, Bureau of Occupational and Adult Education, 1979.

1421. _____, Lambert, R. H., & Gugerty, J. J. *Modifying regular vocational programs and developing curriculum materials for the vocational education of the handicapped. Progress report 1976.* Madison, WI: University of Wisconsin, Center for Studies in Vocational and Technical Education, 1976. (ERIC Document Reproduction Service No. ED 140 541)

1422. *To assure the free appropriate public education of all handicapped children (Public Law 94-142, Section 618).* Executive summary. Washington, D.C.: U.S. Department of Education and U.S. Office of Special Education and Rehabilitative Services, 1980.

1423.   Tobin, I. New York. Effects of federal legislation on physical education in three big cities. *Journal of Physical Education and Recreation*, 1980, *5*(1), 36-38.

1424.   *Tool Kit '76. Head Start services to handicapped children.* Washington, D.C.: Department of Health, Education and Welfare, Office of Child Development, 1976.

1425.   Torres, S. (Ed.). *A primer on individualized education programs for handicapped children.* Reston, VA: The Foundation for Exceptional Children, 1977. (ERIC Document Reproduction Service No. ED 136 453)

1426.   _____. *Special education administrative policies manual.* Reston, VA: The Council for Exceptional Children, 1977. (ERIC Document Reproduction Service No. ED 148 064)

1427.   Tractenberg, P. L. A response to Dunn and Cole. *Educational Leadership*, 1979, *36*, 306-307.

1428.   *A transportable professional development module for mainstreaming students into vocational education.* Louisville, KY: University of Louisville, n.d. (ERIC Document Reproduction Service No. ED 172 003)

1429.   Traylor, E. B., & Schoff, M. J. *Mainstreaming: Ethnography of the emerging role of special education teachers.* Paper presented at the Annual Meeting of the American Educational Research Association, Toronto, Ontario, Canada, March 1978. (ERIC Document Reproduction Service No. ED 154 554)

1430.   Trippe, M. *Love of life, love of truth, love of others.* Paper presented at the 48th Annual Convention of the Council for Exceptional Children, Chicago, IL, April 1970. (ERIC Document Reproduction Service No. ED 039 383)

1431.   Trotter, S. Labeling: It hurts more than it helps. *APA Monitor*, 1974, *13*(3), 2-3.

1432.   Trudeau, E., Nye, R., & Bolick, N. *State laws and administration procedures relating to the placement of exceptional children.* Arlington, VA: State and Federal Information Clearinghouse for Exceptional Children, 1973. (ERIC Document Reproduction Service No. ED 081 125)

1433.   Turnbull, A. P., & Blacher-Dixon, J. Preschool mainstreaming: An empirical and conceptual review. In P. Strain & M. M. Kerr (Eds.), *Mainstreaming of handicapped children in schools: Research and programmatic issues.* New York, NY: Academic Press, 1981.

1434.   _____, & Schulz, J. B. *Mainstreaming handicapped students: A guide for the classroom teacher.* Boston, MA: Allyn & Bacon, 1979.

1435.   _____, Stickland, B., & Goldstein, S. Training professionals and parents in developing and implementing the IEP. *Education and Training of the Mentally Retarded*, 1978, *13*, 414-423.

1436.   Turnbull, H. R. III. The past and future impact of court decisions in special education. *Phi Delta Kappan*, 1978, *59*, 523-527.

1437.   _____. Recent federal legislation on educating the handicapped. *School Law Bulletin*, 1977, *8*(3), 1-11.

1438.   _____, & Turnbull, A. *Free appropriate public education: Law and implementation.* Denver, CO: Love Pub., 1978.

1439.   Turner, R. M., & Macy, D. J. *A five-year longitudinal study of IEP implementation.* Paper presented at the Council for Exceptional Children National Topical Conference on Individualized Education Program Planning, Albuquerque, NM, 1978. (ERIC Document Reproduction Service No. ED 170 973)

1440.   Turney, D. A view from the bridge?: Mainstream or quiet eddy? *Contemporary Education*, 1975, *46*(2), 146.

1441.   Tutalo, A. J. *Staff development program. Maxi I practicum.* Unpublished doctoral dissertation, Nova University, 1975. (ERIC Document Reproduction Service No. ED 119 451)

1442.   *Unbiased assessment: Guidelines, procedures, and forms for the SEA's implementation of Public Law 94-142.* Salt Lake City, UT: Southwest Regional Resource Center, 1977. (ERIC Document Reproduction Service No. ED 138 024)

1443.   U.S. Congress. House. Committee on Conference. *Education of handicapped children: Report to Accompany S.6,* 94th Cong., 1st sess., 1975, H. Rept. 664.

1444.   _____. House. Committee on Education and Labor. *Education for All Handicapped Children Act of 1975: Report to Accompany H.R. 7217,* 94th Cong., 1st sess., 1975, H. Rept. 332.

1445.   _____. House. Committee on Education and Labor. *Financial assistance for improved educational services for handicapped children,* 93rd Cong., 2nd sess., 6, 7, 18, 22 March 1974.

1446.   _____. House. Committee on Labor and Public Welfare. *Extension of Education of the Handicapped Act, Part 10,* 94th Cong., 1st sess., 9, 10 April, 9 June 1975.

1447.   _____. House. *Congressional Record,* 94th Cong., 1st sess., 1975, *121*, pt. 18: 23701.

1448.   _____. House. *Congressional Record,* 94th Cong., 1st sess., 1975, *121*, pt. 20: 25526.

1449. _____. House. *Congressional Record*, 94th Cong., 1st sess., 1975, *121*, pt. 29: 37023.

1450. _____. Senate. Committee on Conference. *Education of handicapped children: Report to Accompany S.6*, 94th Cong., 1st sess., 1975, S. Rept. 455.

1451. _____. Senate. Committee on Labor and Public Welfare. *Education for All Handicapped Children Act: Report to Accompany S.6*, 94th Cong., 1st sess., 1975, S. Rept. 168.

1452. _____. Senate. Committee on Labor and Public Welfare. *Education for all handicapped children, 1973-74, Part 1*, 93rd Cong., 1st sess., 9 April, 7 May 1973.

1453. _____. Senate. Committee on Labor and Public Welfare. *Education for all handicapped children, 1973-74, Part 2*, 93rd Cong., 1st sess., 14 May 1973.

1454. _____. Senate. Committee on Labor and Public Welfare. *Education for all handicapped children, 1973-74, Part 3*, 93rd Cong., 1st sess., 19 October 1973, 93rd Cong., 2nd sess., 18 March 1974.

1455. _____. Senate. Committee on Labor and Public Welfare. *Education for all handicapped children, 1973-74, Part 4*, 93rd Cong., 2nd sess., 17, 24 June 1974.

1456. _____. Senate. Committee on Labor and Public Welfare. *Education of all handicapped children, 1975*, 94th Cong., 1st sess., 8, 9, 15 April 1975.

1457. _____. Senate. *Congressional Record*, 94th Cong., 1st sess., 1975, *121*, pt. 15: 19478.

1458. _____. Senate. *Congressional Record*, 94th Cong., 1st sess., 1975, *121*, pt. 29: 37409.

1459. U.S. President. Statement. "Education for All Handicapped Children Act of 1975." *Weekly Compilation of Presidential Documents*, vol. 11, no. 49, 2 December 1975.

1460. U.S. *Statutes at Large*, vol. 89. (Education for All Handicapped Children Act of 1975)

1461. Univer, I. O. The other handicap mandate—P.L. 94-142. *American School and University*, 1978, *50*(5), 35-36, 38.

1462. Upshur, B. L. Comparison of the self-concept and personality factors of maladjusted junior high school students in a special classroom setting with maladjusted students in a regular program (Doctoral dissertation, Fordham University, 1976). *Dissertation Abstracts International*, 1976, *37*, 2756A. (University Microfilms No. 76-25803)

1463.   Vacc, N. A. Preservice programs deficient in special education courses. *Journal of Teacher Education*, 1978, *29*(6), 42-43.

1464.   Valletutti, P. Integration vs. segregation: A useless dialect. *Journal of Special Education*, 1969, *3*, 405-408.

1465.   Vandivier, S. S., & Vandivier, P. L. To sink or swim in the mainstream. *Clearinghouse*, 1979, *52*, 277-279.

1466.   Van Dyke, M. *Crisis-resource teacher training project.* Paper presented at the Special Study Institute, Washington, D.C., October, 1971. (ERIC Document Reproduction Service No. ED 060 609)

1467.   Van Witsen, B. Attitudes of regular elementary school teachers toward teachers of special classes (Doctoral dissertation, Columbia University, 1968). *Dissertation Abstracts*, 1968, *30*, 973A. (University Microfilms No. 69-15174)

1468.   Veldman, D. J., & Scheffield, J. R. *GUESS WHO: The scaling of sociometric nominations.* Paper presented at the Annual Meeting of the American Education Research Association, Washington, D.C., March-April 1975. (ERIC Document Reproduction Service No. ED 106 360)

1469.   Vergason, G. A., Smith, Jr., F. V., & Wyatt, K. E. Questions for administrators about special education. *Theory into Practice*, 1975, *14*, 99-104.

1470.   Vlahos, P. N. Developing legal rights for handicapped citizens. *Volta Review*, 1977, *79*, 270-274.

1471.   Vlasak, J. W. Relationships between elementary school principals' skills and attitudes of classroom teachers toward programming for mildly handicapped students within regular classrooms (Doctoral dissertation, The University of Texas at Austin, 1974). *Dissertation Abstracts International*, 1974, *35*, 5180A. (University Microfilms No. 75-04470)

1472.   Vodola, T. M. *Education for handicapped children: Rationale, concerns and recommendations.* Unpublished paper, 1978. (ERIC Document Reproduction Service No. ED 164 493)

1473.   _____. *Guidelines for complying with Public Law 94-142 and Section 504 of the Rehabilitation Act of 1973.* Unpublished paper, 1978. ERIC Document Reproduction Service No. ED 164 494)

1474.   Volknor, C., & Langstaff, A. *Bibliography on mainstreaming.* Los Angeles, CA: California Regional Resource Center, 1975.

1475.   Walden, S. B., Meyers, R., Moran, S., Jordan, T., & Phillips, D. *Special service personnel: A source of help for the teacher.* Des Moines, IA: Special Education Curriculum Development Center, University of Iowa, 1971. (ERIC Document Reproduction Service No. ED 054 555)

1476. Walker, C. W. What's happening in New Jersey? *Today's Education*, 1980, 69(2), 49-52.

1477. Walker, H. M., & Hops, H. Use of normative peer data as a standard for evaluating classroom treatment effects. *Journal of Applied Behavior Analysis*, 1976, 9(2), 159-168.

1478. Walker, M. L., & Pomeranz, J. College/Rehab collaboration for 504 compliance. *Journal of College Student Personnel*, 1979, 20, 115-121.

1479. Walker, V. S. Model for preparing regular classroom teachers for mainstreaming. *Exceptional Children*, 1973, 39, 471-472.

1480. Wallin, J. E. W. To set the historical record straight. *Exceptional Children*, 1958, 25, 175-177.

1481. Walsh, E. Handicapped and science: Moving into the mainstream. *Science*, 1977, 196(4297), 1424-1426.

1482. Walters, P. B., Vogel, R. J., Brandis, M. R., & Thouvenelle, S. *Evaluation of the process of mainstreaming handicapped children into Project Head Start. Phase I. Final report.* Silver Spring, MD: Applied Management Sciences, 1978. (ERIC Document Reproduction Service No. ED 168-239)

1483. Ward, M. J., Arkell, R. N., Dahl, H. G., & Wise, J. H. *Everybody counts! A workshop manual to increase awareness of handicapped people.* Reston, VA: The Council for Exceptional Children, 1979. (ERIC Document Reproduction Service No. ED 172 463)

1484. Warfield, C. J. (Ed.). *Mainstream currents: Reprints from Exceptional Children, 1968-1974.* Reston, VA: The Council for Exceptional Children, 1974. (ERIC Document Reproduction Service No. ED 102 759)

1485. Wargo, W. D. Teaching special needs students: Individualizing instruction. *Industrial Education*, 1977, 66(8), 20, 24.

1486. Warnat, W. I. In-service education: Key to P.L. 94-142's service to handicapped children and youth. *Educational Leadership*, 1978, 35, 474-479.

1487. Warnock, N. J. Making general education special. *Education and Training of the Mentally Retarded*, 1976, 11, 304-308.

1488. Warrick, D. B. *Personnel training to facilitate mainstreaming: The educational resource centers model.* Paper presented at the 55th Annual International Convention of the Council for Exceptional Children, Atlanta, GA, April 1977. (ERIC Document Reproduction Service No. ED 139 210)

1489.   _____, & Isaacson, S. *Mainstreaming: The educational resource centers model.* Medford, OR: Jackson County Education Service District, 1978. (ERIC Document Reproduction Service No. ED 145 501 and ED 169 744)

1490.   Wasserman, T., & Adamany, N. Day treatment and public schools: An approach to mainstreaming. *Child Welfare,* 1976, *55*(2), 117-124.

1491.   Watkins, A. V. An assessment of the status of special education students who have returned to regular classrooms for intellectually normal pupils (Doctoral dissertation, Claremont Graduate School, 1975). *Dissertation Abstracts International,* 1975, *36,* 4411A. (University Microfilms No. 75-25838)

1492.   Weber, D. L., & Weber, M. B. *A suggested evaluation strategy for P.L. 94-142.* Paper presented at the Annual meeting of the Eastern Educational Research Association, Kiawah, SC, February 1979). (ERIC Document Reproduction Service No. ED 172 493)

1493.   Weckler, E. *IMPACT: Instructional model program for all children and teachers. Annual evaluation report, 1975-76.* Berrien Springs, MI: Berrien Springs Public Schools, 1976. (ERIC Document Reproduction Service No. ED 144 324)

1494.   _____, Roberts, K., & Youngberg, M. *Impact—did today matter? Part I. Mainstreaming in the classroom; Part II. Student teacher training at the university.* Paper presented at the 21st Annual Meeting of the International Reading Association, Anaheim, CA, May 1976. (ERIC Document Reproduction Service No. ED 122 205)

1495.   Weiderholt, J. L. Planning resource rooms for the mildly handicapped. *Focus on Exceptional Children,* 1974, *5*(8), 1-10.

1496.   Weinberg, R. A., & Wood, F. H. (Eds.). *Observation of pupils and teachers in mainstream and special education settings: Alternative strategies.* Minneapolis, MN: University of Minnesota, College of Education, 1975. (ERIC Document Reproduction Service No. ED 108 423)

1497.   Weiner, B. B. (Ed.). *Periscope: Views of the individualized education program.* Reston, VA: The Council for Exceptional Children, 1978. (ERIC Document Reproduction Service No. ED 159 872)

1498.   Weininger, O. Integrate or isolate: A perspective on the whole child. *Education,* 1973, *94*(2), 139-147.

1499.   Weintraub, F. J. The people, yes, revisited. *Exceptional Children,* 1969, *36,* 47-49.

1500. _____. Recent influences of law regarding the identification and educational placement of children. *Focus on Exceptional Children,* 1972, *4*(2), 1-11.

1501. _____. Understanding the Individualized Education Program (IEP). *Amicus,* 1977, *2*(3), 26-31.

1502. _____. What you need to know about P.L. 94-142. *Early Years,* 1977, *7*(9), 36-37.

1503. _____, & Abeson, A. New education policies for the handicapped. *Education Digest,* 1974, *40,* 13-16.

1504. _____, & Abeson, A. New education policies for the handicapped—the quiet revolution. *Phi Delta Kappan,* 1974, *55,* 526-529, 569. Also in J. W. Schifani (Ed.), *Contemporary issues in mainstreaming.* Dubuque, IA: Kendall/Hunt Pub., 1976.

1505. _____, Abeson, A., Ballard, J., & Lavor, M. (Eds.). *Public policy and the education of exceptional children.* Reston, VA: The Council for Exceptional Children, 1976. (ERIC Document Reproduction Service No. ED 116 403)

1506. _____, Abeson, A., & Braddock, D. L. *State law and education of handicapped children: Issues and recommendations.* Reston, VA: State and Federal Information¹ Clearinghouse for Exceptional Children, The Council for Exceptional Children, 1971. (ERIC Document Reproduction Service No. ED 056 452)

1507. Weisberg, P. Implications of "The Education of All Handicapped Children Act of 1975" for the exceptional parent. *Journal for Special Education of the Mentally Retarded,* 1977, *14,* 52-54.

1508. Weisenstein, G. R. Changing patterns of teacher preparation: A look at the influence of mainstreaming. *Lutheran Education,* 1977, *112,* 267-275.

1509. _____, & Gall, M. D. Adapting teacher education to include mainstreaming: Deans' Grant Projects. *Journal of Teacher Education,* 1978, *29*(6), 22-24.

1510. Weisgerber, R. *Mainstreaming the handicapped in vocational education. Developing a general understanding.* Palo Alto, CA: American Institutes for Research in the Behavioral Sciences, 1977. (ERIC Document Reproduction Service No. ED 142 769)

1511. _____. *Mainstreaming the handicapped in vocational education. Developing a plan for action.* Palo Alto, CA: American Institute for Research in the Behavioral Sciences, 1977. (ERIC Document Reproduction Service No. ED 142 747)

1512. _____ (Ed.). *Vocational education: Teaching the handicapped in regular classes.* Reston, VA: The Council for Exceptional Children, 1978. (ERIC Document Reproduction Service No. ED 159 852)

1513.   Weisgerber, R. A. Individualizing for the handicapped child in the regular classroom. *Educational Technology*, 1974, *14*(11), 33-35.

1514.   Wendel, F. C. Progress in mainstreaming. *Phi Delta Kappan*, 1977, *59*, 58.

1515.   Wenokor, S. A comparative study of teacher and principal role expectations in regular and alternative secondary schools (Doctoral dissertation, Columbia University, Teachers College, 1976). *Dissertation Abstracts International*, 1976, *37*, 1483A. (University Microfilms No. 76-21041)

1516.   Wentling, T. L. Teaching special needs students/Article 9: Measurement and evaluation. *Industrial Education*, 1978, *67*(5), 29-30, 32.

1517.   _____, & Phelps, L. A. An interview with Rupert N. Evans and Maynard C. Reynolds. *Journal of Industrial Teacher Education*, 1977, *14*(4), 9-18.

1518.   Wessel, J. A., Carmichael, D. L., & Elder, J. K. *Planning, implementing and evaluating physical education and recreation for the exceptional child.* Paper presented at the 1st World Congress on Future Special Education, Stirling, Scotland, June 1978. (ERIC Document Reproduction Service No. ED 158 479)

1519.   _____, Vogel, P., & Plack, J. *Physical education (skill) performance objectives, elementary and secondary.* Madison, WI: Wisconsin State Department of Public Instruction, 1974. (ERIC Document Reproduction Service No. ED 096 281)

1520.   West, T. L. *Individualized teacher training for mainstreaming using a computer assisted goal setting procedure.* Paper presented at the 57th Annual International Convention of the Council for Exceptional Children, Dallas, TX, April 1979. (ERIC Document Reproduction Service No. ED 171 005)

1521.   Westervelt, V.D., & McKinney, J. D. Effects of a film on nonhandicapped children's attitudes toward handicapped children. *Exceptional Children*, 1980, *46*, 294-296.

1522.   Westling, D. L., & Joiner, M. D. Consulting with teachers of handicapped children in the mainstream. *Elementary School Guidance and Counseling*, 1979, *13*, 207-213.

1523.   What is "mainstreaming"? *Exceptional Children*, 1975, *42*, 174.

1524.   What the laws and regulations require. *Todays Education*, 1977, *66*(4), 54-56.

1525.   White, A. H. *NCEMMH report on needs in special education.* Columbus, OH: National Center for Educational Media and Materials for the Handicapped, n.d. (ERIC Document Reproduction Service No. ED 101 523)

1526. Whiteford, E. B. *Special needs students in regular home economics programs: 1977 report on Minnesota secondary in-service teacher education.* St. Paul, MN: University of Minnesota, Division of Home Economics Education, 1977. (ERIC Docoument Reproduction Service No. ED 147 556)

1527. _____, & Anderson, D. H. Mainstreaming of special needs students: Home ec teachers are coping. *American Vocational Journal,* 1977, *52,* 42-44.

1528. Whitfield, E. Experiments on tape. *Science and Children,* 1976, *13*(6), 47.

1529. Widlake, P. The education of disadvantaged children. *Aspects of Education,* 1975, *20,* 48-53.

1530. Wiener, W. K., & Rudisill, M. S. *Collecting baseline data for the least restrictive alternative.* Paper presented at the Annual Meeting of the Midwestern Association of Behavior Analysis, Chicago, IL, 1976. (ERIC Document Reproduction Service No. ED 125 053)

1531. Wilderson, F. *Coping power of the mainstream educator—critical issues and problems.* Paper presented at the 4th Annual Invitational Special Education Leadership Conference, Minneapolis, MN, December 1974. In R. A. Johnson, R. F. Weatherman, & A. M. Rehman (Eds.). *Special education leadership series. Vol. IV: Handicapped youth and the mainstream educator.* Minneapolis, MN: AudioVisual Extension Service, University of Minnesota, 1974.

1532. Williams, H. A., Jr. Education for all handicapped children. *Parents Magazine,* 1976, *51,* 20.

1533. Williams, R. J. An investigation of regular class teachers' attitudes toward the mainstreaming of four categories of mildly handicapped students (Doctoral dissertation, The Pennsylvania State University, 1977). *Dissertation Abstracts International,* 1977, *38,* 2708A. (University Microfilms No. 77-23290)

1534. Williams, W., Brown, L., & Certo, N. Basic components of instructional programs. *Theory into Practice,* 1975, *14,* 123-136.

1535. Wilson, G. A. Legal concerns in special education. *Theory into Practice,* 1975, *14,* 69-72.

1536. Wilson, H. H. Mainstreaming sensitivity session for IA teachers. *School Shop,* 1979, *39,* 38-39.

1537. Winnick, J. P. Techniques for integration. *Journal of Physical Education and Recreation,* 1978, *49*(6), 22.

1538. Winzer, M. Swimming upstream: A new concept in mainstreaming. *Orbit,* 1980, *11,* 12.

1539. Wircenski, J. L. *Handbook for the identification and assessment of disadvantaged learners.* University Park, PA: Pennsylvania State University, Division of Occupational and Vocational Studies, n.d. (ERIC Document Reproduction Service No. ED 177 344)

1540. Wirtz, M. A. *An administrator's handbook of special education; a guide to better education for the handicapped.* Springfield, IL: C. C. Thomas, 1977.

1541. Wolfensberger, W., & Mirje, B. *The principle of normalization in human services.* Toronto, Ontario, Canada: National Institute on Mental Retardation, 1972.

1542. Woodward, J. E. Peer acceptance for the handicapped: Myth or reality? *Phi Delta Kappan,* 1980, *61,* 715.

1543. Woodward, R. E. The handicap mandate. *American School and University,* 1977, *50*(1), 35-36, 38, 40.

1544. Woodworth, D., Jr. In the mainstream—Rick's a part of the team. *Instructor,* 1977, *87*(3), 202-203.

1545. Woolfolk, A. E. P. Increasing student attention; a learning theory approach with an emphasis on transfer to the regular classroom (Doctoral dissertation, University of Texas at Austin, 1972). *Dissertation Abstracts International,* 1972, *33,* 4961A. (University Microfilms No. 73-07680)

1546. Worcester Public Schools, Massachusetts. *Mainstreaming: The integration of children with special needs into a regular classroom environment.* Bedford, MA: Institute for Educational Services, 1974.

1547. Wordlaw, J. Mainstreaming that works. In P. H. Mann (Ed.), *Shared responsibility for handicapped students: Advocacy and programming.* Coral Gables, FL: University of Miami Training and Technical Assistance Center, 1976.

1548. Wright, B. A. Changes in attitudes toward people with handicaps. *Rehabilitation Literature,* 1973, *34,* 354-357.

1549. Wright, R. G. Special—but not separate. *Education,* 1967, *87,* 554-557.

1550. Wullschleger, P., & Gavin, R. T. *A secondary resource room program. A practical and applied model for efffective mainstreaming.* Paper presented at the 57th Annual Convention of the Council for Exceptional Children, Dallas, TX, April 1979. (ERIC Document Reproduction Service No. ED 171 092)

1551. Wynne, S., Brown, J. K., Dakof, G., & Ulfelder, L. S. *Mainstreaming and early childhood education for handicapped children; a guide for teachers and parents. Final report.* Washington, D.C.: Wynne Assoc., 1975. (ERIC Document Reproduction Service No. ED 119 445)

1552. _____, Ulfelder, L. S., & Dakof, G. *Mainstreaming and early childhood education for handicapped children. Review and implications of research.* Washington, D.C.: Wynne Associates, 1975. (ERIC Document Reproduction Service No. ED 108 426)

1553. Yang, D. Welcome the handicapped to your classroom and enrich it; an interview. *Teacher,* 1975 *93*(4), 13, 20-21.

1554. Yarger, S. J., & Schmieder, A. A. A promising approach to staff development. *Today's Education,* 1978, *67*(2), 70-71.

1555. Yates, J. R. A model for preparing regular classroom teachers for "mainstreaming." *Exceptional Children,* 1973, *39,* 471-472.

1556. Yates, N. R. How MTA helped teachers get ready. *Today's Education,* 1976, *65*(2), 28-29.

1557. Yoshida, R. K. Out-of-level testing of special education students with a standardized achievement battery. *Journal of Educational Measurement,* 1976, *13,* 215-221.

1558. _____, Fenton, K. S., & Kaufman, M. J. Evaluation of education for the handicapped. *Phi Delta Kappan,* 1977, *59,* 59-60.

1559. _____, Fenton, K. S., Kaufman, M. J., & Maxwell, J. P. Parental involvement in the special education pupil planning process: The school's perspective. *Exceptional Children,* 1978, *44,* 531-534.

1560. _____, Schensul, J. J., Pelto, P. J., & Fenton, K.S. The principal and special education placement. *National Elementary Principal,* 1978, *58,* 34-38.

1561. Young, M. A. *Teaching children with special learning needs—a problem-solving approach. John Day Books in Special Education series.* New York: John Day, 1967. (ERIC Document Reproduction Service No. ED 018 038)

1562. *Your rights under the Education for All Handicapped Children Act (P.L. 94-142).* Washington, D.C.: The Children's Defense Fund, 1976.

1563. Ysseldyke, J. E., & Regan, R. R. Nondiscriminatory assessment: A formative model. *Exceptional Children,* 1980, *46,* 465-466.

1564. Zakariya, S. B. Helping children understand disabilities. *National Elementary Principal,* 1978, *58,* 46-47.

1565. Zelinka, M. The state of mathematics in our schools. *American Mathematical Monthly,* 1980, *86,* 428-432.

1566. Zemanek, D. H., & Lehrer, B. E. The role of university departments of special education in mainstreaming. *Exceptional Children,* 1977, *43,* 377-379.

1567. Zettel, J. J., & Weintraub, F. J. P.L. 94-142: Its origin and implications. *National Elementary Principal*, 1978, *58*, 10-13.

1568. Zinar, R. Music in the mainstream. *Teacher*, 1978, *95*(7), 54-56.

1569. Zufall, D. L. Exceptional person: Approaches to integration. *Journal of School Health*, 1976, *46*, 142-144.

II. GIFTED

1570. Alam, S. J. A comparative study of gifted students enrolled in separate and regular curriculums (Doctoral dissertation, Wayne State University, 1968). *Dissertation Abstracts*, 1968, *29*, 3354A. (University Microfilms No. 69-06057)

1571. Albright, A. D. *Southern high school programs for advanced standing and accelerated college progression.* Fulton County, GA: Southern Association of Colleges and Secondary Schools, n.d. (ERIC Document Reproduction Service No. ED 001 302)

1572. Barbe, W. B., & Norris, D. N. Special classes for gifted children in Cleveland. *Exceptional Children*, 1954, *21*, 55-57, 71.

1573. Boston, B. O. (Ed.) *Gifted and talented: Developing elementary and secondary school programs.* Reston, VA: Council for Exceptional Children, 1975. (ERIC Document Reproduction Service No. ED 117 886)

1574. _____. *A resource manual of information on educating the gifted and talented.* Reston, VA: Council for Exceptional Children, 1975. (ERIC Document Reproduction Service No. ED 117 885)

1575. DeHaan, R. F., & Havighurst, R. J. *Educating gifted children.* Chicago: University of Chicago Press, 1961.

1576. Doe, B. Russian streaming in retreat after great debateski? *Times Educational Supplement (London)*, October 6, 1978, no. 3301, p. 6.

1577. Duncan, A. D. W. Behavior rates of gifted and regular elementary school children (Doctoral dissertation, University of Kansas, 1968). *Dissertation Abstracts*, 1968, *29*, 3920A. (University Microfilms No. 69-05080)

1578. Dunlap, J. M. Gifted children in an enriched program. *Exceptional Children*, 1955, *21*, 135-137.

1579. Flowman, P. D., & Rice, J. P. *Demonstration of differential programming in enrichment acceleration. Counseling and special classes for gifted pupils to grades 1-9. Final report.* Sacramento: California State Department of Education, 1967. (ERIC Document Reproduction Service No. ED 019 763)

1580. Gourley, T. J. Jr. Programs for gifted students: A national survey. *Talents and Gifts,* June 1976, pp. 31-32.

1581. Grupe, A. J. Adjustment and acceptance of mentally superior children in regular and special fifth grade classes in a public school system (Doctoral dissertation, University of Illinois at Urbana-Champaign, 1961). *Dissertation Abstracts,* 1961, *22,* 1508. (University Microfilms No. 61-04301)

1582. Henson, F. O. *Mainstreaming the gifted.* Austin, TX: Learning Concepts, 1976.

1583. Hildreth, G. H. *Educating gifted children at Hunter College Elementary School.* New York: Harper, 1952.

1584. Joyce, J. V. *A comparative study of the social position of retarded and gifted children in regular grades and in segregated groups.* Unpublished doctoral dissertation, Syracuse University, 1954.

1585. Kane, B. Tinker toys: The education of the gifted and talented. *National Elementary Principal,* 1978, *58*(1), 25-29.

1586. Kaplan, S. *Providing programs for the gifted and talented—a handbook.* Reston, VA: Council for Exceptional Children, 1975. (ERIC Document Reproduction Service No. ED 104 093)

1587. Karnes, M. B. *Identifying and programming young gifted/talented handicapped children.* Paper presented at the First World Congress on Future Special Education, Stirling, Scotland, June-July 1978. (ERIC Document Reproduction Service No. ED 157 313)

1588. _____, & Bertschi, J. D. Identifying and educating gifted/talented nonhandicapped and handicapped preschoolers. *Teaching Exceptional Children,* 1978, *10*(4), 114-119.

1589. Kester, E. P.L. 94-142: "Spread the alarm!" *Creative Child and Adult Quarterly,* 1978, *3*(2), 117-121.

1590. Ketcham, W. A. Can instruction for the gifted be improved? Thoughts on a basic design for gifted education. *Innovator,* 1975, *7*(2), 8-11.

1591. Leonard, J. E., & Cansler, D. P. Serving gifted/handicapped preschoolers and their families: A demonstration project. *Roeper Review,* 1980, *2*(3), 39-41.

1592. Lewis, C. L., & Kanes, L. G. Gifted IEPS: Impact of expectations and perspectives. *Journal for the Education of the Gifted,* 1979, *2*(2), 61-69.

1593. Luttrell, J. S. A comparative investigation of the academic achievement and personality development of gifted sixth grade pupils in a special class and in regular classrooms in the public schools of Greensboro, North Carolina (Doctoral dissertation, University of North Carolina at Chapel Hill, 1958). *Dissertation Abstracts,* 1958, *19,* 2536. (University Microfilms No. 59-00052)

1594.   Maker, C. J. *Providing programs for the gifted handicapped.* Reston, VA: Council for Exceptional Children, 1977. (ERIC Document Reproduction Service No. ED 133 942)

1595.   Mulhern, J. D. The gifted child in the regular classroom. *Roeper Review,* 1978, *1*(1), 3-6.

1596.   Orloff, J. H. (Ed.). *Realizing their potential. Proceedings of the 3rd Northern Virginia Council for Gifted/Talented Education, Manassas, VA, March 1978.* (ERIC Document Reproduction Service No. ED 165 358)

1597.   O'Rourke, R. H. A study of the creative thinking abilities, attitudes and achievement of academically talented students in the honors program and regular classes at Cooley High School, 1962-1965 (Doctoral dissertation, Wayne State University, 1968). *Dissertation Abstracts International,* 1968, *30*, 962A. (University Microfilms No. 69-14679)

1598.   Pearlman, L. A. A comparison of selected characteristics of gifted children enrolled in major work and regular curriculums (Doctoral dissertation, Kent State University, 1971). *Dissertation Abstracts International,* 1971, *32*, 4846A. (University Microfilms No. 72-09276)

1599.   Peters, D. *An individualized education plan (IEP) for the gifted child.* Unpublished manuscript, 1978. (ERIC Document Reproduction Service No. ED 166 899)

1600.   Schauer, G. H. An analysis of the self-report of fifth and sixth-grade regular class children and gifted class children (Doctoral dissertation, Kent State University, 1975). *Dissertation Abstracts International,* 1975, *36*, 6001A. (University Microfilms No. 76-04943)

1601.   Scheifele, M. *The gifted child in the regular classroom.* New York: Bureau of Publications, Teachers College, Columbia University, 1953.

1602.   Schible, D. Right to education for all exceptional school-age persons, including gifted, made part of Pennsylvania school code. *Talents and Gifts,* November 1975, p. 22.

1603.   Schreffler, R. H. Six year study of three groups of students screened for sixth grade major work classes: special and regular class students of high Binet IQ, and pseudogifted students (Doctoral dissertation, The Pennsylvania State University, 1968). *Dissertation Abstracts,* 1968, *29*, 3473A. (University Microfilms No. 69-05585)

1604.   Stark, J. B. Program development and the gifted area service centers. *Illinois Libraries,* 1977, *59*, 480-485.

1605. Stevens, D. F. *An experimental study of a program of enrichment for the gifted child in a regular fifth grade class at the Oyster Bay Elementary School.* Unpublished doctoral dissertation, Columbia University, 1959.

1606. Stovall, B. J., & Tongue, C. *The itinerant resource teacher: A manual for programs with gifted children.* Raleigh: North Carolina State Department of Public Instruction/Division of Special Education, 1970. (ERIC Document Reproduction Service No. ED 053 506)

1607. *Suggested solutions to problems teachers encounter with their gifted students.* St. Paul: Minnesota State Department of Education, Division of Instruction, 1972. (ERIC Document Reproduction Service No. ED 071 217)

1608. Svebak, S. *Models for educational integration of retarded, normal and gifted children.* Bergen, Norway: University of Bergen, 1972.

1609. Syphers, D. F. *Gifted and talented children: Practical programming for teachers and principals.* Reston, VA: Council for Exceptional Children, 1972.

1610. *Teaching the gifted and talented in the regular classroom.* Boston: National Association of Independent Schools, 1978.

1611. Tempest, N. R. Gifted—and handicapped? *Special Education: Forward Trends,* 1974, *1*(1), 14-16.

1612. Torrance, E. P. *Gifted children in the classroom.* New York: Mac-Millan, 1965.

1613. Trahin, T. R. Caring for the needs of mentally gifted children in a regular classroom (Doctoral dissertation, University of Arkansas, 1959). *Dissertation Abstracts,* 1959, *20,* 1290. (University Microfilms No. 59-03045)

1614. Trezise, R. L. The gifted child: Back in the limelight. *Phi Delta Kappan,* 1976, *58,* 241-244.

1615. Van Tassel, J. The role of the library in gifted child education. *Illinois Libraries,* 1977, *59,* 498-500.

1616. Zettel, J. J., & Ballard, J. A need for increased Federal effort for the gifted and talented. *Exceptional Children,* 1978, *44,* 261-267.

III. HEARING IMPAIRED

1617. Advisory Council for the Deaf. *A comprehensive plan for the education of hearing impaired children and youth in Massachusetts.* Boston: Massachusetts Department of Education, Division of Special Education, 1975.

1618.   Alexander, D. Some observations on the integration of deaf chil-
        dren into normal schools in Queensland. *Australian Teacher of the
        Deaf,* 1961, 4(1), 4.

1619.   Allen, J. C. A challenge to parents. *Volta Review,* 1977, 79,
        297-302.

1620.   _____. Parents' role in public law 94-142. *Volta Review,* 1977,
        79, 202-203.

1621.   Anderson, G. B., & Bowe, F. G. Racism within the deaf community.
        American Annals of the Deaf, 1972, 117, 617-619.

1622.   Anderson, N. O. Wyoming's unique program for the hearing
        impaired. *Volta Review,* 1964, 66, 537-539.

1623.   Auble, L. F. The integrated superintendent: Normalization can be
        a reality. In W. H. Northcott (Ed.), *The hearing impaired child in a
        regular classroom.* Washington, D.C.: Alexander Graham Bell
        Association for the Deaf, 1973.

1624.   _____. Mainstreaming in Southwestern Michigan. In G. W. Nix
        (Ed.), *Mainstream education for hearing impaired children and
        youth.* New York, NY: Grune & Stratton, 1976.

1625.   _____. Normalization can be a reality. *Volta Review,* 1972, 74,
        481-486.

1626.   Austin, G. F. (Ed.). *Proceedings of the Utah Conference, Profes-
        sional Rehabilitation Workers with the Adult Deaf (PRWAD), Salt
        Lake City, UT, July 1976.* (ERIC Document Reproduction Service
        No. ED 159 834). Also in *Journal of Rehabilitation of the Deaf,*
        1977, 11(1), 1-78.

1627.   Avery, C. B. The education of children with impaired hearing. In
        W. M. Cruickshank, & G. O. Johnson (Eds.), *Education of excep-
        tional children and youth.* 3d. ed. Englewood Cliffs, NJ: Prentice-
        Hall, 1975.

1628.   _____. The social competence of preschool acoustically handi-
        capped children. *Journal of Exceptional Children,* 1948, 25, 71-73.

1629.   Baldwin, C. P., & Baldwin, A. L. *Personality and social develop-
        ment of handicapped children.* Ithaca, NY: Cornell University,
        1972. (ERIC Document Reproduction Service No. ED 079 895)

1630.   Balow, B., Fulton, H., & Peploe, E. Reading comprehension skills
        among hearing-impaired adolescents. *Volta Review,* 1971, 73,
        113-119.

1631.   Bangs, T. E. Where should the deaf child be educated? *Volta
        Review,* 1954, 56, 298-300.

1632.   Beckman, C. Mainstreaming: Hearing-impaired students. *Journal of Home Economics,* 1978, 70(2), 34-38.

1633.   Beebe, H. H. Deaf children can learn to hear. In Nix, G. W. (Ed.), *Mainstream education for hearing impaired children and youth.* New York: Grune & Stratton, 1976.

1634.   Behre, A. *New York speaks to the mainstream issue.* Paper presented at the 47th Biennial Convention of the American Instructors of the Deaf, Greensboro, NC, June, 1975.

1635.   Behrens, T. R. *Demonstration project for the initiation of summer curriculum with special emphasis upon languge acceleration for hearing impaired children: Final report.* Washington, D.C.: Kendall School for the Deaf/Galludet, 1967. (ERIC Document Reproduction Service No. 031 853)

1636.   Bell, A. A tape recorder "takes notes" in a junior high science class. *Volta Review,* 1968, 70, 348-349.

1637.   Bellefleur, P. A. An open letter to my colleagues. *American Annals of the Deaf,* 1974, 119, 29-33.

1638.   Berg, F. S. A model for a facilitative program for hearing impaired college students. *Volta Review,* 1972, 74, 370-375.

1639.   Bernstein, H. W. Special approaches in learning processes for the deaf. *Volta Review,* 1974, 76, 42-51.

1640.   Biklen, D. P. Deaf children vs. the Board of Education. *American Annals of the Deaf,* 1975, 120, 382-386.

1641.   Bilek, S. The integrated teacher. In W. H. Northcott (Ed.), *The hearing impaired child in a regular classroom.* Washington, D.C.: Alexander Graham Bell Association for the Deaf, 1973.

1642.   Birch, J. W. *Hearing impaired pupils in the mainstream.* Minneapolis, MN: University of Minnesota, Leadership Training Institute/Special Education, 1976. (ERIC Document Reproduction Service No. ED 117 904)

1643.   _____. Mainstream education for hearing-impaired pupils: Issues and interviews. *American Annals of the Deaf,* 1976, 121, 69-71.

1644.   Birdsong, M. B. Tad. *Volta Review,* 1967, 69, 265-266.

1645.   Bitter, G. B. Mainstream education for the hearing impaired—Promises to keep. In Nix, G. W. (Ed.), *Mainstream education for hearing impaired children and youth.* New York, NY: Grune & Stratton, 1976.

1646.   _____. Maximum cultural involvement for the hearing impaired: Environmental impact. In Nix, G. W. (Ed.), *Mainstream education for hearing impaired children and youth.* New York, NY: Grune & Stratton, 1976.

1647.   _____. Whose schools—educational expediency/educational integrity? In G. W. Nix (Ed.), *Mainstream education for hearing impaired children and youth.* New York, NY: Grune & Stratton, 1976.

1648.   _____, Johnston, K. A., & Sorensen, R. G. *Project NEED, integration of the hearing-impaired: Educational issues.* Salt Lake City, UT: University of Utah, Department of Special Education, 1973.

1649.   _____, & Mears, E. G. Facilitating the integration of hearing impaired children into regular public school classes. *Volta Review,* 1973, *75,* 13-22.

1650.   Black, P., & Bolin, T. D. *On including an elementary hearing-impaired program in a regular elementary school and integrating hearing impaired children into the student body.* Paper presented at the Alexander Graham Bell National Convention, St. Louis, MO, June 1978.

1651.   Blair, F. X. Programming for auditorially disabled children. *Exceptional Children,* 1969, *36,* 259-264.

1652.   Blake, G. D. Effects of integrated training experiences on the attitudes of hearing adults toward deaf adults and deafness (Doctoral dissertation, University of Arkansas, 1971). *Dissertation Abstracts International,* 1971, *32,* 809A. University Microfilms No. 71-19536)

1653.   Blake, T. E. Friends and hobbies. *Volta Review,* 1967, *69,* 264-266.

1654.   Bloom, F. Deafness termed a social handicap. *Volta Review,* 1967, *69,* 67-70.

1655.   Bloom, J. L. An investigation of the effect of presenting a sex education course to high school students who have been removed from the regular classroom situation because of severe emotional or physical problems (Doctoral dissertation, New York University, 1968). *Dissertation Abstracts International,* 1968, *30,* 483A. (University Microfilms No. 69-11738)

1656.   Blumberg, C. A. A school for the deaf facilitates integration. In W. H. Northcott (Ed.), *The hearing impaired child in a regular classroom.* Washington, D.C.: Alexander Graham Bell Association for the Deaf, 1973.

1657.   Boatner, E. B. The vocational rehabilitation program of the American School for the Deaf. *Journal of Rehabilitation of the Deaf,* 1969, *3* (1), 69-79.

1658.   Bosch, B. Letter to his former schoolmates. *Volta Review,* 1976, *78,* 44-46.

1659. Bothwell, H. Special feature on the physically handicapped: The aurally handicapped child. *Today's Education*, 1967, *56*(8), 33-48.

1660. _____. What the classroom teacher can do for the child with impaired hearing. *Today's Education*, 1967, *56*, 44-46.

1661. Bowling, W. C. Day classes for the deaf-Covina plan. *Volta Review*, 1967, *69*, 54-57.

1662. Bowman, E. A resource room program for hearing impaired students. In W. H. Northcott (Ed.), *The hearing impaired child in a regular classroom*. Washington, D.C.: Alexander Graham Bell Association for the Deaf, 1973.

1663. _____. A resource room program for hearing impaired students. *Volta Review*, 1973, *75*, 208-213.

1664. Bowyer, L. R., & Gillies, J. The social and emotional adjustment of deaf and partially deaf children. *British Journal of Educational Psychology*, 1972, *42*, 305-308.

1665. _____, Marshall, A., & Weddell, K. The relative personality adjustment of severely deaf and partially deaf children. *British Journal of Educational Psychology*, 1963, *33*, 85-87.

1666. Brackett, D., & Henniges, M. Communicative interaction of preschool hearing impaired children in an integrated setting. *Volta Review*, 1976, *78*, 276-285.

1667. Braddock, M. J. Integrating the deaf and hard of hearing student. *Volta Review*, 1962, *64*, 500-501.

1668. Bradway, K. The social competence of deaf children. *American Annals of the Deaf*, 1937, *82*, 122-140.

1669. Breunig, H. L., & Nix, G. W. Historical and educational perspectives. *Volta Review*, 1977, *79*, 263-269.

1670. Brill, R. G. Mainstreaming: Format or quality? *American Annals of the Deaf*, 1975, *120*, 377-381. Also in *Maryland Bulletin*, 1976, *96*(4) 49-53, & in *Audiology and Hearing Education*, 1976, *32*, 13-16.

1671. Brooks, D. K. *Counseling the hearing impaired child in the public schools: Techniques and strategies*. Paper presented at the American Personnel and Guidance Association Convention, Washington, D.C., March 1978. (ERIC Document Reproduction Service No. ED 160 912)

1672. Bruce, W. The parent's role from an educator's point of view. In W. H. Northcott (Ed.), *The hearing impaired child in the regular classroom*. Washington, D.C.: Alexander Graham Bell Association for the Deaf, 1973.

1673. _____. Social integration and effectiveness of speech. *Volta Review*, 1960, *62*, 368-372.

1674. Bruininks, R. H., & Kennedy, P. Social status of hearing impaired children in regular classrooms. *Exceptional Children*, 1974, *40*, 336-342.

1675. Burroughs, J. R., & Powell, F. W. Can we systematically meet the needs of all deaf children. *Peabody Journal of Education*, 1974, *53*, 171-179.

1676. Carruth, K. J., Krueger, A. H., Lesar, D. J., & Redding, A. J. Possible effects of integration of the deaf within a typical vocational school setting. *Journal of Rehabilitation of the Deaf*, 1971, 4(4), 30-41.

1677. Carver, R. L. A parent speaks out on integration in the schools. *Volta Review*, 1966, *68*, 580-583.

1678. Chambers, P. *Team teaching in an integrated elementary school.* Paper presented at the Alexander Graham Bell Association for the Deaf National Convention, St. Louis, MO, June 1978.

1679. Claussen, H. W. *The forgotten child-the needs of the hard of hearing child: Part II.* Paper presented at the First World Congress on Future Special Education, Stirling, Scotland, June-July 1978. (ERIC Document Reproduction Service No. ED 157 310)

1680. Cloud, D. T. Where should the deaf child be educated? Remarks of a representative of a public residential school. *Volta Review*, 1954, *56*, 301-302.

1681. Cohen, O. P. An integrated summer recreation program. *Volta Review*, 1969, *71*, 233-237.

1682. Cole, N. Hear the wind blow. *Volta Review*, 1971, *73*, 36-41. Also in W. H. Northcott (Ed.), *The hearing impaired child in a regular classroom.* Washington, D.C.: Alexander Graham Bell Association for the Deaf, 1973.

1683. Coleman, P. G., Eggleston, K. K., Collins, J. F., Holloway, B. D., & Reider, S. K. A severely hearing impaired child in the mainstream. *Teaching Exceptional Children*, 1975, *8*, 6-9.

1684. Collea, F. P. Science in sounds. *Science and Children*, 1976, *13*(6), 34.

1685. Community College of Denver provides integrated programs. *Volta Review*, 1971, *73*, 190.

1686. Condon, K., & Dahlstrom, M. *Development and implementation of an effective early childhood handicapped program.* Paper presented at the 58th Annual International Convention of the Council for Exceptional Children, Philadelphia, PA, April 1980. (ERIC Document Reproduction Service No. ED 187 079)

1687.   Connor, L. E. Administrative concerns for mainstreaming. In
         G. W. Nix (Ed.), *Mainstream education for hearing impaired
         children & youth*. New York: Grune & Stratton, 1976.

1688.   _____. Deaf and hearing children at the Lexington School for the
         Deaf or—mainstreaming the special school. In G. W. Nix (Ed.),
         Mainstream education for hearing impaired children & youth. New
         York: Grune & Stratton, 1976.

1689.   _____. Mainstreaming a special school: Lexington School for the
         Deaf, New York. *Teaching Exceptional Children*, 1976, *8*, 76-80.

1690.   _____. *New directions in infant programs for the deaf. Two
         recent Lexington School studies show need for integration of
         subject-oriented infant program with "therapeutic" program*.
         Washington, D.C.: Alexander Graham Bell Association for the
         Deaf, n.d.

1691.   _____. The president's opinions: Integration. *Volta Review*,
         1972, *74*, 207-209.

1692.   Cosper, C. H., Jr. The mainstreaming of the junior high and high
         student. In G. W. Nix (Ed.), *Mainstream education for hearing
         impaired children & youth*. New York: Grune & Stratton, 1976.

1693.   _____. An oral deaf adult speaks: On activities of teenage chil-
         dren. *Volta Review*, 1971, *73*, 240-242.

1694.   Council on Education of the Deaf. Resolution on individualized
         educational programming for the hearing impaired (deaf and hard-
         of-hearing). *Volta Review*, 1976, *78*, 302.

1695.   Craig, W. N. Curriculum: Its perspectives and prospects. *Volta
         Review*, 1976, *78*, 52-59.

1696.   _____, & Salem, J. M. Partial integration of deaf with hearing
         students: Residential school perspectives. *American Annals of the
         Deaf*, 1975, *120*, 28-36.

1697.   _____, Salem, J. M., & Craig, H. B. Mainstreaming and partial
         integration of deaf with hearing students. *American Annals of the
         Deaf*, 1976, *121*, 63-68.

1698.   Croft, J. C. A look at the future for a hearing impaired child of
         today. *Volta Review*, 1974, *76*, 115-122.

1699.   Culham, B. R., & Curwin, R. There's a deaf child in my class.
         Learning, 1978, *7*(2), 111-117.

1700.   Dale, D. M. C. Units for deaf children. *Volta Review*, 1966, *68*,
         496-499.

1701.   Davis, J. (Ed.). *Our forgotten children: Hard-of-hearing pupils in the regular classroom.* Minneapolis, MN: Audio Visual Library Services, Leadership Training Institute, University of Minnesota, 1977.

1702.   Deaf graduates of hearing schools. *Volta Review,* 1969, *71,* 34-63.

1703.   Deaf graduates of hearing schools—1966. *Volta Review,* 1967, *69,* 15-35.

1704.   Deaf graduates of schools for the hearing. *Volta Review,* 1971, *73,* 282-288, 290-319.

1705.   Deninger, M. L. *The IEP and deaf children.* Paper presented at the American Personnel and Guidance Association Convention, Washington, D.C., March 1978. (ERIC Document Reproduction Service No. ED 159 837)

1706.   DeSalle, J. M., and Ptasnik, J. Some problems and solutions: High school mainstreaming of the hearing impaired. *American Annals of the Deaf,* 1976, *121,* 533-536.

1707.   A discussion on children with severe hearing impairments in schools with hearing children. A panel discussion at the 1956 summer meeting of the Alexander Graham Bell Association for the Deaf, Los Angeles, June 1956. *Volta Review,* 1957, *59,* 53-63, 84-85.

1708.   Doehring, D. F., Bonnycas, D. E., & Ling, A. H. Rapid reading skills of integrated hearing-impaired children. *Volta Review,* 1978, *80,* 399-409.

1709.   Education for hearing-impaired pupils in Illinois. *Volta Review,* 1972, *74,* 299-302.

1710.   The education of partially deaf children in units attached to ordinary schools. *Teacher of the Deaf,* 1960, *58,* 430-432.

1711.   Eichstaedt, C. B., & Seiler, P. J. Signing. *Journal of Physical Education and Recreation,* 1978, *49*(5), 19-21.

1712.   Elliott, H. How to succeed in college without really hearing. *Volta Review,* 1970, *72,* 157-160.

1713.   Elser, R. P. The social position of hearing handicapped children in the regular grades (Doctoral dissertation, George Peabody College for Teachers, 1958). *Dissertation Abstracts,* 1958, *19,* 2804. (University Microfilms No. 59-01095). Also in *Exceptional Children,* 1959, *27,* 305-309.

1714.   Emerton, R. G., & Rothman, G. *A study of attitudes toward deafness and its implications for mainstreaming.* Paper presented at the annual meeting of the American Educational Research Association, New York, April 1977. (ERIC Document Reproduction Service No. ED 140 524)

1715. Estes, J. Children develop language to relate to the hearing world. *Volta Review*, 1974, *76*, 559-561.

1716. Ewoldt, C. *Mainstreaming the hearing-impaired child: Process not goal.* 1979. (ERIC Document Reproduction Service No. ED 168 275)

1717. Ezold, E. E., & Boss, M. S. You want me to do what? Reflections on our integration program. *Volta Review*, 1978, *80*, 155-159.

1718. Fallis, J. R. The key to integrated learning for children who are hearing impaired. *Volta Review*, 1975, *77*, 363-367.

1719. Fellendorf, G. W. Hearing impaired graduates of regular schools. *Volta Review*, 1973, *75*, 232-255.

1720. _____. NTID—after one year. *Volta Review*, 1969, *71*, 296-307.

1721. _____. Technical training for deaf students at a community college. *Volta Review*, 1970, *72*, 296-302.

1722. Fisher, B. Hearing-impaired children in ordinary schools. *Teacher of the Deaf*, 1971, *69*, 161-174.

1723. _____. A review of two New Zealand research theses about units for deaf children in ordinary schools. *Teacher of the Deaf*, 1974, *72*, 316-318.

1724. Ford, F. C. Reactions of the hearing impaired child to school situations. *Peabody Journal of Education*, 1968, *46*, 177-179.

1725. Frick, E. Adjusting to integration: Some difficulties hearing impaired children have in public schools. *Volta Review*, 1973, *75*, 36-46.

1726. Gantenbein, A. R. Components for normalization of hearing impaired children in a public school setting. In G. W. Nix (Ed.), *Mainstream education for hearing impaired children & youth.* New York, NY: Grune & Stratton, 1976.

1727. Garrett, C., & Stovall, E. M. A parent's views on integration. *Volta Review*, 1972, *74*, 338-344.

1728. Garstecki, D. C. *The mainstreamed hearing-impaired child.* Paper presented at the 55th Annual International Convention, Council for Exceptional Children, Atlanta, GA, April 1977. (ERIC Document Reproduction Service No. ED 139 156)

1729. Gatty, J. C., Meagher, K., & Boothroyd, A. *The Clark School integrated nursery.* Paper presented at the Alexander Graham Bell Association for the Deaf National Convention, St. Louis, MO, June 1978.

1730. Gildston, P. *The hard of hearing child in the classroom—a guide for the classroom teacher. A useful summary of do's and don'ts.* Washington, D.C.: Alexander Graham Bell Association for the Deaf, n.d.

1731.   Glover, K. K. *Facilitating educational integration of the hearing-impaired child: A proposed integration program.* St. Louis, MO: Central Institute for the Deaf, 1973.

1732.   Godsave, B. F. What not to do for the hearing impaired child. *Learning,* 1978, 7(2) 117-118.

1733.   Goldin, G. J., Margolin, R. J., Stotsky, B. A., & Zalk, A. W. Some attitudes of deaf high school students toward attendance at college with normally hearing students. *Volta Review,* 1969, 71, 409-414.

1734.   Golf, H. R. What do you do if the mainstreamed hearing impaired child fails? or Mainstreaming: Sink or swim. In G. W. Nix (Ed.), *Mainstream education for hearing impaired children & youth.* New York, NY: Grune & Stratton, 1976.

1735.   Goodman, M. J. *The deaf student in your class: An index to problems, solutions and shortcuts, and practical information about deaf people for college and high school instructors.* Unpublished manuscript, 1978. (ERIC Document Reproduction Service No. ED 160 163)

1736.   Green, R. Counseling parents of the hearing impaired. *Highlights,* 1972, 52, 18-19.

1737.   _____. The hard of hearing child at home. *Highlights,* 1971, 50, 5-7.

1738.   Green, R. A. *Development and implementation of procedures to maximize instructional time in an itinerant special education setting.* Ft. Lauderdale, FL: Nova University, 1978. (ERIC Document Reproduction Service No. ED 166 878)

1739.   Green, R. R. Psycho-social aspects of mainstreaming for the child and family. In G. W. Nix (Ed.), *Mainstream education for hearing impaired children & youth.* New York: Grune & Stratton, 1976.

1740.   Hadary, D. E., & Cohen, S. H. *Laboratory science and art for blind, deaf, and emotionally disturbed children: A mainstreaming approach.* Baltimore, MD: University Park Press, 1978.

1741.   Hannapel, K. Within the magic circle; program at the Florida School for the Deaf and Blind. *American Education,* 1976, 12(8), 35-36.

1742.   Hanners, B. A. The audiologist as educator: The ultimate hearing aide. In G. W. Nix (Ed.), *Mainstream education for hearing impaired children & youth.* New York: Grune & Stratton, 1976.

1743.   Harrington, J. D. The integration of deaf children and youth through educational strategies. Why? When? How? *Highlights,* 1974, 53, 6-8.

1744. Hayes, G. Feasibility of assigning deaf students to regular classes. *Proceedings of the International Conference on Oral Education of the Deaf,* 1967, *1,* 406-423.

1745. Hayes, G. M., & Griffing, B. L. *A guide to the education of the deaf in the public schools of California.* Sacramento, CA: California State Department of Education, Bureau for Physically Exceptional Children, 1967. (ERIC Document Reproduction Service No. ED 022 292)

1746. Healy, W. C. Integrated education. *Volta Review,* 1976, *78,* 68-75.

1747. Hedgecock, D. Facilitating integration at the junior high level. In W. H. Northcott (Ed.), *The hearing impaired child in a regular classroom.* Washington, D.C.: Alexander Graham Bell Association for the Deaf, 1973.

1748. _____. Facilitating integration at the junior high level: Observations of a teacher-tutor. *Volta Review,* 1974, *76,* 182-188.

1749. Hedrich, V. Applying technology to special education. *American Education,* 1972, *8*(1), 22-25.

1750. Hefele, T. J. The role of teacher interpersonal communication factors in the graduate education of prospective teachers of the deaf and the influence of such factors on the academic achievement of deaf students (Doctoral dissertation, State University of New York at Buffalo, 1970). *Dissertation Abstracts International,* 1970, *31,* 4598A. (University Microfilms No. 71-6076)

1751. Hehir, R. *Mainstreaming and continuum of educational services for the hearing impaired.* Paper presented at the 47th Biennial Convention of the American Instructors of the Deaf, Greensboro, NC, June 1975.

1752. Hehir, R. G. Integrating deaf students for career education. *Exceptional Children,* 1973, *39,* 611-618.

1753. Heinricks, E. L. Where should the deaf child be educated? The day school. *Volta Review,* 1954, *56,* 302-303.

1754. Hemmings, I. A survey of units for hearing-impaired children in schools for normally hearing children. *Teacher of the Deaf,* 1972, *70,* 445-446.

1755. Heys, A. Current trends in the education of the partially deaf. *Teacher of the Deaf,* 1962, *60,* 206-215.

1756. Higgs, R. W. Attitudes toward persons with physical disabilities as a function of information level and degree of contact. (Doctoral dissertation, University of Minnesota, 1971). *Dissertation Abstracts International,* 1971, *32,* 4450A. (University Microfilms No. 72-5537)

1757. Hill, K. A. The model high school for the deaf. *Volta Review,* 1967, *69,* 279-280.

1758. Hine, W. D. The abilities of partially hearing children. *British Journal of Educational Psychology,* 1970, *40,* 171-178.

1759. Hoemann, H. W. The development of communication skills in deaf and hearing students. *Child Development,* 1972, *43,* 990-1003.

1760. Hogue, I. Classes for deaf children attached to classes in regular schools. *The New Zealand Journal for Teachers of the Deaf,* 1966, *1,* 28-30.

1761. Holcomb, R. K., & Corbett, E. E., Jr. Mainstream—the Delaware approach. Newark, DE: Newark School District (Sterck School), 1975.

1762. How to integrate hearing-impaired children in regular classrooms. *Special Education Report,* 1975, *510,* 1-4.

1763. Hubbard, T. L., Frankfurt, L. A., Hubbard, S., Maclaurin, P. L., & Packard, P. A. *To each his own: Presentation of four individualized learning programs at the Montreal Oral School for the Deaf.* Paper presented at the Alexander Graham Bell Association for the Deaf National Convention, St. Louis, MO, June 1978.

1764. Hughes, S. *Student residence hall life: A review of literature, research, and experience pertinent to planning residence-based programs for post-secondary deaf and hearing students.* Rochester, NY: National Technical Institute for the Deaf, 1973. (ERIC Document Reproduction Service No. 084 748)

1765. Hughes, V., Wilkie, F., & Murphy, H. J. The use of interpreters in an integrated liberal arts setting. *Journal of Rehabilitation of the Deaf,* 1974, *7*(3), 17-19.

1766. Hurwitz, S. N. Social enrichment of the deaf. *Hearing and Speech News,* 1970, *38*(5), 4-7.

1767. Hus, Y. The socialization process of hearing-impaired children in a summer camp. *Volta Review,* 1979, *81,* 146-156.

1768. *The integration of deaf children in a hearing class. Publication No. 4.* New York, NY: Bureau of Educational Research/New York City Board of Education, 1956.

1769. The integration of deaf children in a New York Public school. *Volta Review,* 1957, *59,* 355-356.

1770. International Parents' Organization. The value of integration. *Volta Review,* 1968, *70,* 253.

1771. Is there really any point in talking about higher education for deaf youngsters in colleges for the hearing? *Volta Review,* 1965, *67,* 616.

1772. Jackson, C. C. An evaluation of a unit scheme for deaf children. *Teacher of the Deaf,* 1969, *67,* 495-498.

1773. Johnson, E. W. Let's look at the child—not the audiogram. *Volta Review,* 1967, *69,* 306-310. Also in W. N. Northcott (Ed.), *The hearing impaired child in a regular classroom.* Washington, D.C.: Alexander Graham Bell Association for the Deaf, 1973.

1774. Johnson, I. The social acceptance of hearing impaired children in schools and some possible factors affecting this acceptance. *Australian Teacher of the Deaf,* 1961, *2,* 2-5.

1775. Johnson, J. C. *Educating hearing impaired children in ordinary schools.* Manchester, England: Manchester University Press, 1962.

1776. Johnston, K. A. Perspective on integration of children with limited hearing: Consideration of current needs. *Language, Speech and Hearing Services in Schools,* 1974, *5*(2), 79-84.

1777. Jones, B. L. The audiologist in the educational environment. In W. H. Northcott (Ed.), *The hearing impaired child in the regular classroom.* Washington, D.C.: Alexander Graham Bell Association for the Deaf, 1973.

1778. Jones, M. C., & Byers, V. W. Classification of hearing impaired children in the classroom: A theoretical model. *Journal of Learning Disabilities,* 1971, *4,* 51-54.

1779. Jones, R. L., & Murphy, H. J. The Center of Deafness at California State University, Northridge. *PRWAD Annual,* 1974, 245-246.

1780. _____, & Murphy, H. J. Integrated education for deaf college students. *Phi Delta Kappan,* 1974, *55,* 542.

1781. _____, & Murphy, H. J. The Northridge plan for higher education of the deaf. *American Annals of the Deaf,* 1972, *117,* 612-616.

1782. Justman, J., & Maskowitz, S. *The integration of deaf children in a hearing class: The second year.* Publication No. 5. New York, NY: Bureau of Educational Research/New York City Board of Education, 1957.

1783. Karchmer, M. A., & Trybus, R. J. *Who are the deaf children in "mainstream" programs?* Paper presented at the 48th Convention of American Instructors of the Deaf, Los Angeles, June 1977. (ERIC Document Reproduction Service No. ED 148 073)

1784. Katz, L., Mathis, S. L., & Merrill, E. C., Jr. *The deaf child in the public schools. A handbook for parents of deaf children.* Danville, IL: Interstate Printers & Publishers, 1974.

1785.   Keaster, J. How shall the deaf child be educated? *Volta Review*, 1954, *56*, 293-297.

1786.   Kennedy, A. E. C. The effects of deafness on personality: A discussion based on the theoretical model of Erik Erikson's eight stages of man. *Journal of Rehabilitation of the Deaf*, 1973, *6*(3), 22-23.

1787.   _____. Operation chatterbox. *Hearing and Speech Action*, 1975, *43*(3), 24-25.

1788.   Kennedy, P. *Mainstreaming the hearing impaired child: Critical variables. Position paper.* Paper presented at the 54th Annual International Convention of the Council for Exceptional Children Chicago, April 1976. (ERIC Document Reproduction Service No. ED 122 541)

1789.   _____, & Bruininks, R. H. Social status of hearing impaired children in regular classrooms. *Exceptional Children*, 1974, *40*, 336-342.

1790.   _____, McCauley, R., Bruininks, R., & Northcott, W. H. *Results of a follow-up sociometric research study and summary of longitudinal and cross sectional data on hearing impaired children enrolled in regular classrooms.* Paper presented at the 54th Annual International Convention of the Council for Exceptional Children, Chicago, April, 1976. (ERIC Document Reproduction Service No. ED 125 203)

1791.   _____, Northcott, W. H., & McCauley, R. *Results of longitudinal and cross-sectional data on hearing impaired children in regular classes: elementary school years.* Paper presented at the International Congress of Instructors for the Deaf, Tokyo, Japan, 1975.

1792.   _____, Northcott, W. H., McCauley, R., & Myklbye, S. Longitudinal sociometric and cross-sectional data on mainstreaming hearing impaired children. Implications for preschool programming. *Volta Review*, 1976, *78*, 71-81.

1793.   Kilpatrick, I. D. *Mainstreaming the hearing impaired child: Critical variables.* Paper presented at the 54th Annual International Convention of the Council for Exceptional Children, Chicago, April 1976. (ERIC Document Reproduction Service No. ED 122 542)

1794.   Kindred, E. M. Integration at the secondary school level. *Volta Review*, 1976, *78*, 35-43.

1795.   _____. *Mainstreaming teenagers with care!* Paper presented at the 57th Annual International Convention of the Council for Exceptional Children, Dallas, April 1979. (ERIC Document Reproduction Service No. ED 171 042)

1796. Kodman, F. Educational status of hard of hearing children in the classroom. *Journal of Speech and Hearing Disorders,* 1963, *28,* 297-299.

1797. Kolzak, J. *Implementing the IEP via the team approach: School, parents, and service agencies.* Paper presented at the Alexander Graham Bell Association for the Deaf National Convention, St. Louis, MO, June 1978.

1798. Kopchick, E. Mainstreaming deaf students using team teaching. *American Annals of the Deaf,* 1977, *122,* 522-524.

1799. Kopp, H. G. Adolescence: Adjustment or rebellion? In W. H. Northcott (Ed.), *The hearing impaired child in a regular classroom.* Washington, D.C.: Alexander Graham Bell Association for the Deaf, 1973.

1800. Kowalsky, M. Integration of a severely hard of hearing child in a normal first grade program: A case study. *Journal of Speech and Hearing Disorders,* 1962, *24,* 349-358.

1801. LaPorta, R. A., McGee, D. I., Simmons-Martin, A., Vorce, E., Saaz von Hippel, C., & Donovan, J. *Mainstreaming preschoolers: Children with hearing impairment. A guide for teachers, parents, and others who work with hearing impaired preschoolers.* Belmont, MA: Contract Research Corp., 1978. (ERIC Document Reproduction Service No. ED 164 109)

1802. Lawrenson, T. J. An investigation into the social maturity of two different groups of girls with profoundly impaired hearing and a group of institutionalized girls with normal hearing. A comparison of the social maturity of girls with profoundly impaired hearing in a school for the deaf with girls with profoundly impaired hearing in regular community schools and with institutionalized girls with normal hearing (Doctoral dissertation, New York University, 1963). *Dissertation Abstracts,* 1963, *24,* 2785. (University Microfilm No. 64-00259)

1803. Layman, E. Children who hear aid the hearing impaired. *Volta Review,* 1974, *76,* 36-41.

1804. Leckie, D. J. Creating a receptive climate in the mainstream program. In W. H. Northcott (Ed.), *The hearing impaired child in a regular classroom.* Washington, D.C.: Alexander Graham Bell Association for the Deaf, 1973. Also in *Volta Review,* 1973, *75,* 23-27.

1805. Leigh, D. The deaf child enrolled in a hearing school. *Volta Review,* 1963, *65,* 312.

1806. Leslie, P. T. A rationale for a mainstream education for the hearing impaired. In G. W. Nix (Ed.), *Mainstream education for hearing impaired children & youth.* New York: Grune & Stratton, 1976.

1807. Lewis, D. N. Lipreading skills of hearing impaired children in regular schools. *Volta Review,* 1972, *74,* 303-311. Also in *Highlights,* 1971, *50*(2), 4-8.

1808. Lexington School for the Deaf. Giving deaf children needed experiences with the hearing world. *Audio-Visual Instruction,* 1969, *14*(9), 89-99.

1809. Ling, D., Ling, A. H., & Pflaster, G. Individualized educational programming for hearing impaired children. *Volta Review,* 1977, 79, 204-230.

1810. Linn, M. C., Hadary, D., Rosenberg, R., & Haushalter, R. *Science education for the deaf: Comparison of ideal resource and mainstream settings.* Paper presented at the Annual Meeting of the American Educational Research Association, Toronto, Ontario, Canada, March 1978. (ERIC Document Reproduction Service No. 154 569) Also in *Journal for Research in Science Teaching,* 1979, *16,* 305-316.

1811. Lloyd, G. T. Proposal for better educational opportunity for the deaf child. *American Annals of the Deaf,* 1967, *112,* 18-19.

1812. Lorain, Ohio starts a pilot program. *Volta Review,* 1966, *68,* 583-585.

1813. Lowe, A. Difficulties facing the integration of hearing-impaired children into regular educational programs in the Federal Republic of Germany. *Scandinavian Audiology,* 1972, *2,* 9-12.

1814. _____. Mainstream education for deaf pupils. *Special Education: Forward Trends,* 1978, *5*(4), 19.

1815. _____. Some basic requirements for an integration of hearing-impaired children into regular education programs. *Scandinavian Audiology,* 1972, *2,* 83-87.

1816. Lubovsky, V. I. Defectology: The science of handicapped children. *International Review of Education,* 1974, *20,* 298-305.

1817. Lynch, E. J. *Program for hearing impaired adolescents. Secondary school phase, Maxi II practicum report.* Ft. Lauderdale, FL: Nova University, 1976. (ERIC Document Reproduction Service No. ED 127 770)

1818. McAndrew, H. Rigidity and isolation: A study of the deaf and blind. *Journal of Abnormal and Social Psychology,* 1948, *63,* 476-494.

1819. McCauley, R., Bruininks, R. H., & Kennedy, P. *The observed behavior of hearing impaired children in regular classrooms.* Paper presented at the 52nd Annual International Convention of the Council for Exceptional Children, New York, April 1974.

1820.   _____, Kennedy, P., & Bruinicks, R. Behavioral interactions of hearing impaired children in regular classrooms. *Journal of Special Education*, 1976, *10*, 277-284.

1821.   McClure, A. T. Academic achievement of mainstreamed hearing-impaired children with congenital rubella syndrome. *Volta Review*, 1977, *79*, 379-384.

1822.   McCormick, M. Gradual integration of a group of deaf children into a hearing situation. *Volta Review*, 1963, *65*, 92-94.

1823.   McGee, D. I. The benefits of educating deaf children with hearing children. *Teaching Exceptional Children*, 1970, *2*, 133-137.

1824.   _____. *Critical variables in the mainstreaming of hearing impaired children.* Paper presented at the 54th Annual International Convention of the Council for Exceptional Children, Chicago, April, 1976. (ERIC Document Reproduction Service No. ED 122 540)

1825.   _____. Mainstreaming problems and procedures: Ages 6-12. In G. W. Nix (Ed.), *Mainstream education for hearing impaired children & youth.* New York: Grune & Stratton, 1976.

1826.   McIndoe, C. J. *The role of an auditory/learning disabilities specialist in a public school program for hearing-impaired students.* Paper presented at the Alexander Graham Bell Association for the Deaf National Convention, St. Louis, MO, June 1978.

1827.   Macklin, F. Mainstreaming: The cost issue. *American Annals of the Deaf*, 1976, *121*, 364-365.

1828.   McLaughlin, H. F. Integration of deaf children into hearing society. In A. Ewing (Ed.), *The modern educational treatment of deafness.* Manchester, England: Manchester University Press, 1960.

1829.   Madebrink, R. Integration of the deaf—a must? *Scandinavian Audiology*, 1972, *2*, 13.

1830.   Mangan, K. What is a realistic curriculum for deaf children in regular classes? *Volta Review*, 1960, *62*, 386-387.

1831.   Mangen, T. Integration of the hearing impaired into community programs. In J. Maestas (Ed.), *Education of the Deaf: Some practical considerations.* Minneapolis, MN: University of Minnesota, 1975.

1832.   Martin, P. I, too, want to be a real person. *Volta Review*, 1975, *77*, 375-380.

1833.   Mathas, C., & Morehouse, W. A work-study program for hearing impaired students. *Volta Review*, 1969, *71*, 553-556.

1834. Matter, G. M. In the current—with only one oar. In G. W. Nix
       (Ed.), *Mainstream education for hearing impaired children &
       youth.* New York: Grune & Stratton, 1976.

1835. _____. *Mainstreaming the hearing impaired child: Critical vari-
       ables: Or integration . . . . for whom?* Paper presented at the 54th
       Annual International Convention of the Council for Exceptional
       Children, Chicago, April 1976. (ERIC Document Reproduction
       Service No. ED 122 543)

1836. _____. Teachers' forum: Using pre-typed lecture notes and over-
       head film projector. *Volta Review,* 1963, *65,* 313.

1837. Mayer, C. A. *Understanding young children: The handicapped
       child in the normal preschool class.* Anchorage, AL: Treatment
       Center for Crippled Children and Adults, Inc., 1974. (ERIC Docu-
       ment Reproduction Service No. ED 092 257)

1838. Mecham, S. R., & Van Dyke, R. C. Pushing back the walls between
       hearing and hearing impaired children. *Volta Review,* 1971, *73,*
       359-364.

1839. Medart, J. R. Where should the deaf child be educated? Opinions
       of a graduate of a school for the deaf. *Volta Review,* 1954, *56,*
       304-305.

1840. Miles, D. L. Integrated rehabilitation services for the deaf. *Journal
       of Rehabilitation of the Deaf,* 1967, *1*(3), 16-23.

1841. Miller, A. G. Actor and observer perceptions of the learning of a
       task. *Journal of Experimental Social Psychology,* 1975, *11,* 95-111.

1842. Miller, A. S. Academic preparation to insure adjustment into
       classes with hearing students. *Volta Review,* 1964, *66,* 414-425.

1843. Miller, J. K., Munson, H. L., Gargantiel, C. W., & Huang, J.
       *Mainstreaming the deaf in occupational education: Knowledge and
       attitudes in the school environment.* Paper presented at the Annual
       Meeting of the American Educational Research Association, Toronto,
       Ontario, Canada, March 1978. (ERIC Document Reproduction Ser-
       vice No. ED 154 570)

1844. _____, Munson, H. L., Gargantiel, C. W., & Huang, J. Occupa-
       tional training of the hearing impaired. *Exceptional Children,*
       1980, *46,* 424-431.

1845. _____, Munson, H. L., Gargantiel, C. W., & Huang, J. *Philo-
       sophic consideration in mainstreaming the hearing impaired in
       occupational education programs: An empirically based discussion
       of goals and objectives.* Paper presented at the Annual Meeting of
       the American Educational Research Association, Toronto, March
       1978. (ERIC Document Reproduction Service No. ED 154 571)

1846. Model high school for the deaf. *Volta Review*, 1967, *69*, 279-281.

1847. Monaghan, A. Educational placement for the multiply handi-capped hearing impaired child. *Volta Review*, 1964, *66*, 383-387.

1848. _____. Pressures for change in teaching hearing handicapped children. *Volta Review*, 1966, *68*, 500-505.

1849. Montague, H. The parents talk it over: A deaf child's problems with hearing children. *Volta Review*, 1956, *58*, 363-365.

1850. Morris, J. *Mainstreaming the hearing impaired child, K-6. Escam-bia County*. Pensacola, FL: Escambia County Board of Public Instruction, 1975. (ERIC Document Reproduction Service No. ED 115 008)

1851. Mulholland, A. M., & Fellendorf, G. W. *Final report: National research conference on day programs for hearing impaired children*. Washington, D.C.: Alexander Graham Bell Association for the Deaf, 1968.

1852. Murphy, C. H. S. Where should the deaf child be educated? A parent speaks. *Volta Review*, 1954, *56*, 305-306.

1853. Murphy, H. J. *Affective support services for deaf college students in an integrated setting*. Paper presented at the Alexander Graham Bell Association National Convention, St. Louis, MO, June 1978.

1854. _____. *Campus services for the deaf: Support services for deaf students at California State University, Northridge*. Paper pre-sented at the International Congress of the Deaf, Tokyo, Japan, August 1975.

1855. _____. Comparative studies of academic achievement between hearing impaired and non-hearing impaired students at California State University, Northridge. *American Annals of the Deaf*, 1976, *121*, 305-308.

1856. _____. *Research and evaluation studies relating to the integration of deaf students at California State University, Northridge*. Paper presented at the 7th World Conference of the World Federation of the Deaf, Washington, D.C., 1975.

1857. _____. *Selected issues associated with delivery of support services to hearing-impaired students at California State University, North-ridge*. Paper presented at the 47th Biennial Convention of Ameri-can Instructors of the Deaf, Greensboro, NC, June 1975.

1858. _____. *A study of the achievement of deaf students in an inte-grated situation*. Paper presented at the 47th Biennial Convention of American Instructors of the Deaf, Greensboro, NC, June 1975.

1859. _____. *Support services for deaf students at California State University, Northridge.* Paper presented at the 47th Biennial Convention of American Instructors of the Deaf, Greensboro, NC, June 1975.

1860. _____. (Ed.). *Selected readings in the integration of deaf students at CSUN. Number 1.* Northridge, CA: Center of Deafness, California State University, 1976. (ERIC Document Reproduction Service No. ED 123 812)

1861. Nance, L. M. Deaf and bright. *Volta Review,* 1968, *70,* 43-44.

1862. National College of Teachers of the Deaf. Enquiry regarding placement of children in partially hearing units. *Teacher of the Deaf,* 1965, *63,* 113-120.

1863. Neyhus, A. I. Assessment for individualized education programming. *Volta Review,* 1978, *80,* 286-295.

1864. Nix, G. W. The least restrictive environment. *Volta Review,* 1977, *79,* 286-296.

1865. _____. Mainstream placement question/checklist. *Volta Review,* 1977, *79,* 345-346.

1866. _____ (Ed.). *Mainstream education for hearing impaired children & youth.* New York: Grune & Stratton, 1976.

1867. _____ (Ed.). *The rights of hearing-impaired children.* Washington, D.C.: Alexander Graham Bell Association for the Deaf, 1978.

1868. Nober, E. H., Nober, L., & Murphy, H. Assessment of a higher education mainstreamed deaf program. *Volta Review,* 1980, *82,* 50-57.

1869. Nober, L. W. Getting ready for P.L. 94-142: A model for support services to mainstreamed hearing-impaired children. *Volta Review,* 1977, *79,* 231-237.

1870. _____. *The hearing impaired formal inservice program (HI-FI).* Amherst, MA: Northeast Regional Media Center for the Deaf, n.d. (ERIC Document Reproduction Service No. ED 096 787) Also in *Language, Speech, and Hearing Services in Schools,* 1975, *6,* 187-190.

1871. _____. An inservice program for integrating hearing impaired children. *Volta Review,* 1975, *77,* 173-175.

1872. _____. *A model for support services to mainstreamed hearing impaired children.* Paper presented at the 54th Annual International Convention of the Council for Exceptional Children, Chicago, April 1976. (ERIC Document Reproduction Service No. ED 127 752)

1873. Northcott, W. H. The academic tutor and the hearing impaired child. In W. H. Northcott (Ed.), *The hearing impaired child in a regular classroom.* Washington, D.C.: Alexander Graham Bell Association for the Deaf, 1973.

1874. _____. Candidate for integration: A hearing-impaired child in a regular nursery school. *Young Children,* 1970, *25*, 367-380.

1875. _____. Competencies needed by teachers of hearing-impaired infants, birth to three years, and their parents. *Volta Review,* 1973, *75*, 532-544.

1876. _____. *Critical variables in mainstreaming the hearing-impaired child: Or integration . . . . for whom? Summary statements.* Paper presented at the 54th Annual International Convention of the Council for Exceptional Children, Chicago, April 1976. (ERIC Document Reproduction Service No. ED 122 546)

1877. _____. *Curriculum guide: Hearing-impaired children, birth to three years, and their parents.* Washington, D.C.: Alexander Graham Bell Association for the Deaf, 1978.

1878. _____. An experimental summer school: Impetus for successful integration. *Volta Review,* 1970, *72*, 498-507.

1879. _____. Head start program—implications for deaf children. *Volta Review,* 1968, *70*, 106-113.

1880. _____. A hearing-impaired pupil in the classroom. *Volta Review,* 1972, *74*, 105-108.

1881. _____. Implementing programs for young hearing impaired children. *Exceptional Children,* 1973, *39*, 455-463.

1882. _____. Integrating the preprimary hearing impaired child—an examination of the process, product, and rationale. In M. J. Guralnick (Ed.), *Early intervention and the integration of handicapped and nonhandicapped children.* Baltimore, MD: University Park Press, 1978.

1883. _____. The integration of young deaf children into ordinary educational programs. *Exceptional Children,* 1971, *38*, 29-32.

1884. _____. Mainstreaming the preprimary hearing-impaired child, 0-6—practices—progress—problems. In G. W. Nix (Ed.), *Mainstream education for hearing impaired children & youth.* New York: Grune & Stratton, 1976.

1885. _____. Normalization of the preschool child with hearing impairment. *The Otolaryngologic Clinics of North America,* 1975, *8*(2), 159-186.

1886. _____. Reading list on integration. *Volta Review,* 1973, *75*, 33-35.

1887.   _____. A speech clinician as multidisciplinary team member. In W. H. Northcott (Ed.), *The hearing impaired child in a regular classroom*. Washington, D.C.: Alexander Graham Bell Association for the Deaf, 1973.

1888.   _____. Tutoring a hearing impaired student in the elementary grades. *Volta Review*, 1972, *74*, 432-435.

1889.   _____ (Ed.). *The hearing impaired child in a regular classroom: Preschool, elementary and secondary years*. Washington, D.C.: Alexander Graham Bell Association for the Deaf, 1973.

1890.   _____, Nelson, J. V., & Fowler, S. A. UNISTAPS: A family oriented infant/preschool program for hearing impaired children and their parents. *Peabody Journal of Education*, 1974, *51*, 192-196.

1891.   Northeast Regional Media Center for the Deaf. *Hearing impaired formal in-service program*. Amherst, MA: Author, 1973. (ERIC Document Reproduction Service No. ED 096 787)

1892.   Nuernberger, J. The role of the psychologist: Evaluating potential for integration. In W. H. Northcott (Ed.), *The hearing impaired child in a regular classroom*. Washington, D.C.: Alexander Graham Bell Association for the Deaf, 1973.

1893.   Numbers, M.E. Educational, vocational, and social experiences of the graduates of the Clarke School for the Deaf. In A. Ewing (Ed.), *The modern educational treatment of deafness*. Manchester, England: Manchester University Press, 1960.

1894.   O'Connor, C. D. Integration of graduates of the Lexington School for the Deaf in programmes for the normal hearing. In A. Ewing (Ed.), *The modern educational treatment of deafness*. Manchester, England: Manchester University Press, 1960.

1895.   _____. The integration of the deaf in schools for the normally hearing. *American Annals of the Deaf,* 1961, *106*, 229-232. Also in I. S. Fuseld (Ed.), *A handbook of readings in education of the deaf and post-school implications*. Springfield, IL: C. C. Thomas, 1967.

1896.   _____, Connor, L. E. A study of the integration of deaf children in regular classrooms. *Exceptional Children*, 1961, *27*, 483-486.

1897.   Orlansky, J. Z. *Mainstreaming the hearing impaired child: An educational alternative*. Austin, TX: Learning Concepts, 1977.

1898.   Osguthorpe, R. T., Whitehead, B. D., & Bishop, M. E. Training and managing paraprofessionals as tutors and notetakers for mainstreamed deaf students. *American Annals of the Deaf,* 1978, *123*, 563-571.

1899.   Owsley, P. J. Can a residential school program students into public schools? *Volta Review*, 1973, *75*, 28-31.

1900.   _____. *Readings in the education of hearing impaired children.* Mt. Airy, PA: Pennsylvania School for the Deaf, 1965.

1901.   Parker, B. L. The St. Paul TVI program for deaf students. *Deaf American*, 1975, *28*, 9-14.

1902.   Parsons, M. Patterns of integration to meet the needs of hearing handicapped children. *New Zealand Journal for Teachers of the Deaf*, 1968, *2*, 118-128.

1903.   Paul, R. L. A resource room for hard of hearing children in the public schools. *Volta Review*, 1963, *65*, 200-202.

1904.   _____, & Young, B. *The hard of hearing child in the regular classroom. ESEA Title III Project.* Pontiac, MI: Oakland Public Schools, 1974.

1905.   Payne, R., & Murray, C. Principals' attitudes toward integration of the handicapped. *Exceptional Children*, 1974, *41*, 123-125.

1906.   Perkins, C. E. Music to their ears. *Instructor*, 1979, *89*(4), 134-136.

1907.   Peterson, M. K. Achievement of hard-of-hearing students in regular public schools (Doctoral dissertation, Wayne State University, 1972). *Dissertation Abstracts International*, 1972, *33*, 2165B. (University Microfilms No. 72-28509)

1908.   Pettyman, E. Education of the deaf in Toronto. *Volta Review*, 1965, *67*, 420-421.

1909.   Pflaster, G. A factor analytic study of hearing impaired children integrated into regular schools (Doctoral dissertation, Columbia University, Teachers College, 1976). *Dissertation Abstracts International*, 1976, *37*, 2115A. (University Microfilms No. 76-21780)

1910.   Pinter, R. An adjustment test with normal and hard of hearing children. *Journal of Genetic Psychology*, 1940, *56*, 367-381.

1911.   Pitchers, B. I. The educational treatment of deafness in Kent. *Volta Review*, 1968, *70*, 577-580.

1912.   Poitras, B. The case for the deaf child in the regular school. *Volta Review*, 1961, *63*, 16-17, 43.

1913.   Pollack, D. Denver's acoupedic program. *Peabody Journal of Education*, 1974, *51*, 180-185.

1914.   _____, & Ernst, M. Don't set limits: Expectations for preschool children. *Volta Review*, 1973, *75*, 359-367. Also in W. H. Northcott (Ed.), *The hearing impaired child in a regular classroom.* Washington, D.C.: Alexander Graham Bell Association for the Deaf, 1973.

1915.   _____, & Ernst, M. Learning to listen in an integrated preschool. *Volta Review,* 1973, *75,* 359-367.

1916.   Pollock, M. B., & Pollock, K. C. Letter to the teacher of a hard-of-hearing child. *Childhood Education,* 1971, *47,* 206-209.

1917.   Porter, G. The missing vital dimension in successful integration: Cooperative program at Oralingua School for the Hearing Impaired, Whittier, California. *Volta Review,* 1975, *77,* 416-422.

1918.   Powers, G. W. Helping the hearing-impaired child. *Pennsylvania School Journal,* 1976, *125,* 74-76.

1919.   Pratt, G. T. Where should the deaf child be educated? The private residential school. *Volta Review,* 1954, *56,* 307-309.

1920.   *P.L. 94-142 and deaf children.* Washington D.C.: Alumni Office, Gallaudet College, 1977.

1921.   A public school program for multiply handicapped deaf children. *Volta Review,* 1970, *72,* 552-559.

1922.   Quigley, S. P. Higher education for deaf persons in regular institutions. *Journal of Rehabilitation of the Deaf,* 1969, *3*(1), 34-43.

1923.   _____, Jenne, W., & Phillips, S. *Deaf students in colleges and universities.* Washington, D.C.: Alexander Graham Bell Association for the Deaf, 1968.

1924.   _____, & Thomure, F. E. *Some effects of hearing impairment upon school performance.* Urbana, IL: University of Illinois, Institute of Research for Exceptional Children, 1969. (ERIC Document Reproduction Service No. ED 044 869)

1925.   Randle, W. E. A junior high program for hearing impaired pupils. *Volta Review,* 1969, *71,* 279-283.

1926.   Rankhorn, B. *Some effects of reverse integration on the language environment of hearing impaired children.* New York: Lexington School for the Deaf, 1974.

1927.   Raviv, S., Sharan, S., & Strauss, S. Intellectual development of deaf children in different educational environments. *Journal of Communication Disorders,* 1973, *6,* 29-36.

1928.   Reich, C. Models of integration. *British Columbia Journal of Special Education,* 1978, *2*(3), 215-225.

1929.   _____, & Hambleton, D. *Integration of hearing handicapped children in regular school settings: Research design.* Toronto, Ontario, Canada: Board of Education, City of Toronto, 1974. (ERIC Document Reproduction Service No. ED 133 937)

1930.   _____, Hambleton, D., & Klein, B. The integration of hearing impaired children in regular classrooms. *American Annals of the Deaf,* 1977, *122,* 534-543.

1931.   Reineke, M. E. Junior high—a cooperative venture. *Volta Review,* 1966, *68,* 284-288.

1932.   *Report of the study committee on statewide planning for the education of the deaf and severely hard of hearing in California Public Schools.* Sacramento, CA: California State Department of Education, 1970. (ERIC Document Reproduction Service No. ED 046 190)

1933.   Research on integration of deaf children in a New York public school. *Volta Review,* 1957, *59,* 353-356.

1934.   Resources list—for parents to implement P.L. 94-142. *Volta Review,* 1977, *79,* 349-351.

1935.   Reynolds, L. The school adjustment of children with minimal hearing loss. *Journal of Speech and Hearing Disorders,* 1955, *20,* 380-384.

1936.   Rhodes, M. J. From a parent's point of view. *Deaf American,* 1971, *24,* 20-22.

1937.   Risley, G. W. *The effects of mainstreaming and self-contained education for hearing impaired students.* Los Altos, CA: Los Altos School District, 1977. (ERIC Document Reproduction Service No. ED 150 762)

1938.   Rister, A. Deaf children in mainstream education. *Volta Review,* 1975, *77,* 279-290.

1939.   Rodda, M. Social adjustment of hearing impaired adolescents. *Volta Review,* 1966, *68,* 279-283, 318.

1940.   Rosenthal, C. Social adjustment of hearing handicapped children. *Volta Review,* 1966, *68,* 293-297.

1941.   Ross, M. Assessment of the hearing impaired prior to mainstreaming. In G. W. Nix (Ed.), *Mainstream education for hearing impaired children & youth.* New York: Grune & Stratton, 1976.

1942.   _____. Model educational cascade for hearing impaired children. In G. W. Nix (Ed.), *Mainstream education for hearing impaired children & youth.* New York: Grune & Stratton, 1976.

1943.   _____. *Position paper; Mainstream education of the hearing impaired child: Audiological considerations.* Paper presented at the 54th Annual International Convention of the Council for Exceptional Children, Chicago, April 1976. (ERIC Document Reproduction Service No. ED 122 544)

1944.   _____, & Calvert, D. R. The semantics of deafness. In W. H. Northcott (Ed.), *The hearing impaired child in a regular classroom.* Washington, D.C.: Alexander Graham Bell Association for the Deaf, 1973. Also in *Volta Review,* 1967, *69,* 644-649.

1945.   Rudy, J. P. & Nance, J. G. A transitional instrument: Selection of hearing impaired students for integration. In W. H. Northcott (Ed.), *The hearing impaired child in a regular classroom.* Washington, D.C.: Alexander Graham Bell Association for the Deaf, 1973.

1946.   Russell, G. The place of the social worker in integration. In W. H. Northcott (Ed.), *The hearing impaired child in a regular classroom.* Washington, D.C.: Alexander Graham Bell Association for the Deaf, 1973.

1947.   Salem, J. M. Deaf students in a "hearing" college. *Volta Review,* 1967, *69,* 36-40.

1948.   _____. Deaf students in a "hearing" college—a follow up. *Volta Review,* 1969, *71,* 435-437.

1949.   _____. Partial integration at the high school level. *Volta Review,* 1971, *73,* 42-46.

1950.   _____, & Herward, P. A survey to determine the impact of P.L. 94-142 on residential schools for the deaf. *American Annals of the Deaf,* 1978, *123,* 524-527.

1951.   Sanders, D. Residual hearing—the yeast of communication. In G. W. Nix (Ed.), *Mainstreaming education for hearing impaired children & youth.* New York: Grune & Stratton, 1976.

1952.   Sansone, J. J., Jr. A study to determine the relationship of sociometric status and reading achievement and selection variables for integrated hearing impaired children (Doctoral dissertation, University of Colorado, 1975). *Dissertation Abstracts International,* 1976, *36,* 4409A. (University Microfilms No. 76-225)

1953.   Scheeline, A. Integrating deaf children into public schools. *Volta Review,* 1971, *73,* 370-373.

1954.   Scheeline (Mrs. Isaiah), Jr. Jan in junior high. *Volta Review,* 1966, *68,* 453-455.

1955.   Schlesinger, H. S., & Meadow, K. P. Development of maturity in deaf children. *Exceptional Children,* 1972, *38,* 461-467.

1956.   Schlesinger, I. M., & Namir, L. (Eds.). *Sign language of the deaf: Psychological linguistic and sociological perspectives.* New York: Academic Press, 1978.

1957.   Schwartz, M. G. A deaf child in my hearing class. *Volta Review,* 1964, *66,* 627-630.

1958.   Schwartzberg, J. G. *Mainstreaming the hearing impaired child: A parent's experience. Montessori and some comparisons.* Paper presented at the 54th Annual International Convention of the Council for Exceptional Children, Chicago, April 1976. (ERIC Document Reproduction Service No. ED 122 545)

1959.   Seltz, A. In-service training: Maxi-model. In W. H. Northcott (Ed.), *The hearing impaired child in a regular classroom.* Washington, D.C.: Alexander Graham Bell Association for the Deaf, 1973.

1960.   Shellgrain, E. The case for the day school. *Volta Review,* 1957, *59,* 58-60.

1961.   Shepherd, B. D. Parent potential. *Volta Review,* 1973, *75,* 220-224.

1962.   Singler, L. P. *Mainstreaming the deaf in a metropolitan setting: A critique.* Paper presented at the 48th Biennial Convention of the American Instructors of the Deaf, Los Angeles, June 1977. (ERIC Document Reproduction Service No. ED 154 544).

1963.   Simmons-Martin, A. The Central Institute for the Deaf Home Demonstration Home Program. In G. W. Nix (Ed.), *Mainstream education for hearing impaired children & youth.* New York: Grune & Stratton, 1976.

1964.   _____. The oral/aural procedure: Theoretical basis and rationale. *Volta Review,* 1972, *74,* 541-551.

1965.   Simon, A. B. The deaf college student in 1984. *Volta Review,* 1966, *68,* 289-292.

1966.   _____. A deaf man's experiences in a hearing world. *Volta Review,* 1967, *69,* 652-655.

1967.   _____. Factors in influencing the hearing impaired college student. *Volta Review,* 1969, *71,* 501-504.

1968.   Stack, P. M. (Sister). In our program—everyone gets into the act. *Volta Review,* 1973, *75,* 425-430.

1969.   Stassen, R. A. I have one in my class who's wearing hearing aids. In W. H. Northcott (Ed.), *The hearing impaired child in a regular classroom.* Washington, D.C.: Alexander Graham Bell Association for the Deaf, 1973.

1970.   Stern, V. W. Fingerpaint on the hearing aid. *Volta Review,* 1969, *71,* 149-154. Also in W. H. Northcott (Ed.), *The hearing impaired child in a regular classroom.* Washington, D.C.: Alexander Graham Bell Association for the Deaf, 1973.

1971.   Stewart, B. Education of the partially hearing child outside special school. *Teacher of the Deaf,* 1964, *62,* 29-34.

1972.   Stinson, M. Group communication for the deaf. *Volta Review,* 1972, *74,* 52-54.

1973.   Stone, L. J., Fiedler, M. F., & Fine, C. G. Preschool education of deaf children. *Journal of Speech and Hearing Disorders,* 1961, *26,* 45-60.

1974. Stovall, E. H., & Garrett, C. A parent's view on integration. *Volta Review,* 1972, *74,* 338-344.

1975. Strattner, M. J. Deaf and hearing children learn together—an Australian model. *Young Children,* 1974, *29,* 231-234.

1976. Streng, A. Public school programmes for children with impaired hearing in small school systems. *Exceptional Children,* 1958, *25,* 71-76.

1977. _____, & Kirk, S. The social competence of deaf and hard of hearing children in a public day school. *American Annals of the Deaf,* 1938, *83,* 244-254.

1978. Stuckles, E. R. *A notetaking procedure for deaf students in regular classes.* Rochester, NY: Rochester Institute of Technology, National Technical Institute for the Deaf, 1969. (ERIC Document Reproduction Service No. ED 040 530)

1979. _____, & Enders, M. *A study of selected support services for postsecondary deaf students in regular classes.* Rochester, NY: Rochester Institute of Technology, National Technical Institute for the Deaf, 1971. (ERIC Document Reproduction Service No. 060 600)

1980. Sugrue, T. J. New York City's high school program for the deaf. *Volta Review,* 1967, *69,* 247-252.

1981. Suliver, M. E. *Assisting the hearing impaired in the classroom.* Madison, WI: Wisconsin State Department of Public Instruction/ Bureau for Handicapped Children, 1968.

1982. Sullivan, C. D. Deafness is not insurmountable. *Volta Review,* 1967, *69,* 262-263.

1983. Taussig, E. Where should the deaf child be educated? The day school—a state programme. *Volta Review,* 1954, *56,* 309-310.

1984. Taylor, M. J. The program in the Compton Aural Education Department. *Volta Review,* 1957, *59,* 54-57.

1985. Teel, P. L. Tacoma's program for intermediate hearing impaired children. *Volta Review,* 1971, *73,* 557-560, 564.

1986. Teller, H. E., Jr. The relationship of parent attitudes with the successful integration of hearing-impaired children into regular classrooms (Doctoral dissertation, University of Alabama, 1974). *Dissertation Abstracts International,* 1974, *36,* 821A. (University Microfilms No. 75-18310)

1987. Testus, E. W., & Baldwin, R. L. Educational options. *Volta Review,* 1977, *79,* 281-286.

1988. Thompson, R. E. Adjustment in high school with normally hearing contemporaries. *Volta Review,* 1960, *62,* 414-417.

1989. Timberlake, J. Why do some deaf students succeed among hearing students? *Volta Review,* 1940, *42,* 756-764.

1990. Van der Horst, A. Defective hearing, school achievement and school choice. *Teacher of the Deaf,* 1971, *69,* 398-414.

1991. Van Wyk, M. K. Integration—a look at the total picture. *Volta Review,* 1960, *62,* 69-71.

1992. _____. Integration? Yes, if. *Volta Review,* 1959, *61,* 59-62.

1993. Vaughn, G. R. *Education of deaf and hard of hearing adults in established facilities for the normally hearing. Final report.* Pocatello, ID: Idaho State University/Department of Speech Pathology and Audiology, 1967. (ERIC Document Reproduction Service No. 015 306)

1994. _____. Hearing impaired students benefit from supportive programs. *Volta Review,* 1968, *70,* 14-23, 58-66.

1995. Vernon, B., & Billingslea, H. Hard of hearing children in a public setting. *Maryland Teacher,* 1973, *30.*

1996. Vernon, M. Editorial: Integration or mainstreaming: *American Annals of the Deaf,* 1975, *120,* 15-16.

1997. _____. Major current trends in rehabilitation and education of the deaf and hard of hearing. *Rehabilitation Literature,* 1975, *36,* 102-107.

1998. _____, & Athey, J. The Holcomb plan; a creative approach to mainstreaming deaf and hard of hearing children. *Instructor,* 1977, *86*(5), 136-137.

1999. _____, & Prickett, J., Jr. Mainstreaming: Issues and a model plan. *Audiology and Hearing Education,* 1976, *2,* 5-6, 10-11.

2000. Wall, E. R. The peripatetic service for children with defective hearing in Lancashire. *Teacher of the Deaf,* 1960, *58,* 394-401.

2001. Warnke, E. F. Integration of hearing impaired with normal hearing students. *Hoergeschaedigte Kinder,* 1972, *9,* 57-59.

2002. Watkins, C. Peripatetic teaching services for hearing impaired children. *Teacher of the Deaf,* 1965, *63,* 55-76.

2003. _____. Some suggestions for teachers of the deaf working with hearing impaired children in partially hearing units and peripatetic services. *Teacher of the Deaf,* 1965, *63,* 319-329.

2004. Watson, T. J. Integration of hearing impaired children in nursery schools in England. In W. H. Northcott (Ed.), *The hearing impaired child in a regular classroom.* Washington, D.C.: Alexander Graham Bell Association for the Deaf, 1973.

2005. _____. Research in the education of the deaf outside the United States. *Volta Review,* 1963, *65,* 535-541.

2006. Wedenberg, E. Experience from 30 years' auditory training. *Volta Review,* 1967, *69,* 588-594.

2007. Weinstein, G. W. Nursery school with a difference—deaf and normal children in New York. *Parents' Magazine,* 1968, *43,* 66-69, 147.

2008. Weiss, J. Integrating the hearing handicapped. *Instructor,* 1968, *78*(3), 102.

2009. Werner, R. J. *P.L. 94-142, one year later.* A short course presented at the 1978 Alexander Graham Bell Association National Convention, St. Louis, MO, June 1978.

2010. Whorton, G. P. The hard of hearing child: A challenge to educators. *Volta Review,* 1966, *68,* 351-353.

2011. Wilkison, A. G. (Mrs.). A mother of a deaf child comments. *Volta Review,* 1967, *69,* 280-281.

2012. Williams D. M. L., Darbyshire, J. O., & Campbell, S. M. *Play patterns and abilities in hearing impaired children: Integrated nursery.* Kingston, Ontario, Canada: Queens University, 1974.

2013. Witcher, B. She's not deaf, she's hard of hearing. *Volta Review,* 1974, *76,* 428-434.

2014. Woodburn, V., & Schuster, M. Mike was our first deaf student. *Today's Education,* 1968, *67*(2), 76-78.

2015. Wooden, H. Z., & Willard, L. L. Project LIFE; language improvement to facilitate education of hearing impaired children. *American Annals of the Deaf,* 1965, *110,* 541-552.

2016. Worthington, A. M. Psychological implications of integration of deaf children with hearing children. *American Annals of the Deaf,* 1958, *103,* 467-472.

2017. Yater, V. V. The hearing clinician program. In W. H. Northcott (Ed.), *The hearing impaired child in a regular classroom.* Washington, D.C.: Alexander Graham Bell Association for the Deaf, 1973.

2018. _____. *Mainstreaming of children with a hearing loss: Practical guidelines and implications.* Springfield, IL: C. C. Thomas, 1977.

2019. _____. Parents write about integration. *Volta Review,* 1972, *74,* 554g-554h.

2020. _____. St. Louis County Hearing Clinician Program. *Volta Review,* 1972, *74,* 247-255.

2021. Yingling, P. S. Mainstreaming the hearing impaired child. *Maryland Teacher,* 1976, *33*(3), 11-14, 25-26.

IV. LEARNING DISABLED AND EMOTIONALLY DISTURBED

2022. Acker, F. Left-handed scissors; the integration of disabled children into a primary school. *Times Educational Supplement (London)*, May 9, 1975, no. 3128, p. 29.

2023. Adamson, G. The educational modulation center; an overview. *Kansas Studies in Education*, 1969, *19*(3), 1-3.

2024. Adelman, H. W. *Learning problems and classroom instruction.* Riverside, CA: University of California, Department of Education, n.d. (ERIC Document Reproduction Service No. ED 090 744)

2025. Almond, P., Rodgers, S., & Krug, D. Mainstreaming: A model for including elementary students in the severely handicapped. *Teaching Exceptional Children*, 1979, *11*, 135-139.

2026. Andersen, L. H., Barner, S. L., & Larson, H. J. Evaluation of written individualized education programs. *Exceptional Children*, 1978, *45*, 207-208.

2027. Anderson, R. Mainstreaming is the name for a new idea: Getting the problem child back into a regular classroom. *School Management*, 1973, *17*(7), 28-30, 52.

2028. Anderson, S. M. *A diagnostic and prescriptive approach to teaching through observation.* Buffalo, NY: State University of New York, Faculty of Professional Studies, 1974. (ERIC Document Reproduction Service No. ED 094 538)

2029. Ascione, F. R., & Borg, W. R. Effects of a training program on teacher behavior and handicapped children's self-concept. *Journal of Psychology*, 1980, *104*, 53-65.

2030. Baldwin, C. P., & Baldwin, A. L. *Personality and social development of handicapped children.* Ithaca, NY: Cornell University, 1972. (ERIC Document Reproduction Service No. ED 079 895)

2031. Bauch, M. Some thoughts about mainstreaming. *National Association of Secondary School Principals. Bulletin*, 1979, *63*, 77-80.

2032. Bauer, H. The resource teacher; a teacher consultant: Helping special students integrated in the mainstream. *Academic Therapy*, 1975, *10*, 299-304.

2033. Becker, L. D., & Snider, M. A. Teachers' ratings and predicting special class placement. *Journal of Learning Disabilities*, 1979, *12*, 96-99.

2034. Berryman, C., & Perry B. *A manual for teachers of learning disabled children.* Unpublished manuscript, n.d. (ERIC Document Reproduction Service No. ED 085 958)

2035.   Bersoff, D. N., Kabler, M., Fiscus, E., & Ankney, R. Effectiveness of special class placement for children labeled neurologically handicapped. *Journal of School Psychology,* 1972, *10,* 157-163.

2036.   Bettelheim, B. *Love is not enough: The treatment of emotionally disturbed children.* New York: Avon Books, n.d.

2037.   Binkley, B., DePriest, G., & Wieties, A. *In-service training for general education teachers in compliance with P.L. 94-142 under the Tennessee State Plan.* Paper presented at the 57th Annual International Convention of the Council for Exceptional Children, Dallas, TX, April 1979. (ERIC Document Reproduction Service No. ED 171 075)

2038.   Bloom, J. L. An investigation of the effect of presenting a sex education course to high school students who have been removed from the regular classroom situation because of severe emotional or physical problems (Doctoral dissertation, New York University, 1968). *Dissertation Abstracts International,* 1968, *30,* 483A. (University Microfilms No. 69-11738)

2039.   Bloomer, C. The LD tightrope. *Teacher,* 1975, *92*(7), 54-58.

2040.   Boeck, D. G., & Foster, G. G. The effectiveness of a learning disabilities inservice program. *Psychology in the Schools,* 1975, *12,* 409-411.

2041.   Bradfield, R. H., Brown, J., Kaplan, P., Rickert, E., & Stannard, R. The special child in the regular classroom. *Exceptional Children,* 1973, *39,* 384-390.

2042.   Brown, G. *An educational model for autistic children.* Orlando, FL: Orange County Public Schools, n.d. (ERIC Document Reproduction Service No. ED 113 922)

2043.   _____. A study of the critical factors that are associated with success of emotionally handicapped students in regular secondary grades in Detroit (Doctoral dissertation, The University of Michigan, 1972). *Dissertation Abstracts International,* 1972, *33,* 5957A. (University Microfilms No. 73-11053)

2044.   Brown, L., Bellamy, T., & Sontag, E. *The development and implementation of a public school prevocational training program for trainable level retarded and severely emotionally disturbed students. Vol. I.* Madison, WI: Madison Public Schools, 1971.

2045.   _____, & Sontag, E. *Toward the development and implementation of an empirically based public school program for trainable mentally retarded and severely emotionally disturbed students. Vol. II.* Madison, WI: Madison Public Schools, 1972.

2046.   Bruninks, V. L. Actual and perceived peer status of learning disabled students in mainstream programs. *The Journal of Special Education,* 1978, *12,* 51-58.

2047.   Bryan, T. H. Peer popularity of learning disabled children. *Journal of Learning Disabilities,* 1974, *7,* 621-625.

2048.   Bunch, G. Emotionally disturbed children in the regular classroom. *Special Education in Canada,* 1970, *44*(3), 29-33.

2049.   Bushlow, P. A., & Sudwarth, C. A. Underachievers profit from pilot project in John Eaton School. *Delta Kappa Gamma Bulletin,* 1970, *36*(3), 45-48.

2050.   Byrnes, M. A. Positive attitudes: A must for special programs in public schools. *Teaching Exceptional Children,* 1976, *8,* 82-84.

2051.   Cahn, L. D., & Nolan, C. E. Learning disabled adolescents: Creating a climate for learning. *National Association of Secondary School Principals. Bulletin,* 1976, *60,* 16-20.

2052.   Calabree, J. M., Kelley, B. W., Miller, B. K., & Newell, T. J. Addendum to prescriptive teaching workshop resource manual. New Providence, NJ: New Providence Board of Education, 1973. (ERIC Document Reproduction Service No. ED 117 891)

2053.   Calhoun, G., Jr. Classroom behavior and self-esteem of EMR, ED, LD and regular pupils: A three year study. *Mental Retardation,* 1977, *15,* 65-66.

2054.   _____. Hyperactive emotionally disturbed and hyperkinetic learning disabilities: A challenge for the regular classroom. *Adolescence,* 1978, *13,* 335-338.

2055.   _____. A longitudinal investigation of classroom behavior and self-esteem of EMR, ED, LD and regular pupils. *Journal for Special Educators of the Mentally Retarded,* 1978, *14,* 91-96.

2056.   _____, & Elliott, R. N., Jr. Self concept and academic achievement of educable retarded and emotionally disturbed pupils. *Exceptional Children,* 1977, *43,* 379-380.

2057.   Carman, G. O., Kosberg, B., & McDonald, E. *PROJECT ORPHEUS: Complying with the Education for All Handicapped Children Act at the Orchard School, an innovative approach to utilizing educational technology.* Paper presented at the 57th Annual International Convention of the Council for Exceptional Children, Dallas, TX, April 1979. (ERIC Document Reproduction Service No. ED 171 099)

2058.   Carroll, J., Katz, S. G., Waters, C., & Zaremba, S. *An effective model for mainstreaming emotionally impaired students.* Paper presented at the 56th Annual Convention of the Council for Exceptional Children, Kansas City, MO, May 1978. (ERIC Document Reproduction Service No. ED 153 406)

2059. Cawley, J. F. *Mainstream: A program of analysis and achievement for children with learning disabilities and behavioral disorders.* Wallingford, CT: Educational Sciences, 1973.

2060. Chaiken, W. E., & Harper, M. J. *Mainstreaming the learning disabled adolescent: A staff development guide.* Springfield, IL: C. C. Thomas, 1979.

2061. Christoplos, F. Keeping exceptional children in regular classes. *Exceptional Children,* 1973, *39,* 569-572.

2062. Connor, E. M., & Muldoon, J. F. Resource programming for emotionally disturbed teenagers. *Exceptional Children,* 1967, *34,* 261-265.

2063. Consilia, M. USA in the 70's—a look at the learning-disabled child. *Academic Therapy,* 1974, *9,* 301-308.

2064. Cook, J. M. M. Programmed tutoring in reading, a study of the use of out-of-school neighborhood youth corps enrollees as tutors to low-achieving behaviorally disordered children in the regular classrooms of an inner-city elementary school (Doctoral dissertation, University of Kentucky, 1973). *Dissertation Abstracts International,* 1973, *34,* 4034A. (University Microfilms No. 74-01406)

2065. Cotterell, G. C. Suggestions for helping the dyslexic child in the ordinary classroom. *Dyslexia Review,* 1974, *11,* 15-17.

2066. Cross, D. P. The effects of a systematic group language development program with low-achieving and regular class third grade subjects (Doctoral dissertation, University of Kansas, 1968). *Dissertation Abstracts,* 1968, *29,* 1819A. (University Microfilms No. 68-17372)

2067. Cruickshank, W. M. Myths and realities in learning disabilities. *Journal of Learning Disabilities,* 1977, *10,* 51-58.

2068. Csapo, M. G. Utilization of normal peers as behavior change agents for reducing the inappropriate behavior of emotionally disturbed children in regular classroom environments (Doctoral dissertation, University of Kansas, 1971). *Dissertation Abstracts International,* 1971, *32,* 1940A. (University Microfilms 71-27137)

2069. Dangel, H. L., Erickson, J., Haltom, C., & Molinaro, A. *An integrated model for individualizing services to children with learning problems.* Paper presented at a Special Conference on Emerging Models of Special Education for Sparsely Populated Areas, Memphis, TN, December 1971. (ERIC Document Reproduction Service No. ED 057 511)

2070. DeBlassie, R. R., & Lebsock, M. S. Counseling with handicapped children. *Elementary School Guidance and Counseling,* 1979, *13,* 199, 206.

2071. Decker, R. J., & Decker, L. A. Mainstreaming the LD child: A cautionary note. *Academic Therapy,* 1977, *12,* 353-356.

2072. Deem, M. A., & Porter, W. R. *Development of a program for the re-education and rehabilitation of emotionally handicapped male adolescents within a public school setting.* Rockville, MD: Montgomery County Public Schools, 1965. (ERIC Document Reproduction Service No. ED 010 265)

2073. *Demonstration models Garden City resource room-helping teacher team. For school year 1972-73.* Garden City, MI: Garden City Public Schools, 1973. (ERIC Document Reproduction Service No. ED 098 739)

2074. Deno, E. N. *Mainstreaming: Learning disabled, emotionally disturbed, and socially maladjusted children in regular classes.* Minneapolis, MN: Leadership Training Institute/Special Education, 1978.

2075. Dupont, H. *Educating emotionally disturbed children: Readings.* 2d. ed. Clifton, NJ: Holt, Rinehart & Winston, 1975.

2076. Ebersole, M., Dephart, N. D., & Ebersole, J. *Steps to achievement for the slow learner in the classroom.* Columbus, OH: C. E. Merrill, 1969.

2077. Edelmann, A. M. *A pilot study in exploring the use of mental health consultants to teachers of socially and emotionally maladjusted pupils in regular classes.* Philadelphia, PA: Mental Health Association of Southeast Pennsylvania and the Philadelphia Public Schools, 1966. (ERIC Document Reproduction Service No. ED 026 292)

2078. Edgington, R. Public school programming for children with learning disabilities. *Academic Therapy,* 1967, *2,* 166-169, 196.

2079. *Education for children with epilepsy: The Education for All Handicapped Children Act.* Washington, D.C.: Epilepsy Foundation of America, n.d.

2080. Eubanks, L. L. A study of slow learning children in regular and specially designed classes (Doctoral dissertation, The University of Oklahoma, 1969). *Dissertation Abstracts International,* 1969, *30,* 1773A. (University Microfilms No. 69-18449)

2081. *An exploratory study of children with neurological handicaps in school districts of Los Angeles County.* Los Angeles, CA: Los Angeles County Superintendent of Schools, 1963. (ERIC Document Reproduction Service No. ED 026 757)

2082. Faber, W. L. Conceptual tempo of elementary age learning disabled, slow-learning, and regular class boys (Doctoral dissertation, Case Western Reserve University, 1975). *Dissertation Abstracts International,* 1975, *36,* 4346A. (University Microfilms No. 75-27903)

2083. Fairchild, T. N., & Henson, F. O. *Mainstreaming children with learning disabilities.* Austin, TX: Learning Concepts, 1976.

2084. _____. *Managing the hyperactive child in the classroom.* Austin, TX: Learning Concepts, 1976.

2085. Farrald, R. R., & Schamber, R. G. *A diagnostic and prescriptive technique: A mainstream approach to identification, assessment and amelioration of learning disabilities.* Sioux Falls, SD: Adapt Press, 1973.

2086. Federlein, A. C. *A study of play behaviors and interactions of preschool children in mainstreamed and segregated settings.* Paper presented at the 57th Annual International Convention of the Council for Exceptional Children, Dallas, TX, April 1979. (ERIC Document Reproduction Service No. ED 171 048)

2087. _____. *A year long study of the frequency of play interactions of handicapped preschoolers in mainstreamed and segregated classrooms.* Paper presented at the 58th Annual International Convention of the Council for Exceptional Children, Philadelphia, PA, April 1980. (ERIC Document Reproduction Service No. ED 188 426)

2088. Flynn, N. M., & Rapoport, J. L. Hyperactivity in open and traditional classroom environments. *Journal of Special Education,* 1976, *10,* 285-290.

2089. Follman, D. E. A comparison of learning disabled students with regular class students on conformity (Doctoral dissertation, University of Northern Colorado, 1974). *Dissertation Abstracts International,* 1974, *35,* 2803A. (University Microfilms No. 74-24482)

2090. Foster, S. L., & O'Leary, K. D. Teacher attitudes toward educational and psychological services for conduct problem children. *Journal of Abnormal Child Psychology,* 1977, *5,* 101-111.

2091. Fotos, J. P. *A model program to meet the needs of the learning disabled child.* Ft. Lauderdale, FL: Nova University, 1976. (ERIC Document Reproduction Service No. ED 132 815)

2092. Fox, B. *Secondary special education. Part I: The "stepping stone model" designed for secondary learning disabled students. Part II: Adapting materials and curriculum.* Paper presented at the 58th Annual International Convention of the Council for Exceptional Children, Philadelphia, PA, April 1980. (ERIC Document Reproduction Service No. ED 188 389)

2093. Gallistel, E. R. Setting goals and objectives for LD children—process and problems. *Journal of Learning Disabilities,* 1978, *11,* 177-184.

2094.   Gearhart, B. R. *Teaching the learning disabled: A combined task-process approach.* St. Louis, MO: Mosby, 1976.

2095.   Glavin, J. P. *Behavioral strategies for classroom management.* Columbus, OH: C. E. Merrill, 1974.

2096.   _____. Behaviorally oriented resource rooms: A follow-up. *Journal of Special Education,* 1974, *8,* 337-347.

2097.   _____. Follow up behavioral research in resource rooms. *Exceptional Children,* 1973, *40,* 211-213.

2098.   Goodman, L., & Price, M. BEH final regulations for learning disabilities: Implications for the secondary school. *Learning Disability Quarterly,* 1978, *1*(4), 73-79.

2099.   Griffiths, A. N., Gillen, J. F., & Dankel, R. Leave dyslexics in the classroom. *Academic Therapy,* 1972, *8,* 57-65.

2100.   Grosenick, J. K. Assessing the reintegration of exceptional children into regular classes. *Teaching Exceptional Children,* 1970, *2,* 113-119.

2101.   Grzynkowicz, W. M. *Meeting the needs of learning disabled children in the regular class.* Springfield, IL: C. C. Thomas, 1974.

2102.   Gunderson, L. Who is that stranger? *Academic Therapy,* 1978, *14,* 99-102.

2103.   Hadary, D. E., & Cohen, S. H. *Laboratory science and art for blind, deaf, and emotionally disturbed children: A mainstreaming approach.* Baltimore, MD: University Park Press, 1978.

2104.   Haddad, J., & Ferguson, E. The wall chart and individualization. *Academic Therapy,* 1976, *11,* 297-300.

2105.   *Handicapped and normal children learning together. Summary of project, 1970-73.* Washington, D.C.: Federal Way School District 210, 1973. (ERIC Document Reproduction Service No. ED 088 262)

2106.   Hannah, E. P., & Parker, R. M. Mainstreaming vs. the special setting. *Academic Therapy,* 1980, *15,* 271-278.

2107.   Haring, N. G., & Fargo, G. A. Evaluating programs for preparing teachers of emotionally disturbed children. *Exceptional Children,* 1969, *36,* 157-164.

2108.   Harris, P. *Operation mainstream. (Training teachers to teach handicapped students). A practicum.* Ft. Lauderdale, FL: Nova University, 1976. (ERIC Document Reproduction Service No. ED 125 232)

2109.   Hawkins, D. A. The relative effects of mainstream and segregated programs on the primary learning disabled students' acquisition of prerequisite reading skills and growth of self-concept (Doctoral dissertation, University of Wisconsin-Madison). *Dissertation Abstracts International,* 1975, *36,* 7836A.

2110.   _____. *The relative effects of mainstreamed and segregated programs on the primary learning disabled students' acquisition of reading skills and growth of self-concept.* Paper presented at the 54th Annual International Convention of the Council for Exceptional Children, Chicago, IL, April 1976. (ERIC Document Reproduction Service No. ED 122 505)

2111.   Hayball, H. L., & Dilling, H. J. *Study of students from special classes who have been returned to regular classes.* Scarborough, Ontario, Canada: Scarborough Board of Education, 1969. (ERIC Document Reproduction Service No. ED 050 508)

2112.   Hayden, A. H., Smith, R. K., Saaz von Hippel, C., & Baer, S. A. *Mainstreaming preschoolers: Children with learning disabilities. A guide for teachers, parents, and others who work with learning disabled preschoolers.* Belmont, MA: Contract Research Corp., 1978. (ERIC Document Reproduction Service No. ED 164 110)

2113.   Hays, J. Diagnostic class for children with learning disabilities. *Pointer,* 1974, *19*(2), 140-141.

2114.   Heidmann, M. A. *The slow learner in the primary grades.* Columbus, OH: C. E. Merrill, 1973.

2115.   Hendrickson, B. Teachers make mainstreaming work. *Learning,* 1978, 7(2), 104-110.

2116.   Hennon, M. L. *Identifying handicapped children for child development programs.* Atlanta, GA: Humanics Press, 1973.

2117.   Henson, F. O., & Fairchild, T. N. *Mainstreaming children with learning disabilities.* Austin, TX: Learning Concepts, 1976.

2118.   Heron, T. E. Punishment: A review of the literature with implications for the teacher of mainstreamed children. *Journal of Special Education,* 1978, *12,* 243-252.

2119.   Hertel, P. N., & Hertel, N. W. *Getting into the mainstream: Learning disabilities.* St. Louis, MO: Milliken Pub., 1977.

2120.   Heule, G. R., & Zukowski, P. A. An overview of a secondary level program for emotionally disturbed adolescents. *Bureau Memorandum,* 1978, *19*(3), 9-14.

2121.   Hewett, F. M. *The emotionally disturbed child in the classroom: A developmental strategy for educating children with maladaptive behavior.* Boston, MA: Allyn & Bacon, 1968.

2122. _____. *The emotionally disturbed child in the classroom: The orchestration of success.* Boston, MA: Allyn & Bacon, 1980.

2123. _____, Artuso, A. A., Taylor, F. D., & Stillwell, R. J. *The Santa Monica Project: Demonstration and evaluation of an engineered classroom design for emotionally disturbed children in the public school: Phase one. Elementary level.* Santa Monica, CA: Santa Monica Unified School District, 1969. (ERIC Document Reproduction Service No. ED 031 026)

2124. _____, Artuso, A. A., Taylor, F. D., & Stillwell, R. J. *The Santa Monica Project: Demonstration and evaluation of an engineered classroom design for emotionally disturbed children in the public school: Phase two. Primary and secondary level. Final report.* Santa Monica, CA: Santa Monica Unified School District, 1969. (ERIC Document Reproduction Service No. ED 038 809)

2125. Horne, M. D. An investigation of teacher and peer attitudes and the effect of achievement on self-concepts and status of learning disabled and non-learning disabled pupils in regular elementary classrooms (Doctoral dissertation, Boston University School of Education, 1975). *Dissertation Abstracts International,* 1975, *36,* 1436A. (University Microfilms No. 75-18538)

2126. Houck, C., & Houck, E. *Investigation of the relationships between academic achievement and self-concept in children with specific learning disabilities.* Paper presented at the 54th Annual International Convention of the Council for Exceptional Children, Chicago, IL, April 1976. (ERIC Document Reproduction Service No. ED 125 204)

2127. Hoyt, J. H. Georgia's Rutland Center. *American Education,* 1978, *14*(1), 27-32.

2128. Introduction: Federal definition of LD: Last chance to make your input. *Journal of Learning Disabilities,* 1977, *10,* 66-67.

2129. Jackson, J. T. Teacher influence and classroom behavior of emotionally disturbed students in regular classes of a junior high school (Doctoral dissertation, University of Minnesota, 1969) *Dissertation Abstracts International,* 1969, *31,* 1102A. (University Microfilms No. 70-15850)

2130. Jensen, B. Close up: On a small school with a big idea . . . removing the stigma from special education. *Children's House,* 1973, *6*(1), 14-16.

2131. Jones, B. Helping teachers teach the LD student. *Today's Education,* 1977, *66*(4), 46-48.

2132. Kaufman, M. J., Semmel, M. I., & Agard, J. A. *Project PRIME: Interim report, year one 1971-1972 (Purpose and procedures)*. Washington, D.C.: BEH/Division of Training Programs, 1973. (ERIC Document Reproduction Service No. ED 106 307)

2133. Kirby, D. F. Renovate, rejuvenate, and release: A plan to abolish the special class. *Pointer*, 1973, *17*(3), 170-175.

2134. Kirsch, G. *Project Harmony—success for the learning disabled in the mainstream*. Mason, MI: Ingham Intermediate School District, 1978. (ERIC Document Reproduction Service No. ED 163 721)

2135. Klein-Konigsberg, E. *Semantic integration in learning disabled children*. Paper presented at the 57th Annual International Convention of the Council for Exceptional Children, Dallas, TX, April 1979. (ERIC Document Reproduction Service No. ED 171 083)

2136. Kosko, K., Grainger, L., & Takacs, T. (Eds.). *Teaching children who learn differently: A course designed for the regular classroom teacher in diagnosing and prescribing for the learning disabled child*. Monmouth, OR: Oregon College of Education, 1978. (ERIC Document Reproduction Service No. ED 165 388)

2137. Kounin, J. S., Friesen, W. V., & Norton, E. Managing emotionally disturbed children in regular classrooms. *Journal of Educational Psychology*, 1966, *57*(1), 1-13.

2138. Kueffer, E. A. Supplementary education—a new direction. *Thrust for Educational Leadership*, 1973, *2*(6), 28-31.

2139. Kunzweiler, C. E. Learning for behaviorally disoriented children in regular classrooms in middle schools. *Journal of Instructional Psychology*, 1974, *1*(3), 11-15.

2140. LaBrie, V. *Learning disabilities activity guide for the elementary classroom*. Augusta, ME: Maine State Department of Educational and Cultural Services, n.d. (ERIC Document Reproduction Service No. ED 117 907)

2141. Lamendola, A. Science and the emotionally disadvantaged child—a case study. *Science and Children*, 1976, *13*(6), 17-18.

2142. Lasher, M. G., Mattick, I., Perkins, F. J., Saaz von Hippel, C., & Hailey, L. G. *Mainstreaming preschoolers: Children with emotional disturbance. A guide for teachers, parents, and others who work with emotionally disturbed preschoolers*. Belmont, MA: Contract Research Corp., 1978. (ERIC Document Reproduction Service No. ED 164 108)

2143. Laurie, T. E., Buchwach, L., Silverman, R., & Zigmond, N. Teaching secondary learning disabled students in the mainstream. *Learning Disability Quarterly*, 1978, *1*(4), 62-72.

2144.   Lazar, A. L. (Ed.). *Aids to psycholinguistic teaching for the regular class teacher with mainstreamed exceptionals.* Palos Verdes, CA: Palos Verdes Estates, PASKI Pub., 1977. (ERIC Document Reproduction Service No. ED 150 819)

2145.   Leahy, M. A. *Level of question as a function of teacher knowledge of perceptual handicaps.* Paper presented at the Second International Scientific Federation of Learning Disabilities, Brussels, Belgium, January 1975. (ERIC Document Reproduction Service No. ED 113 861)

2146.   *Learning disabilities handbook: A guide for classroom teachers in the junior high school.* Richmond, VA: Chesterfield County Public Schools, Learning Disabilities Center, 1975.

2147.   *Learning disabilities reconsidered: A report of the Wayne County Committee for the study of children with learning disabilities, 1967-1969.* Detroit, MI: Wayne County Intermediate School District, 1969. (ERIC Document Reproduction Service No. ED 033 487)

2148.   LeFevre, D. A proposed plan for educating children with learning disabilities. *USU Special Education,* 1973, *8*(2), 3-9.

2149.   Leidy, G. A. A study of asynchrony in auditory and proprioceptive feedback processing in elementary-age learning-disabled and regular-class children (Doctoral dissertation, University of Maryland, 1971). *Dissertation Abstracts International,* 1971, *32*, 5071A. (University Microfilms No. 72-10075)

2150.   Leitch, L. J. *Learning disabilities: Review of the literature and selected annotated bibliography. Reports in education, number 3.* Montreal, Quebec, Canada: McGill University, n.d. (ERIC Document Reproduction Service No. ED 094 540)

2151.   Lerner, J. W. *Children with learning disabilities: Theories, diagnosis, teaching strategies.* Boston, MA: Houghton-Mifflin, 1976.

2152.   Lesiak, W. J., Jr., & Wait, J. A. The diagnostic kindergarten: Initial steps in the identification and programming of children with learning problems. *Psychology in the Schools,* 1974, *11*, 282-290.

2153.   Levin, A. J. A comparison of the responses of selected educators on the effectiveness of specified procedures for reintegrating children with learning and behavioral disorders from special self-contained classes into regular elementary classes (Doctoral dissertation, The Ohio State University, 1974). *Dissertation Abstracts International,* 1974, *35*, 5171A. (University Microfilms No. 75-03122)

2154.   Lewis, A. L. A resource room program for LD pupils. *Academic Therapy,* 1974, *10*, 93-100.

2155. Ley, D., & Metteer, R. The mainstream approach for the SLD child: A public school model. *Bulletin of the Orton Society,* 1974, *24,* 130-134.

2156. Lloyd, J., Sabatino, D., Miller, T., & Miller, S. II. Proposed Federal guidelines: Some open questions. *Journal of Learning Disabilities,* 1977, *10,* 69-71.

2157. Lockwood, A. V. Accommodating learning disabilities: Creating the least restrictive environment. *Illinois Schools Journal,* 1978/79, *58*(4), 33-36.

2158. Lott, L. A., Jr., Hudak, B. J., & Scheetz, J. A. *Strategies and techniques for mainstreaming: A resource room handbook.* Monroe, MI: Monroe County Intermediate School District, 1975. (ERIC Document Reproduction Service No. ED 117 890)

2159. Lovitt, T. C. Managing inappropriate behaviors. *Teacher,* 1978, *95*(5), 81-82.

2160. Lupton, F. D., Jr. The effects of a behavior management training program on counselor performance in regular day camps which include children with behavior problems (Doctoral dissertation, University of Illinois at Urbana-Champaign, 1972). *Dissertation Abstracts International,* 1972, *33,* 2780A. (University Microfilms No. 72-19871)

2161. McCombs, C. B. A study of the visual-motor ability and self-concept of children with learning disabilities in two instructional situations: regular classes and special classes (Doctoral dissertation, The University of Alabama, 1975). *Dissertation Abstracts International,* 1975, *36,* 7852A. (University Microfilms No. 76-13924)

2162. McGraw, J. J. A comparison of mean subtest raw scores on the Wechsler Intelligence Scale for Children of regular and over-achieving readers with under-achieving readers (Doctoral dissertation, The University of Oklahoma, 1966). *Dissertation Abstracts,* 1966, *27,* 1552A. (University Microfilms No. 66-14229)

2163. McIndoe, C. J. *The role of an auditory/learning disabilities specialist in a public school program for hearing-impaired students.* Paper presented at the Alexander Graham Bell Association National Convention, St. Louis, MO, June 1978.

2164. McKinnon, A. J. Parent and pupil perceptions of special classes for emotionally disturbed children. *Exceptional Children,* 1970, *37,* 302-303.

2165. McNutt, G. *Procedures for identifying specific learning disabilities.* Unpublished manuscript, 1978. (ERIC Document Reproduction Service No. ED 161 175)

2166.   Mann, P. H. *Training regular teachers in learning disabilities.* Tallahassee, FL: Florida State University/College of Education, 1972. Paper presented at the Special Study Institute, Washington, D.C., October 1971. (ERIC Document Reproduction Service No. ED 060 609)

2167.   Maryland State Department of Education. *A design for a continuum of special education services including a proposal for a pilot study.* Baltimore, MD: Author, 1969. (ERIC Document Reproduction Service No. ED 036 005)

2168.   Masat, L., Ledebur, J. K., Azzara, C., & Morotz, B. *Transitional strategies for mainstreaming emotionally disturbed (ED) students.* Paper presented at the 58th Annual International Convention of the Council for Exceptional Children, Philadelphia, PA, April 1980. (ERIC Document Reproduction Service No. ED 188 388)

2169.   Mathews, J. B., Bondra, G., Camiros, C., & Gile, L. *Project 3R. End-of-project evaluation report, July 1, 1969 through June 30, 1972.* East Granby, CT: Cooperative Special Services Center, n.d. (ERIC Document Reproduction Service No. ED 088 269)

2170.   Mayer, C. A. *Understanding young children: Emotional and behavioral development and disabilities.* Anchorage, AK: Alaska Treatment Center for Crippled Children and Adults, 1974. (ERIC Document Reproduction Service No. ED 092 258)

2171.   _____. *Understanding young children: The handicapped child in the normal preschool class.* Anchorage, AK: Alaska Treatment Center for Crippled Children and Adults, 1974. (ERIC Document Reproduction Service No. ED 092 257)

2172.   _____. *Understanding young children: Intellectual development and intellectual disabilities.* Anchorage, AK: Alaska Treatment Center for Crippled Children and Adults, 1974. (ERIC Document Reproduction Service No. ED 092 261)

2173.   _____. *Understanding young children: Learning development and learning disabilities.* Anchorage, AK: Alaska Treatment Center for Crippled Children and Adults, 1974. (ERIC Document Reproduction Service No. ED 092 259)

2174.   Meisels, S. J., & Friedland, S. J. Mainstreaming young emotionally disturbed children: Rationale and restraints. *Behavioral Disorders,* 1978, *3,* 178-185.

2175.   Miller, M. B. *Mainstreaming-supportive educational services for the learning disabled (DSEPPS) 1975-1976. Evaluation report.* Brooklyn, NY: Board of Education of the State of New York, Office of Educational Evaluation, 1976. (ERIC Document Reproduction Service No. ED 136 486)

2176. Miller, T. L., & Sabatino, D. A. An evaluation of the teacher consultant model as an approach to mainstreaming. *Exceptional Children*, 1978, *45*, 86-91.

2177. Minskoff, E. H., & Minskoff, J. G. A unified program of remedial and compensatory teaching for children with process learning disabilities. *Journal of Learning Disabilities*, 1976, *9*, 215-222.

2178. Mirkin, P. K., & Deno, S. L. *The effects of selected variations in the components of formative evaluation to improved academic performance*. Paper presented at the 64th Annual Meeting of the American Educational Research Association, Boston, MA, April 1980. (ERIC Document Reproduction Service No. ED 186 489)

2179. *Model for children's learning centers. Second year report*. St. Louis, MO: Affton School District, 1973. (ERIC Document Reproduction Service No. ED 101 509)

2180. *A model program of comprehensive educational services for students with learning problems*. Union, NJ: Union Township Board of Education, 1973. (ERIC Document Reproduction Service No. ED 083 770)

2181. Moracco, J. C. Helping the learning disabled student: What counselors can do. *Journal of Counseling Services*, 1978, *2*(3), 21-24.

2182. Morrissey, P. A., & Semmel, M. I. Instructional models for the learning disabled. *Theory into Practice*, 1975, *14*, 110-122.

2183. Morse, W. C., Cutler, R., & Fink, A. *Public school classes for the emotionally handicapped: A research analysis*. Reston, VA: The Council for Exceptional Children, 1964. (ERIC Document Reproduction Service No. ED 025 056)

2184. Mosby, R. J. A bypass program of supportive instruction for secondary students with learning disabilities. *Journal of Learning Disabilities*, 1979, *12*, 187-190.

2185. _____ (Ed.). *Developmental by-pass techniques for teaching the secondary learning disabled student*. Union, MO: Franklin County Special Education Cooperative, 1977. (ERIC Document Reproduction Service No. ED 153 380)

2186. Murphy, J. F. Learning by listening: A public school approach to learning disabilities. *Academic Therapy*, 1973, *8*, 167-189.

2187. Murphy, J. R. *Listening, language and learning disabilities: A guide for parents and teachers*. Cambridge, MA: Educators Pub. Service, 1970.

2188. Myklebust, H. R. Learning disabilities. *Science and Children*, 1976, *13*(6), 12-13.

2189. Nagrodsky, J. R. The LD/ED child: The practitioner's point of view from a Title I program perspective. *Behavioral Disorders,* 1977, *2,* 152-156.

2190. Nelson, C. M. Differences in measures of locus of control, evaluation style, incentive orientation, academic achievement and overt behavior between conduct disturbed children and their peers in the regular classroom (Doctoral dissertation, University of Kansas, 1969). *Dissertation Abstracts International,* 1969, *30,* 5295A. (University Microfilms No. 70-10986)

2191. Newman, R. G. The assessment of progress in the treatment of hyperaggressive children with learning disturbances within a school setting. *The American Journal of Orthopsychiatry,* 1959, *29,* 633-643.

2192. Nicolaou, A. W. The relation of self-concept and frustration to aggression in emotionally disturbed and normal children in special and regular programs (Doctoral dissertation, The University of Michigan, 1969). *Dissertation Abstracts International,* 1969, *31,* 647A. (University Microfilms No. 70-14606)

2193. Oaks, C. A., Smith, C. R., White, M. A., & Peterson, R. L. *Considerations in the integration of behaviorally disordered students into the regular classroom: Implications for the school principal.* Paper presented at the 57th Annual International Convention of the Council for Exceptional Children, Dallas, TX, April 1979. (ERIC Document Reproduction Service No. ED 171 096)

2194. Orfitelli, M. A. *An approach to mainstreaming the handicapped child with the nonhandicapped child.* Unpublished manuscript, 1978. (ERIC Document Reproduction Service No. ED 164 507)

2195. Orlando, C., & Lynch, J. Learning disabilities or educational casualties? Where do we go from here? *Elementary School Journal,* 1974, *74,* 461-467.

2196. Ozer, M. N., & Dworkin, N. E. The assessment of children with learning problems: An in-service teacher training program. *Journal of Learning Disabilities,* 1974, *7,* 539-544.

2197. Painter, M. *The Santa Cruz Eleven: A comprehensive plan for the education of autistic and seriously emotionally disturbed children.* Santa Cruz, CA: Santa Cruz County Board of Education, 1974. (ERIC Document Reproduction Service No. ED 112 531)

2198. Pappanikou, A. J., & Paul, J. L. (Eds.). *Mainstreaming emotionally disturbed children.* Syracuse, NY: Syracuse University Press, 1977.

2199. Parks, A. L., & Fairchild, T. N. *Behavior disorders: Helping children with behavioral problems.* Austin, TX: Learning Concepts, 1976.

2200.   Pastor, D. L., & Swap, S. M. An ecological study of emotionally disturbed preschoolers in special and regular classes. *Exceptional Children,* 1978, *45,* 213-215.

2201.   Pizzo, J. R., Giannitti, Sr. M. C., Wheeler, R., & Yakimoff, M. *A system approach to the evaluation of children with learning disabilities.* Unpublished manuscript, n.d. (ERIC Document Reproduction Service No. ED 139 754)

2202.   Post, C. K. *The school resource program: Alternative tutoring models for delivering supportive services to LD children in mainstream education.* Paper presented to the International Federation of Learning Disabilities at the Second International Scientific Conference, Brussels, Belgium, January 1975. (ERIC Document Reproduction Service No. ED 113 868)

2203.   *Project FAST.* Essexville, MI: Hampton Public Schools, 1975. (ERIC Document Reproduction Service No. ED 117 923)

2204.   *Project FAST: Final report.* Essexville, MI: Hampton Public Schools, 1975. (ERIC Document Reproduction Service No. ED 117 926)

2205.   *Project FAST (Functional Analysis Systems Training): Adopter/ Facilitator Information.* Essexville, MI: Hampton Public Schools, 1975. (ERIC Document Reproduction Service No. ED 117 925)

2206.   Radko, D. A. A program proposal designed to assist regular classroom teachers with mainstreamed socially maladjusted and emotionally disturbed children (Doctoral dissertation, Rutgers University, The State University of New Jersey, 1976). *Dissertation Abstracts International,* 1976, *39,* 202A. (University Microfilms No. 78-00208)

2207.   Ramey, J. Prescriptions for learning: Resource centers for children with learning disabilities. *Colorado Journal of Education Research,* 1975, *14*(3), 16-21.

2208.   Reger, R. A case study of the effects of labeling. *Journal of Learning Disabilities,* 1974, *7,* 650-651.

2209.   _____. What is a resource room program? *Journal of Learning Disabilities,* 1973, *6,* 609-613.

2210.   _____ (Ed.). Preschool programming of children with disabilities. Springfield, IL: C. C. Thomas, 1970.

2211.   Rhodes, W. C., & Gibbons, S. *Environmental forces impinging upon normal and disturbed children in a regular classroom. Final report.* Unpublished manuscript, 1971. (ERIC Document Reproduction Service No. ED 071 262)

2212.   Rieth, H. J., Jr. Experimental analysis of procedures used to modify the academic and attending behavior of students alternatively placed in regular and special education (Doctoral dissertation, University of Kansas, 1971). *Dissertation Abstracts International,* 1971, *32,* 1949A. (University Microfilms No. 71-27226)

2213.   Ritter, D. R. Surviving in the regular classroom: A follow-up of mainstreamed children with learning disabilities. *Journal of School Psychology,* 1978, *16,* 253-256.

2214.   Rubin, E. Z., Simson, C. B., & Betwee, M. C. *Emotionally handicapped children and the elementary school.* Detroit, MI: Wayne State University Press, 1966.

2215.   Saunders, B. T. The effect of the emotionally disturbed child in the public school classroom. *Psychology in the Schools,* 1971, *8,* 23-26.

2216.   Scarbrough, A. T. *Guiding growth in reading: Reference manual for teachers of children with learning problems in the regular classroom grades 1-4.* Unpublished manuscript, 1973. (ERIC Document Reproduction Service No. ED 090 726)

2217.   Schirmer, G. J. The use of behavior modification techniques to reduce out of seat behaviors in two regular classrooms (Doctoral dissertation, The University of Michigan, 1971). *Dissertation Abstracts International,* 1971, *32,* 6223A. (University Microfilms No. 72-14987)

2218.   Schultz, J. J. Integration of emotionally disturbed students: The role of the director of special education. *Exceptional Children,* 1973, *40,* 39-41.

2219.   Schworm, R. W. Models in special education: Considerations and cautions. *Journal of Special Education,* 1976, *10,* 179-186.

2220.   Seely, T., Durkin, P. B., & Adams, C. D. *Behavior disorders program design.* Douglasville, GA: Douglas County School System, 1974. (ERIC Document Reproduction Service No. ED 108 421)

2221.   Serving the needs of individuals with behavior disorders. *Exceptional Children,* 1977, *44,* 158-164.

2222.   Sheehy, E. Children's perceptions of teachers' expectations among selected able and specifically disabled learners in regular and special classrooms (Doctoral dissertation, University of Southern California, 1974). *Dissertation Abstracts International,* 1974, *35,* 3579A. (University Microfilms No. 74-28464)

2223.   Siegel, E. *Special education in the regular classroom.* New York, NY: John Day, 1969.

2224. Silverman, M. *Beyond the early identification and treatment of the young child: The chronic child patient.* Unpublished manuscript, 1978. (ERIC Document Reproduction Service No. ED 162 484)

2225. _____. Beyond the mainstream: The special needs of the chronic child patient. *American Journal of Orthopsychiatry,* 1979, *49,* 62-68.

2226. Simek, R. *An investigation of the relationship between specific organizational variables and integration of emotionally disturbed and neurologically impaired students.* Paper presented at the 57th Annual International Convention of the Council for Exceptional Children, Dallas, TX, April 1979. (ERIC Document Reproduction Service No. ED 170 999)

2227. Singleton, K. *The role of the resource specialist in increasing positive attitudes toward having individuals with special needs enrolled in the regular classroom. Final report.* Culver City, CA: Culver City Unified School District, 1976. (ERIC Document Reproduction Service No. ED 148 040)

2228. Skindrud, K. In-service preparation for mainstreaming. A continuum of strategies for instructional planning (IEP) teams. *Teacher Education and Special Education,* 1978, *2*(1), 41-52.

2229. Speece, D. L., & Mandell, C. J. Resource room support services for regular teachers. *Learning Disability Quarterly,* 1980, *3*(1), 49-53.

2230. Springmeyer, L. B. Stimulus variation transition from behavior modification treatment to regular classroom (Doctoral dissertation, University of Utah, 1973). *Dissertation Abstracts International,* 1973, *34,* 4009A. (University Microfilms No. 73-31012)

2231. Stearns, K., & Swenson, S. H. The resource teacher: An alternate to special class placement. *Viewpoints in Teaching and Learning,* 1973, *49*(1), 1-12.

2232. Stellern, J., & Vasa, S. F. *A primer of diagnostic-prescriptive teaching and programming.* Laramie, WY: College of Education, University of Wyoming, Center for Research, n.d.

2233. Stephens, E., & Jones, L. *An educator's blueprints: A guide to programs and services K-12.* Homewood, IL: Cook County School District 153, 1975. (ERIC Document Reproduction Service No. ED 101 500)

2234. Stephens, T. M. Teaching learning and behavioral disabled students in least restrictive environments. *Behavioral Disorders,* 1977, *2,* 146-151.

2235. Strain, P. S. & Timm, M. An experimental analysis of social interaction between a behaviorally disordered preschool child and her classroom peers. *Journal of Applied Behavior Analysis,* 1974, *7,* 583-590.

2236. Sulzbacher, S., & Kenowitz, L. A. I: At last, a definition of learning disabilities we can live with? *Journal of Learning Disabilities,* 1977, *10,* 67-69.

2237. Summers, M. Learning disabilities . . . a puzzlement. *Today's Education,* 1977, *66*(4), 40-42.

2238. Sussman, S. *The organization of education for learning handicapped pupils: A review and recommendation.* Toronto, Ontario, Canada: York Borough Board of Education, 1974. (ERIC Document Reproduction Service No. ED 091 912)

2239. Toker, M. L. *Pilot models for mainstreaming secondary students who are mild to moderate behaviorally disordered. Administrator manual.* Lincoln, NB: Nebraska State Department of Education, 1976. (ERIC Document Reproduction Service No. ED 155 854)

2240. _____. *Pilot models for mainstreaming secondary students who are mild to moderate behaviorally disordered. Resource teacher manual.* Lincoln, NB: Nebraska State Department of Education, 1978. (ERIC Document Reproduction Service No. ED 155 853)

2241. _____, & Hoeltke, G. M. *Pilot models for mainstreaming secondary students who are mild to moderate behaviorally disordered.* Paper presented at the 56th Annual International Convention of the Council for Exceptional Children, Kansas City, KS, May 1978. (ERIC Document Reproduction Service No. ED 153 438)

2242. Trembley, P. W., & Clapper, C. H. Deficit grouping—a solution to the segregation of problem learners and their long wait for a relevant program after identification. *Journal of School Psychology,* 1972, *10,* 181-185.

2243. Turner, M. T., & Watkins, C. H. *A three-dimensional approach to learning disabilities in the secondary school.* Paper presented at the 1975 American Educational Research Association Meeting, Washington, D.C., March-April, 1975. (ERIC Document Reproduction Service No. ED 112 578)

2244. Vacc, N. A. Long term effects of special class intervention for emotionally disturbed children. *Exceptional Children,* 1972, *39,* 15-22.

2245. _____. A study of emotionally disturbed children in regular and special classes (Doctoral dissertation, State University of New York at Albany, 1967). *Dissertation Abstracts,* 1967, *28,* 4499A. (University Microfilms No. 68-05274)

2246. _____. A study of emotionally disturbed children in regular and special classes. *Exceptional Children,* 1968, *35,* 197-204.

2247. Vogel, A. L. Integration of nine severe learning-disabled children in a junior high school core program. *Academic Therapy,* 1973, *9,* 99-104. Also in *School Psychology Digest,* 1976, *5,* 54-56.

2248.   Wagoner, E. M. A study of roles and effectiveness of classroom teachers and the learning disability specialist in resource room and regular classroom instruction for students with arithmetic disabilities (Doctoral dissertation, Boston University School of Education, 1975). *Dissertation Abstracts International*, 1975, *36*, 1443A. (University Microfilms No. 75-18544)

2249.   Walker, H. M. Competency-based training issues in the development of behavior management packages for specific classroom behavior disorders. *Behavioral Disorders*, 1976, *1*, 112-122.

2250.   _____, Mattson, R. H., & Buckley, N. K. *Special class placement as a treatment alternative for deviant behavior in children. Section one. Interim report.* Eugene, OR: University of Oregon, 1968. (ERIC Document Reproduction Service No. ED 026 694)

2251.   Watson, D. L., & Hall, D. L. *Self-control of hyperactivity.* LaMesa, CA: Spring Valley School District, 1977.

2252.   Weckler, E., & Youngberg, M. *IMPACT: Mainstreaming learning problems in the classroom. Part I: In classroom; Part II: Dissemination at university.* Paper presented at the 5th Southwestern Regional Conference, Phoenix, AZ, January 1975. (ERIC Document Reproduction Service No. ED 112 559)

2253.   Welch, D. Educational modulation center: Model for education of learning disability children. *Kansas Studies in Education*, 1969, *19*(3), 1-33.

2254.   White, M. A. *Considerations in the integration of behaviorally disordered students into the regular classroom: Teacher concerns and considerations.* Paper presented at the 57th Annual International Convention of the Council for Exceptional Children, Dallas, TX, April 1979. (ERIC Document Reproduction Service No. ED 171 082)

2255.   Williams, M. J., Frost, K., & Tracy, A. *A curriculum guide for industrial arts activities for children with emotional problems.* New Britain, CT: Central Connecticut State College, Division of Technology, 1976. (ERIC Document Reproduction Service No. ED 134 677)

2256.   Wood, M. H. The dyslexic in the general classroom. *Bulletin of the Orton Society*, 1976, *26*, 124-140.

2257.   Young, D. W. G. The effectiveness of an inservice education program for regular classroom primary teachers regarding the recognition and accommodation of children with learning problems (Doctoral dissertation, University of Pittsburgh, 1973). *Dissertation Abstracts International*, 1973, *34*, 3226A. (University Microfilms No. 73-29376).

2258.   Zedler, E. Y. Educating programming for pupils with neurologically based language disorders. *Journal of Learning Disabilities*, 1970, *3*, 618-628.

2259.   Zehm, S. J. Search for solutions to the problems of educating slow learners in American public schools. *Slow Learning Child*, 1975, *22*(1), 32-37.

V. MENTALLY HANDICAPPED

2260.   Adams, C. A program for mainstreaming at Stevens Point. *Bureau Memorandum*, 1972, *13*(3), 9-11.

2261.   Allen, R. M. Note on mixed summer camping with retardates and non-retardates. *Training School Bulletin*, 1957, *54*, 50-51.

2262.   Aloia, G. F. A systematic examination of the stereotypic influence of the label "educable mentally retarded" on the initial expectations of elementary school teachers regarding mainstreamed children (Doctoral dissertation, University of California, Riverside, 1976). *Dissertation Abstracts International*, 1977, *38*, 3410A. (University Microfilms No. 77-27150)

2263.   _____, Beaver, R. J., & Pettus, W. F. Increasing initial interactions among integrated EMR students and their nonretarded peers in a game-playing situation. *American Journal of Mental Deficiency*, 1978, *82*, 573-579.

2264.   Altman, R., & Meyan, E. L. Research implications. *Education and Training of the Mentally Retarded*, 1975, *10*, 276.

2265.   Anderson, S. M., & Dirr, P. J. *Open education and the handicapped; a paper for the Instructional Technology course for teachers.* Buffalo, NY: State University of New York at Buffalo, and Educational Research and Development Complex, 1974. (ERIC Document Reproduction Service No. ED 105 674)

2266.   Anooshian, V. B. *A survey of problems arising from the integration of EMR boys in the California High School regular P.E. class.* Master's thesis, Claremont Graduate School, 1961.

2267.   Aquilina, R. I. Revolutionary legislation for a bicentennial year. *Education and Training of the Mentally Retarded*, 1976, *11*, 189-196.

2268.   Arn, W. J. Verbal language behavior of EMR pupils in relation to regular and special primary class placement (Doctoral dissertation, Kent State University, 1967). *Dissertation Abstracts*, 1967, *28*, 4615A. (University Microfilms No. 68-06203)

2269.   Audette, R. H., & Heiny, R. W. The governance of early education programs: A case in support of public school responsibility for them. *Behavioral Disorders,* 1978, *3,* 168-177.

2270.   Baine, D. Selection and evaluation of instructional programs. *Mental Retardation Bulletin,* 1976, 4(3), 133-138.

2271.   Baker, C. D. The effect of certain student and non-student factors on the adjustment of mildly retarded students in regular classes (Doctoral dissertation, University of Northern Colorado, 1974). *Dissertation Abstracts International,* 1974, *35,* 3547A. (University Microfilms No. 74-24473)

2272.   Baldwin, W. K. *The social position of the educable mentally retarded child in the regular grades in the public school.* Unpublished doctoral dissertation, Columbia University, 1958.

2273.   _____. The social position of the educable mentally retarded child in the regular grades in the public schools. *Exceptional Children,* 1958, *25,* 106-112.

2274.   Ballard, M., Gottlieb, J., Corman, L., & Kaufman, M. J. Improving the social status of mainstreamed retarded children. *Journal of Educational Psychology,* 1977, *69,* 605-611.

2275.   Behrens, R. F., & Berkowitz, A. J. Public education for trainable mentally retarded persons. *Journal for Special Educators of the Mentally Retarded,* 1973, *10,* 21-26.

2276.   Belkin, L. Miracles for the retarded. *AV Guide: The Learning Media Magazine,* 1972, *51*(9), 8-10, 18-19.

2277.   Bessant, H. P. Pen and share it; the mainstream in education. *Education and Training of the Mentally Retarded,* 1974, *9,* 96-97.

2278.   Birch, J. W. Changing relationship between special and regular education; interview; ed. by J. B. Jordan. *Education and Training of the Mentally Retarded,* 1977, *12,* 277-285.

2279.   _____. *Mainstreaming: Educable retarded children in regular classes.* Reston, VA: The Council for Exceptional Children, 1974. (ERIC Document Reproduction Service No. ED 090 724)

2280.   _____. *Retarded pupils in the mainstream: The special education of educable mentally retarded pupils in regular classes.* Reston, VA: The Council for Exceptional Children, 1974.

2281.   _____, & Stevens, G. *Teaching exceptional children in every classroom: Reaching the mentally retarded.* Indianapolis, IN: Bobbs-Merrill, 1955.

2282.   Blatt, B. The nine pillars of mental retardation. *Family Involvement,* 1975, *8*(1), 5-10.

2283.   _____. The physical, personality, academic status of children who are mentally retarded attending regular classes. *American Journal of Mental Deficiency*, 1958, *62*, 310-318.

2284.   _____. The physical, personality, and academic status of children who are mentally retarded attending special classes as compared with children who are mentally retarded attending regular classes (Doctoral dissertation, The Pennsylvania State University, 1956). *Dissertation Abstracts*, 1957, *17*, 265. (University Microfilms No. 00-19333)

2285.   _____. Some persistently recurring assumptions concerning the mentally subnormal. *Training School Bulletin*, 1960, *57*, 48-59.

2286.   Bloom, B. Normalizing the education experience. *Deficience Mentale/Mental Retardation*, 1975, *25*(1), 2-7.

2287.   Blumberg, A. A comparison of the conceptions and attitudes of parents of children in regular classes and parents of mentally retarded children concerning the subgroups of mental retardation (Doctoral dissertation, Syracuse University, 1964). *Dissertation Abstracts*, 1964, *25*, 6407A. (University Microfilms No. 65-03448)

2288.   Bogdan, R., & Taylor, S. The judged, not the judges: An insider's view of mental retardation. *American Psychologist*, 1976, *31*, 47-52.

2289.   Boland, S. K. *Integration: Parent alliance. In-service consultor; volume I, number I.* Greeley, CO: Educational Consultant Enterprises, Inc., 1974.

2290.   Brace, D. K. Physical education and recreation for mentally retarded pupils in public schools. *Research Quarterly*, 1968, *39*, 779-782. Also in *Mental Retardation*, 1968, *6*, 18-20.

2291.   _____. *Physical education and recreation for mentally retarded pupils in public schools.* Washington, D.C.: American Alliance for Health, Physical Education and Recreation, 1966. (ERIC Document Reproduction Service No. ED 080 531)

2292.   Bradfield, R. H., Brown, J., Kaplan, P., Rickert, E., & Stannard, R. The special child in the regular classroom. *Exceptional Children*, 1973, *39*, 384-390.

2293.   Bricker, D. D., & Bricker, W. A. Developmentally integrated approach to early intervention. *Education and Training of the Mentally Retarded*, 1977, *12*, 100-108.

2294.   Brown, A. T., Jr. Integration of trainable students in a regular high school building. *Educational and Training of the Mentally Retarded*, 1976, *11*, 51-52.

2295. Brown, L. Instructional programs for trainable-level retarded students. In L. Mann, & D. A. Sabatino (Eds.), *The first review of special education, vol. 2.* Philadelphia, PA: JSE Press, 1973.

2296. _____, Bellamy, T., & Sontag, E. *The development and implementation of a public school prevocational training program for trainable level retarded and severely emotionally disturbed students. Vol. I.* Madison, WI: Madison Public Schools, 1971.

2297. _____, & Sontag, E. *Toward the development and implementation of an empirically based public school program for trainable mentally retarded and severely emotionally disturbed students. Vol. II.* Madison, WI: Madison Public Schools, 1972.

2298. _____, & York, R. Developing programs for severely handicapped students: Teacher training and classroom instruction. *Focus on Exceptional Children,* 1974, 6(2), 1.

2299. Bruininks, R. H., & Rynders, J. E. Alternatives to special class placement for educable mentally retarded children. *Focus on Exceptional Children,* 1971, 3(1), 1-12. Also in R. L. Jones, & D. C. Macmillan (Eds.), *Special education in transition.* Boston, MA: Allyn & Bacon, 1974.

2300. _____, & Rynders, J. E. *Alternatives to special class placement for educable mentally retarded children. Occasional paper #6.* Minneapolis, MN: University of Minnesota, Research Development and Demonstration Center in Education of Handicapped Children, 1971. (ERIC Document Reproduction Service No. ED 102 803)

2301. _____. Rynders, J. E., & Gross, J. C. Social acceptance of retarded pupils in resource rooms and regular classes. *American Journal of Mental Deficiency,* 1974, 78, 377-383.

2302. Budoff, M. Providing special education without special classes. *Journal of School Psychology,* 1972, 10, 199-205.

2303. _____, & Gottlieb, J. *A comparison of EMR children in special classes with EMR children who have been reintegrated into regular classes.* Cambridge, MA: Research Institute for Educational Problems, 1974. (ERIC Document Reproduction Service No. ED 108 434)

2304. _____, & Gottlieb, J. Special class EMR children mainstreaming: A study of an aptitude (learning potential) treatment interaction. *American Journal of Mental Deficiency,* 1976, 8, 1-11.

2305. Burke, P. J., & Saettler, H. The division of personnel preparation: How funding priorities are established and a personal assessment of the impact of P.L. 94-142. *Education and Training of the Mentally Retarded,* 1976, 11, 361-365.

2306.   Burt, R. A. Judicial action to aid the retarded. In N. Hobbs (Ed.), *Issues in the classification of children* (2 vols.). San Francisco, CA: Jossey-Bass, 1975.

2307.   Butefish, B., & Mattson, B. *What research says about teaching the educable mentally retarded in the classroom.* Lubbock, TX: West Texas School Study Council, Technology Station, 1965. (ERIC Document Reproduction Service No. ED 014 184)

2308.   Calhoun, G., Jr. Classroom behavior and self-esteem of EMR, ED, LD and regular pupils: A three year study. *Mental Retardation,* 1977, *15*, 65-66.

2309.   _____. A longitudinal investigation of classroom behavior and self-esteem of EMR, ED, LD and regular pupils. *Journal for Special Educators of the Mentally Retarded,* 1978, *14*, 91-96.

2310.   _____, & Elliott, R. N., Jr. Self concept and academic achievement of educable retarded and emotionally disturbed pupils. *Exceptional Children,* 1977, *43*, 379-380.

2311.   Carlsson, H., & Sletved, H. (Eds.). *Report from the preCongress seminar on special education and rehabilitation of the mentally retarded, 1973.* Malmo, Sweden: International Association for the Scientific Study of Mental Deficiency, 1973. (ERIC Document Reproduction Service No. ED 108 409)

2312.   Carriker, W. R. *A comparison of postschool adjustments of regular and special class retarded individuals served in Lincoln and Omaha, Nebraska public schools.* Lincoln, NB: Nebraska State Department of Education, 1957. (ERIC Document Reproduction Service No. ED 002 775)

2313.   Carroll, A. W. The effects of segregated and partially integrated school progams on self-concept and academic achievement of educable mental retardates. *Exceptional Children,* 1967, *34*, 93-99.

2314.   Carter, J. L. Effects of a physical education program upon the physical fitness of educable mentally retarded boys. *Texas AHPER Journal,* 1970, *4*, 33.

2315.   _____. The status of educable mentally retarded boys on the AAHPER youth fitness test. *Texas AHPER Journal,* 1966, *1,*8.

2316.   Carvajal, A. L. Predictors of four criteria of self concept in educable mentally retarded adolescents. *Exceptional Children,* 1972, *39*, 239.

2317.   Cassidy, V. M., & Stanton, J. E. *An investigation of factors involved in the educational placement of mentally retarded children.* Columbus, OH: Ohio State University, Bureau of Educational Research & Services, 1959. (ERIC Document Reproduction Service No. ED 002 752)

2318.   Caster, J. A., & Grimes, J. *Current issues in mental retardation: Psychologists' regional in-service meeting.* Des Moines, IA: Iowa State Department of Public Instruction, Division of Special Education, 1974. (ERIC Document Reproduction Service No. ED 098 742)

2319.   Cegelka, P. T. Exemplary projects and programs for the career development of retarded individuals. *Education and Training of the Mentally Retarded,* 1977, *12,* 161-163.

2320.   Cegelka, W. J., & Tyler, J. L. The efficacy of special class placement for the mentally retarded in proper perspective. *Training School Bulletin,* 1970, *67,* 33-68.

2321.   Chaffin, J. D. Will the real "mainstreaming" program please stand up—(or . . . should Dunn have done it?) *Focus on Exceptional Children,* 1974, 6(5), 1-18.

2322.   Charney, L. A comparative study of the suggestibility characteristics of retarded children in regular classes and retarded children in special classes (Doctoral dissertation, Syracuse University, 1959). *Dissertation Abstracts,* 1959, *21,* 304. (University Microfilms No. 60-02599)

2323.   Childs, R. E. A review of the research concerning mainstreaming. *Journal for Special Educators of the Mentally Retarded,* 1975, *11,* 106-112.

2324.   Chinn, P. E., Drew, C. J., & Logan, D. R. *Mental retardation: A life cycle approach.* St. Louis, MO: C. V. Mosby, 1975.

2325.   Clark, G. M. Mainstreaming for the secondary educable mentally retarded: Is it defensible? *Focus on Exceptional Children,* 1975, 7(2), 1-6.

2326.   Clark, R. M. An analysis of the role of a resource teacher for the mainstreamed educable mildly handicapped children in selected Nebraska public schools (Doctoral dissertation, The University of Nebraska-Lincoln, 1977). *Dissertation Abstracts International,* 1977, *38,* 7134A. (University Microfilms No. 78-09150)

2327.   Clifford, M., & McKinney, J. D. *Evaluation of exemplary programs for the educable retarded: ESEA Title III. Final report for 1973-74 budget period.* Chapel Hill, NC: Chapel Hill City Schools and University of North Carolina at Chapel Hill, 1974. (ERIC Document Reproduction Service No. ED 102 776)

2328.   Cohen, S. B., & Plaskon, S. P. Selecting a reading approach for the mainstreamed child. *Language Arts,* 1978, 55(8), 966-70.

2329.   Cole, C. J. *A study of physical fitness and selected sports skills of normal and educable mentally retarded girls enrolled in Levelland Junior High School in Levelland, Texas.* Master's thesis, Texas Woman's University, 1967.

2330. Cole, M. E. P.L. 94-142: A view from the benches, not the trenches. *Mississippi Educator,* 1978, *3*(1), 14-46.

2331. Collister, L. *A comparison of the long-range benefits of graduation from special vs. mainstream school for mildly mentally handicapped students.* Seattle, WA: Seattle Public Schools, Department of Planning, Research and Evaluation, 1975. (ERIC Document Reproduction Service No. ED 117 870)

2332. Combs, R. H., & Harper, J. L. Effects of labels on attitudes of educators toward handicapped children. *Exceptional Children,* 1967, *33*, 399-403.

2333. Cook, I. D., & Engleman, V. Vocational education for the handicapped: Methodology for planning and implementing inservice. *Education and Training of the Mentally Retarded,* 1978, *13*, 294-97.

2334. Cooke, T. P., Apolloni, T., & Cooke, S. A. Normal preschool children as behavioral models for retarded peers. *Exceptional Children,* 1977, *43*, 531-532.

2335. Corcoran, E. L., & French, R. L. Mainstreaming the retarded adult: An organizational model. *Special Children,* 1976, *2*(3), 45-47.

2336. Cormany, R. B. Returning special education students to regular classes. *Personnel and Guidance Journal,* 1970, *48*, 641-646.

2337. Cousins, A. L. *Secondary counselors' perception of role and function of guidance service delivery to mainstreamed, educable mentally retarded pupils.* Unpublished doctoral dissertation, Walden University, 1977. (ERIC Document Reproduction Service No. ED 150 477)

2338. Creswell, D. Integration is a two-way street. *Education Canada,* 1973, *13*(3), 4-7.

2339. Cronk, M. S. *Attitude change toward trainable mentally retarded: Mainstreaming in reverse.* Paper presented at the First World Congress on Future Special Education, Stirling, Scotland, June-July, 1978. (ERIC Document Reproduction Service No. ED 158 509). Also paper presented at the 57th Annual International Convention of the Council for Exceptional Children, Dallas, TX, April 1979. (ERIC Document Reproduction Service No. ED 171 007)

2340. Darrah, J. Diagnostic practices and special classes for the educably mentally retarded—a layman's critical view. *Exceptional Children,* 1967, *33*, 523-527.

2341. DeBlassie, R. R., & Lebsock, M. S. Counseling with handicapped children. *Elementary School Guidance and Counseling,* 1979, *13*, 199-206.

2342.   Deno, E. N. *Instructional alternatives for exceptional children.* Reston, VA: The Council for Exceptional Children, 1973. (ERIC Document Reproduction Service No. ED 074 678)

2343.   Densem, P., & Wilton, K. Social interaction of intellectually handicapped children in integrated and segregated preschools. *Exceptional Children*, 1977, *24*, 165-172.

2344.   Dettre, J. H. *The effect of inservice training and teacher involvement upon teachers' acceptance of integration of EMR students in regular classrooms.* Unpublished doctoral dissertation, The University of New Mexico, 1970.

2345.   Dever, R. B., & Knapczyk, D. *Indiana University School of Education Undergraduate Program for Training Teachers of Moderately, Severely, and Profoundly Retarded Individuals.* Bloomington, IN: Indiana University, Bloomington, School of Education, 1976. (ERIC Document Reproduction Service No. ED 159 135)

2346.   Dietrich, D. J. *Mainstreaming special needs students in vocational education.* Oil City, PA: Venango County Area Vocational-Technical School, 1978. (ERIC Document Reproduction Service No. ED 159 361)

2347.   _____. Work adjustment ratings of educable mentally retarded and non-retarded students enrolled in a mainstreamed area vocational-technical school program (Doctoral dissertation, University of Pittsburgh, 1978). *Dissertation Abstracts International*, 1978, *39*, 1472A. (University Microfilms No. 78-16785)

2348.   Diggs, E. A. A study of change in the social status of rejected mentally retarded children in regular classrooms (Doctoral dissertation, University of Northern Colorado, 1963). *Dissertation Abstracts*, 1963, *25*, 220. (University Microfilms No. 64-04180)

2349.   Dolloway, E. A., & Snell, M. E. Efficacy revisited. *Education and Training of the Mentally Retarded*, 1975, *10*, 276-283.

2350.   Dunn, L. M. Special education for the mildly retarded—is much of it justifiable? *Exceptional Children*, 1968, *35*, 5-24. Also in R. L. Jones & D. C. Macmillan (Eds.), *Special education in transition.* Boston, MA: Allyn & Bacon, 1974. Also in J. W. Schifani (Ed.), *Contemporary issues in mainstreaming handicapped citizens.* Dubuque, IA: Kendall/Hunt Pub., 1976.

2351.   Egg, H. C. M. *Integration of the mentally retarded in society: Their wish or ours?* Paper presented at the First World Congress on Future Special Education, Stirling, Scotland, June-July 1978. (ERIC Document Reproduction Service No. ED 157 277)

2352. Ehrenburg, L. H. *The benefit to educable mentally retarded girls by participation in a physical education program.* Master's thesis, Fresno State College, 1963.

2353. *An exploratory study of children with neurological handicaps in school districts of Los Angeles County.* Los Angeles, CA: Los Angeles County Schools, 1963. (ERIC Document Reproduction Service No. ED 026 757)

2354. Feitler, F. C., & DuBasik, V. *Attitudes of regular classroom teachers toward EMR students.* Paper presented at the Convention of the American Educational Research Association, Toronto, Ontario, Canada, March 1978. (ERIC Document Reproduction Service No. ED 155 857)

2355. Fine, M. J. Clearinghouse: Attitudes of regular and special class teachers toward the educable mentally retarded child. *Exceptional Children,* 1967, *33,* 429-430.

2356. Flynn, T. M., & Flynn, L. A. The effect of a parttime special education program on the adjustment of EMR students. *Exceptional Children,* 1970, *36,* 680-681.

2357. _____. Ratings of educable mentally handicapped students by regular and special teachers. *Exceptional Children,* 1978, *44,* 539-540.

2358. _____. Regular-class adjustment of EMR students attending a part-time special education program. *The Journal of Special Education,* 1974, *8,* 167-173.

2359. Foley, J. M. Effect of labeling and teacher behavior on children's attitudes. *American Journal of Mental Deficiency,* 1979, *83,* 380-384.

2360. Folman, R., & Budoff, M. *Learning potential and family status among special (EMR) and regular class adolescents. Studies in Learning Potential. Vol. 2, No. 37.* Cambridge, MA: Research Institute for Educational Problems, 1971. (ERIC Document Reproduction Service No. ED 085 972)

2361. Forer, A. M., & Zajac, M. *Library services to the mentally retarded.* Harrisburg, PA: Pennsylvania State Library, n.d. (ERIC Document Reproduction Service No. ED 165 728)

2362. Forness, S. R. The mildly retarded as casualties of the educational system. *Journal of School Psychology,* 1972, *10,* 117, 124.

2363. Fountain Valley School District, California. *Children without labels: ESEA, Title III, Project 1232; handicapped children in the regular classroom.* Fountain Valley, CA: Author, n.d. (ERIC Document Reproduction Service No. ED 096 806)

2364.   _____. *Handicapped children in the regular classroom.* Fountain Valley, CA: Author, 1972. (ERIC Document Reproduction Service No. ED 073 592)

2365.   Frick, T. *Application of SIGGS to Project PRIME: A general systems approach to evaluation of mainstreaming.* Bloomington, IN: Indiana University, Bloomington. Center for Innovation in Teaching the Handicapped. 1976. (ERIC Document Reproduction Service No. ED 129 841)

2366.   Fuchigami, R. Y. An investigation of the extent of integration and some related factors affecting the social relationships of educable mentally handicapped children in Illinois (Doctoral dissertation, University of Illinois, Champaign, 1964). *Dissertation Abstracts,* 1965, *25,* 6311A. (University Microfilms No. 65-3586)

2367.   Fullerton, N. H. An analysis of verbal and nonverbal behaviors of teachers of educable mentally retarded students mainstreamed and in special classes (Doctoral dissertation, The University of Tennessee, 1978). *Dissertation Abstracts International,* 1978, *39,* 2865A. (University Microfilms No. 78-15015)

2368.   Gadson, R. D. Queries from the classroom: Should special classes for the educable mentally retarded be disbanded? *Pointer,* 1973, *17*(3), 166-167.

2369.   Gampel, D. H., Gottlieb, J., & Harrison, R. H. *Comparison of classroom behavior of special-class EMR, integrated EMR, low IQ, and nonretarded children. Studies in Learning Potential, Vol. 3, No. 41.* Cambridge, MA: Research Institute for Educational Problems, 1973. (ERIC Document Reproduction Service No. ED 085 964). Also in *American Journal of Mental Deficiency,* 1974, *79,* 16-21.

2370.   _____, Harrison, R. H., & Budoff, M. *An observational study of segregated and integrated EMR children and their nonretarded peers: Can we tell the difference by looking? Studies in Learning Potential, Vol. 2, No. 27.* Cambridge, MA: Research Institute for Educational Problems, 1972. (ERIC Document Reproduction Service No. ED 062 747)

2371.   Gardner, O. S. Out of the classroom: The birth and infancy of the resource center at Hauula. *Exceptional Children,* 1971, *38,* 53-58.

2372.   Garnett, J. "Special" children in a comprehensive. *Special Education: Forward Trends,* 1976, *3,* 8-11.

2373.   Garrison, M., Jr., & Hammill, D. D. Who are the retarded? *Exceptional Children,* 1971, *38,* 13-20.

2374. _____, & Hammill, D. D. *Who are the retarded? Multiple criteria applied to children in educable classes. Final report.* Philadelphia, PA: Temple University, College of Education, 1970. (ERIC Document Reproduction Service No. ED 047 485)

2375. Gilhool, T. K. The uses of litigation: The right of retarded children to a free public education. *Peabody Journal of Education,* 1973, *50,* 120-127.

2376. Gjessing, H. J. Integration of the handicapped: What demands will be made? *Slow Learning Child,* 1972, *19*(1), 28-39.

2377. Gladstein, B. A. *Teacher and peer observations of mainstreamed elementary school pupils: A comparative group study.* Paper presented at the 5th Annual Convention of the Genesee Valley Psychological Association, Rochester, NY, 1978. (ERIC Document Reproduction Service No. ED 168 258)

2378. Goldstein, H. The efficacy of special classes and regular classes in the education of educable mentally retarded children. In J. Zubin, & G. A. Jervis (Eds.), *Psychopathology of mental development.* New York, NY: Grune & Stratton, 1967.

2379. _____, Moss, J. W., & Jordan, L. J. *The efficacy of special class training on the development of mentally retarded children.* Urbana, IL: University of Illinois, Urbana-Champaign, Institute for Research on Exceptional Children, 1964.

2380. _____, Moss, J. W., & Jordan, L. J. *A study of the effects of special class placement on educable mentally retarded children.* Urbana, IL: University of Illinois, Urbana-Champaign, Institute for Research on Exceptional Children, 1965.

2381. Goodman, H., Gottlieb, J., & Harrison, R. H. *Social acceptance of EMRs integrated into a non-graded elementary school.* Cambridge, MA: Research Institute for Educational Problems, 1971. (ERIC Document Reproduction Service No. ED 050 510). Also in *American Journal of Mental Deficiency,* 1972, *76,* 412-417.

2382. Goodman, J. F. Developmental class: Best of both worlds for the mentally retarded. *Psychology in the Schools,* 1976, *13,* 257-265.

2383. Gottlieb, J. Attitudes of Norwegian and American children toward mildly retarded children in special classes. *Journal of Special Education,* 1974, *8,* 313-319.

2384. _____, Agard, J., Kauffman, N., & Semmel, M. Retarded children mainstreamed: Practices as they affect minority group children. In R. L. Jones, & F. B. Wilderson (Eds.), *Mainstreaming and the minority child.* Reston, VA: The Council for Exceptional Children, 1976.

2385. _____, & Budoff, M. *Attitudes toward school by segregated and integrated retarded children: A study and experimental validation. Studies in Learning Potential, Vol. 2, No. 35.* Cambridge, MA: Research Institute for Educational Problems, 1972. (ERIC Document Reproduction Service No. ED 062 751)

2386. _____, Budoff, M. *Social acceptability of retarded children in nongraded schools differing in architecture. Studies in Learning Potential, Vol. 2, No. 28.* Cambridge, MA: Research Institute for Educational Problems, 1972. (ERIC Document Reproduction Service No. ED 062 748). Also in *American Journal of Mental Deficiency,* 1973, *78,* 15-19.

2387. _____, Cohen, L., & Goldstein, L. Social contact and personal adjustment as variables relating to attitudes toward EMR children. *Training School Bulletin,* 1974, *71,* 9-16.

2388. _____, & Corman, L. Public attitudes toward mentally retarded children. *American Journal of Mental Deficiency,* 1975, *80,* 72-80.

2389. _____, & Davis, J. E. Social acceptance of EMR children during overt behavioral interactions. *American Journal of Mental Deficiency,* 1973, *78,* 141-143.

2390. _____, Gampel, D. H., & Budoff, M. *Classroom behavior of retarded children before and after "reintegration" into regular classes. Studies in Learning Potential, Vol. 3, No. 49.* Cambridge, MA: Research Institute for Educational Problems, 1973. (ERIC Document Reproduction Service No. ED 085 967) Also in *Journal of Special Education,* 1975, *9,* 307-315.

2391. Greene, W. R., & Potter, R. E. Overcoming obstacles—the mentally retarded child goes to school. *Journal for Special Educators of the Mentally Retarded,* 1977, *13,* 91-98.

2392. Greenfield, E. R. Teacher acceptance and perception of behavior of educationally handicapped pupils transferred from special to regular classes. Los Angeles Unified School District (Doctoral dissertation, Brigham Young University, 1972). *Dissertation Abstracts International,* 1972, *33,* 2645A. (University Microfilms No. 72-29745)

2393. Griffith, J. R. Mainstreaming EMR students. *Illinois Teacher of Home Economics,* 1977, *21*(2), 72-74.

2394. Gross, E. A. *Survey of physical education for educable mentally retarded children in public schools throughout the United States.* Master's thesis, University of Kansas, 1973.

2395. Gruen, G. E., Ottinger, D. R., & Ollendick, T. H. Probability learning in retarded children with differing histories of success and failure in school. *American Journal of Mental Deficiency,* 1975, *79,* 417-423.

2396. Guerin, G. R. *The differential effects of association and involvement upon the attitudes of regular class students toward educable mentally retarded students.* Unpublished doctoral dissertation, University of California, Berkeley, 1972.

2397. _____, Szatlocky, K. Integration programs for the mildly retarded. *Exceptional Children,* 1974, *41,* 173-179.

2398. *Guidelines for mainstreaming. Maintaining and integrating educable mentally retarded students in regular classes.* Salem, OR: Oregon Department of Education, Special Education and Special Schools Division, 1977.

2399. Gullota, T. P. Teacher attitudes toward the moderately disturbed child. *Exceptional Children,* 1974, *41,* 49-51.

2400. Hahn, H. R. The influence of regular class and special class placement on the reaction to verbal reinforcement and success expectancy of children with low intelligence (Doctoral dissertation, University of Illinois, Urbana-Champaign, 1965). *Dissertation Abstracts,* 1965, *26,* 7155. (University Microfilms No. 66-04192)

2401. Hambleton, D., & Zeigler, S. *The study of the integration of trainable retarded students into a regular elementary school setting.* Toronto, Ontario, Canada: Metropolitan Toronto School Board, 1974.

2402. Hammons, G. W. Educating the mildly retarded: A review. *Exceptional Children,* 1972, *38,* 565-570.

2403. *Handicapped and normal children learning together. Summary of project, 1970-73.* Washington, D.C.: Brigadoon Elementary School, Federal Way School District, 1973. (ERIC Document Reproduction Service No. ED 088 262)

2404. Haring, N. G., & Krug, D. A. Evaluation of a program of systematic instructional procedures for extremely poor retarded children. *American Journal of Mental Deficiency,* 1975, *79,* 627-631.

2405. _____, & Krug, D. A. Placement in regular programs: Procedures and results. *Exceptional Children,* 1975, *41,* 413-417.

2406. Harkleroad, A. D. *The effect of a planned program of physical education upon the motor performance of educable mentally retarded eighth grade boys.* Master's thesis, University of Maryland at College Park, 1966.

2407. Harris, P. *Operation mainstream (Training teachers to teach handicapped students.) A practicum.* Fort Lauderdale, FL: Nova University, 1976. (ERIC Document Reproduction Service No. ED 125 232)

2408. Hartman, R. K., & Hartman, J. A. Two-directional resource room: Report on a pilot project. *Education and Training of the Mentally Retarded,* 1976, *11,* 296-303.

2409. Hawkins-Shepard, C. Perspectives on mainstreaming mildly handicapped at secondary level—conversation. *Education and Training of the Mentally Retarded,* 1977, *12,* 387-395.

2410. _____. Successful secondary school strategies for exceptional youth: A conversation with Ernest A. Gotts and Katherine E. Hargrove. *Education and Training of the Mentally Retarded,* 1979, *14,* 34-38.

2411. Herink, N. *Results of mainstreaming on social interaction of mentally retarded preschoolers.* Paper presented at the 58th Annual International Convention of the Council for Exceptional Children, Philadelphia, PA, April 1980. (ERIC Document Reproduction Service No. ED 187 057)

2412. Heron, T. E. Punishment: A review of the literature with implications for the teacher of mainstreamed children. *Journal of Special Education,* 1978, *12,* 243-252.

2413. Hill, A. D. The effects of social reinforcers on the task persistence of educable mentally retarded children: An implication for mainstreaming (Doctoral dissertation, The American University, 1976). *Dissertation Abstracts International,* 1976, *37,* 2784A. (University Microfilms No. 76-26213)

2414. Hoek, J. H. *Resource room for the educable mentally handicapped and the opportunity group student for school years 1972 and 1973.* Portage, MI: Portage Public Schools, 1972. (ERIC Document Reproduction Service No. ED 094 521)

2415. Hoellein, R. H., Jr. Adaptive behavior assessment of educable mentally retarded children as rated by regular classroom teachers and special education teachers (Doctoral dissertation, The Ohio State University, 1976). *Dissertation Abstracts International,* 1976, *37,* 2742A. (University Microfilms No. 76-24616)

2416. Hoeltke, G. M. Effectiveness of special class placement for educable mentally retarded children (Doctoral dissertation, The University of Nebraska Teachers College, 1966). *Dissertation Abstracts,* 1967, *27,* 3311A. (University Microfilms No. 67-3432)

2417. Holmes, D. L. Mainstreaming exceptional children. *Journal for Special Educators of the Mentally Retarded,* 1976, *13,* 17-25.

2418. Holzberg, R. The educable retarded. *Science and Children,* 1976, *13*(6), 19.

2419. Iano, R. P. Shall we disband special classes? *Journal of Special Education,* 1972, *6,* 167-177.

2420. _____, Ayers, D., Heller, H. B., McGettigan, J. F., & Walker, V. S. Sociometric status of retarded children in an integrative program. *Exceptional Children,* 1974, *40,* 267-271.

2421. Ingold, J. Where handicaps are forgotten. *American Education,* 1972, *8*(2), 25-28.

2422. Jackson, S. E., & Taylor, G. R. Flexibility in placement. In S. E. Jackson, & G. R. Taylor, *School organization for the mentally retarded.* 2d. ed. Springfield, IL: C. C. Thomas, 1973.

2423. _____, & Taylor, G. R. *School organization for the mentally retarded.* 2d. ed. Springfield, IL: C. C. Thomas, 1973.

2424. Jedrysek, E., & Soles, B. *Behavioral and management problems of mentally retarded functioning within the sensori-motor stage.* Paper presented at the 10th Annual Meeting of the Interdisciplinary International Conference, Los Angeles, CA, February 1980. (ERIC Document Reproduction Service No. ED 188 377)

2425. Johnson, F. *Mainstreaming from plan to program: From the perspective of the mainstream coordinator. Rationale for mainstreaming.* Paper presented at the 55th Annual International Convention of the Council for Exceptional Children, Atlanta, GA, April 1977. (ERIC Document Reproduction Service No. ED 139 228)

2426. Johnson, G. O. Special education for the mentally handicapped—a paradox. *Exceptional Children,* 1962, *29,* 62-69.

2427. _____. A study of the social position of mentally handicapped children in regular grades (Doctoral dissertation, The University of Illinois, Urbana-Champaign, 1950). *Dissertation Abstracts,* 1950, *10,* 65. (University Microfilms No. 00-01664). Also in *American Journal of Mental Deficiency,* 1950, *55,* 60-89.

2428. _____, & Kirk, S. A. Are mentally handicapped children segregated in the regular grades? *Exceptional Children,* 1950, *17,* 65-68, 87-88.

2429. Jones, R. L. Labels and stigma in special education. *Exceptional Children,* 1972, *38,* 553-564.

2430. Joyce, J. V. *A comparative study of the social position of retarded and gifted children in regular grades and in segrated groups.* Unpublished doctoral dissertation, Syracuse University, 1954.

2431. Joynt, R. R. A comparison of educable mentally retarded pupils with regular class pupils of the Greeley, Colorado Public Schools on decision-making behavior (Doctoral dissertation, University of Northern Colorado, 1967). *Dissertation Abstracts,* 1967, *28,* 2899A. (University Microfilms No. 68-00431)

2432.   Kaufman, M. J. Mainstreaming: Toward an explication of the construct. *Focus on Exceptional Children*, 1975, 7(3), 1-11.

2433.   _____, Semmel, M. I., & Agard, J. A. *Project PRIME: Interim report, year one 1971-1972 (Purpose and procedures).* Washington, D.C.: BEH/Division of Training Programs, 1973. (ERIC Document Reproduction Service No. ED 106 307)

2434.   Kendall, W. S. *Public Law 94-142 and the minority retarded child: An overview of issues and practices.* Paper presented at the Annual Meeting of the South Central Region of the American Association of Mental Deficiency, Hot Springs, AR, 1978. (ERIC Document Reproduction Service No. ED 169 737)

2435.   _____. *Reading achievement and self-concept of educable retarded boys in three educational settings.* Paper presented at the 55th Annual International Convention of the Council for Exceptional Children, Atlanta, GA, April 1977. (ERIC Document Reproduction Service No. ED 139 135)

2436.   Keogh, B. K., Levitt, M. L., Robson, G., & Chan, K. S. *A review of transition programs in California public schools.* Los Angeles, CA: California State University, Los Angeles and University of California, Los Angeles, School of Education, 1974. (ERIC Document Reproduction Service No. ED 102 794)

2437.   Khadim, G. R. A study of high and low impulsivity among educable mentally retarded boys of regular and special classes (Doctoral dissertation, Indiana University, 1965). *Dissertation Abstracts*, 1965, 26, 5788. (University Microfilms No. 65-14048)

2438.   Kidd, J. W. *Pro—the efficacy of special class placement for educable mental retardates.* Paper presented at the 48th Annual Convention of the Council for Exceptional Children, Chicago, IL, April 1970. (ERIC Document Reproduction Service No. ED 039 383)

2439.   Kirby, D. F. Renovate, rejuvenate, and release: A plan to abolish the special class. *Pointer*, 1973, 17(3), 170-175.

2440.   Klein, G. (Ed.). *COVERT (Children Offered Vital Educational Retraining and Therapy) project. Year I.* Tucson, AZ: Arizona Children's Home, Tucson Child Guidance Clinic, and Tucson Public Schools, 1967. (ERIC Document Reproduction Service No. ED 023 205)

2441.   Knight, O. B. The self-concept of educable mentally retarded children in special and regular classes (Doctoral dissertation, University of North Carolina at Chapel Hill, 1967). *Dissertation Abstracts*, 1967, 28, 4483A. (University Microfilms No. 68-06744)

2442. Kolstoe, O. P. Forum: Programs for the mildly retarded: A reply to the critics. *Exceptional Children*, 1972, *39*, 51-56.

2443. _____. *Implications of research findings on vocational and career education for the mentally handicapped. Occasional paper No. 33.* Columbus, OH: Ohio State University, Center for Vocational Education, 1977. (ERIC Document Reproduction Service No. ED 147 637)

2444. _____. *Mental-retardation: An educational viewpoint.* New York, NY: Holt, Rinehart & Winston, 1972.

2445. Korn, M. The integration of handicapped children with non-handicapped children in a municipal day care center. *Deficience Mentale/Mental Retardation*, 1974, *24*, 26-30.

2446. Kraft, A. Down with (most) special education classes. *Academic Therapy*, 1972, *8*, 207-216.

2447. Lapp, E. R. A study of the social adjustment of slow learning children who were assigned part-time to regular classes. *American Journal of Mental Deficiency*, 1975, *62*, 254-262.

2448. Lawrence, E. A., & Winschel, J. F. Locus of control: Implications for special education. *Exceptional Children*, 1975, *41*, 483-490.

2449. Lawson, C. W. An investigation of a mainstreaming program for elementary urban mildly retarded youth (Doctoral dissertation, Case Western Reserve University, 1978). *Dissertation Abstracts International*, 1978, *39*, 2182A. (University Microfilms No. 78-16472)

2450. Lax, B., & Carter, J. L. Social acceptance of the EMR in different educational placements. *Mental Retardation*, 1976, *14*, 10-13.

2451. Lent, J. R. The realism of level of aspiration displayed by mentally handicapped children in the regular grades and in special classes (Doctoral dissertation, Syracuse University, 1959). *Dissertation Abstracts*, 1959, *21*, 313. (University Microfilms No. 60-02603)

2452. Levy, R. D. Curriculum development procedures for mainstreaming educable mentally retarded students: A proposal. *Clearinghouse*, 1976, *49*, 325-327.

2453. Levy, W. K., Webster, R. E., & Schenck, S. J. Too retarded to be retarded. *Education and Training of the Mentally Retarded*, 1979, *14*, 56-59.

2454. Lombardi, T. P. Changing institutional structures for effective special education programs. *Education and Training of the Mentally Retarded*, 1972, *7*, 99-103.

2455. _____, & Balch, P. E. Science experiences and the mentally retarded. *Science and Children*, 1976, *13*(6), 20.

2456.   Long, K. *Johnny's such a bright boy, what a shame he's retarded.*
        Boston, MA: Houghton Mifflin, 1977.

2457.   Lott, L. A., Jr., Hudak, B. J., & Scheetz, J. A. *Strategies and techniques for mainstreaming: A resource room handbook.* Monroe,
        MI: Monroe County Intermediate School District, 1975. (ERIC
        Document Reproduction Service No. ED 117890)

2458.   Lynch, E. W., Simms, B. H., Saaz von Hippel, C., & Shuchat, J.
        *Mainstreaming preschoolers: Children with mental retardation; a
        guide for teachers, parents and others who work with mentally
        retarded preschoolers.* Belmont, MA: Contract Research Corp.,
        1978. (ERIC Document Reproduction Service No. ED 164 103)

2459.   Lynch, W. W., & Ames, C. *A comparison of teachers' cognitive
        demands on special EMR and regular elementary classes. Final
        report.* Bloomington, IN: Indiana University, Bloomington, Center for Innovation in Teaching the Handicapped, 1972. (ERIC
        Document Reproduction Service No. ED 067 809)

2460.   MacMillan, D. L. The problems of motivation in the education of
        the mentally retarded. *Exceptional Children,* 1971, *37,* 579-586.
        Also in R. L. Jones, & D. C. Macmillan (Eds.), *Special education in
        transition.* Boston, MA: Allyn & Bacon, 1974.

2461.   _____. Special education for the mildly retarded: Servant or
        savant. *Focus on Exceptional Children,* 1971, *2*(9), 1-11.

2462.   _____, Jones, R. L., & Aloia, G. F. The mentally retarded label:
        A theoretical analysis and review of research. *American Journal of
        Mental Deficiency,* 1974, *79,* 241-261.

2463.   _____, Jones, R. L., & Meyer, C. E. Mainstreaming the mildly
        retarded: Some questions, cautions and guidelines. *Mental Retardation,* 1976, *14,* 3-10.

2464.   _____, Meyers, C. E., & Yoshida, R. K. Regular class teachers'
        perceptions of transition programs for EMR students and their
        impact on students. *Psychology in the Schools,* 1978, *15,* 99-103.

2465.   Martin, E. W. Mental retardation: A changing perspective. *Education and Training of the Mentally Retarded,* 1976, *11,* 287-292.

2466.   Martin, M. A. *Social acceptance and attitudes toward school of
        mentally retarded pupils in regular classes.* Unpublished doctoral
        dissertation, University of Southern California, 1953.

2467.   Melone, R. A. Little things mean a lot: Implementing a program to
        meet the needs of the retarded. *School Counselor,* 1972, *20,* 53-56.

2468.   Mercer, J. R. *Labeling the mentally retarded.* Berkeley, CA: University of California Press, 1973.

2469. Meyerowitz, J. H. Self-derogations in young retardates and special class placement. *Child Development*, 1962, *33*, 443-451.

2470. Meyers, C. E. The school psychologist and mild retardation: Report of an ad hoc committee. *Mental Retardation*, 1973, *11*, 15-20.

2471. _____, & Lombardi, T. P. Definition of the mentally retarded: Decision time for AAMD. *Mental Retardation*, 1974, *12*, 43.

2472. _____, MacMillan, D. L., & Yoshida, R. K. *Correlates of success in transition of MR to regular class. Vol. I. (Appendix). Final report.* Los Angeles, CA: University of California, Los Angeles, and Pomona, CA: Neuropsychiatric Institute, & Pacific State Hospital, 1975. (ERIC Document Reproduction Service No. ED 116 441)

2473. _____, MacMillan, D. L., & Yoshida, R. K. *Correlates of success in transition of MR to regular class. Vol. II. (Appendix). Final report.* Los Angeles, CA: University of California, Los Angeles, and Pomona, CA: Neuropsychiatric Institute, & Pacific State Hospital, 1975. (ERIC Document Reproduction Service No. ED 116 442)

2474. _____, Sitkei, E. G., & Watts, C. A. Attitudes toward special education and the handicapped in two community groups. *American Journal of Mental Deficiency*, 1966, *71*, 78-84.

2475. Mient, L. E. *A model of vocational education providing for the mainstreaming of educable mentally retarded students.* Unpublished doctoral dissertation, University of Pittsburgh, 1978.

2476. Miller, T. L., & Sabatino, D. A. An evaluation of the teacher consultant model as an approach to mainstreaming. *Exceptional Children*, 1978, *45*, 86-91.

2477. Mirkin, P. K., & Deno, S. L. *The effects of selected variations in the components of formative evaluation to improved academic performance.* Paper presented at the 64th Annual Meeting of the American Educational Research Association, Boston, MA, April 1980. (ERIC Document Reproduction Service No. ED 186 489)

2478. Monroe, J. D., & Howe, C. E. The effects of integration and social class on the acceptance of retarded adolescents. *Education and Training of the Mentally Retarded*, 1971, *6*, 20-24.

2479. Moore, J., & Fine, M. J. Regular and special class teachers' perceptions of normal and exceptional children and their attitudes toward mainstreaming. *Psychology in the Schools*, 1978, *15*, 253-259.

2480. Muehlberger, C. E. Factors related to the acceptance of special classes within the public schools. *Mental Retardation*, 1970, *6*, 104-108.

2481. Mullen, F. A., & Itkin, W. *Achievement and adjustment of educable mentally handicapped children in special classes and in regular grades, parts I-VI.* Chicago, IL: Chicago Board of Education, 1961. (ERIC Document Reproduction Service No. ED 002 991)

2482. Myers, J. K. The efficacy of the special day school for EMR pupils. *Mental Retardation,* 1976, *14,* 3-11.

2483. National Education Association. *The educable mentally retarded student in the secondary school. What Research Says to the Teacher Series.* Washington, D.C.: Author, 1975.

2484. _____. *Mainstreaming the educable mentally retarded.* Washington, D.C.: Author, n.d.

2485. Nazzaro, J. Mental retardation in the Soviet Union. *Education and Training of the Mentally Retarded,* 1973, *8,* 166-171.

2486. Novotny, P. A. *Mainstreaming the EMR is neither a panacea nor a simple solution: A research study.* Unpublished manuscript, 1974. (ERIC Document Reproduction Service No. ED 101 522)

2487. O'Connor, K. H. *Removing roadblocks to reading: A guidebook for teaching perceptually handicapped children for regular classroom teachers of primary and upper grades.* St. Petersburg, FL: Johnny Reads, Inc., 1976.

2488. Ohrtman, W. F. One more instant solution coming up. *Journal of Special Education,* 1972, *6,* 377-381.

2489. Orfitelli, M. A. *An approach to mainstreaming the handicapped child with the nonhandicapped child.* Unpublished manuscript, 1978. (ERIC Document Reproduction Service No. ED 164 507)

2490. Panagoplos, N. A. Mainstreaming exceptional students in the typewriting program. *Business Education World,* 1977, *58*(1), 11, 31.

2491. Parkin, A. E. Mainstreaming the educable mentally retarded student. *Bureau Memorandum,* 1972, *13*(3), 3-5.

2492. Parks, A. L., & Fairchild, T. N. *Mainstreaming the mentally retarded child.* Austin, TX: Learning Concepts, 1976.

2493. Paul, J. L., Turnbull, A. P., & Cruickshank, W. M. *Mainstreaming: A practical guide.* Syracuse, NY: Syracuse University Press, 1977. (ERIC Document Reproduction Service No. ED 157 606)

2494. Payne, J. S. Mainstreaming mentally retarded students in the public schools. *Mental Retardation,* 1979, *17,* 45-46.

2495. Peck, C. A., Apolloni, T., Cooke, T. P., & Cooke, S. R. Teaching developmentally delayed toddlers and preschoolers to imitate the free-play behavior of non-retarded classmates: Trained and generalized effects. In M. J. Guralnick (Ed.), *Early intervention and the integration of handicapped and nonhandicapped children*. Baltimore, MD: University Park Press, 1978.

2496. Polloway, E. A., & Snell, M. E. Efficacy revisited. *Education and Training of the Mentally Retarded*, 1975, *10*, 276-282.

2497. Porter, R. B., & Milazzo, T. C. A comparison of mentally retarded adults who attended a special class with those who attended regular school classes. *Exceptional Children*, 1958, *24*, 410-412, 420.

2498. Post, J. O., Jr., & Petzy, V. J. A career accessibility model for special needs individuals. *Career Education Quarterly*, 1977, *2*(4), 6-14.

2499. Power, E. M. Integration: Problems and promises. *Mental Retardation*, 1975, *13*, 42.

2500. Presland, J. Who should go to E.S.N. schools? *Special Education*, 1970, *59*(1), 11-16.

2501. Prillaman, D. An analysis of placement factors in classes for the educable mentally retarded. *Exceptional Children*, 1975, *42*, 107-108.

2502. Pruess, L. A. *The status of physical education programs for mentally handicapped children in the State of Wisconsin*. Master's thesis, University of Colorado, 1972.

2503. Pumphrey, M. W., Goodman, M. B., Kidd, J. W., & Peters, E. N. Participation of retarded children in regular recreational activities at a community center. *Exceptional Children*, 1970, *36*, 453-458.

2504. Rapp, W. E. Tele-lecture inservice instruction teaching regular classroom teachers about mental retardation, utilizing tele-lecture instruction (Doctoral dissertation, University of Colorado, 1964). *Dissertation Abstracts*, 1964, *25*. (University Microfilms No. 65-04778)

2505. Rarick, G. L., Dobbins, D. A., & Broadhead, G. D. *The motor domain and its correlates in educationally handicapped children*. Englewood Cliffs, NJ: Prentice-Hall, 1976.

2506. *Recreation and physical activity for the mentally retarded*. Reston, VA: The Council for Exceptional Children, and Washington, D.C.: American Alliance for Health, Physical Education and Recreation, 1966. (ERIC Document Reproduction Service No. ED 017 088)

2507. Reese-Dukes, J. L., & Stokes, E. H. Social acceptance of elementary educable mentally retarded pupils in the regular classroom. *Education and Training of the Mentally Retarded*, 1978, *13*, 356-361.

2508. Reger, R. *The efficacy of special placement for the educable mental retardates.* Paper presented at the 48th Annual Convention of the Council for Exceptional Children, Chicago, IL, April 1970. (ERIC Document Reproduction Service No. ED 039 383)

2509. Renz, P., & Simenson, R. J. The social perception of normals toward their EMR grade-mates. *American Journal of Mental Deficiency,* 1969, *74,* 405-408.

2510. Rice, J. W., Jr. Interrelationship between teacher knowledge of and attitude toward exceptionality and behavioral interaction with educable mentally retarded and nonretarded children integrated in elementary school classrooms (Doctoral dissertation, University of Connecticut, 1975). *Dissertation Abstracts International,* 1975, *35,* 7133A. (University Microfilms No. 75-10662)

2511. Richman, V. C. Meeting the needs of the special child in the regular classroom. *Journal for Special Educators of the Mentally Retarded,* 1977, *13,* 165-168.

2512. Risler, W. P., & Mefford, J. P. Public school education for the severely mentally retarded. *Viewpoints in Teaching and Learning,* 1973, *49*(1), 13-24.

2513. Rodriguez, J., & Lombardi, T. P. Legal implications of parental prerogatives for special class placement of the MR. *Mental Retardation,* 1973, 11, 29-31.

2514. Rose, C. The placement of T.M.R. students in the regular elementary school: An analysis of teacher and student attitudes. *British Columbia Journal of Special Education,* 1978, *2,* 293-299.

2515. Roselli, C. J. Career education vs. resource room—mainstreaming and socialization for handicapped children. *Journal for Special Educators of the Mentally Retarded,* 1978, *14,* 83-85.

2516. Rosenkranz, C. Another look at mainstreaming. *Bureau Memorandum,* 1973, *14*(2), 31-34.

2517. _____. An experimental program for mainstreaming in three types of elementary schools. *Bureau Memorandum,* 1972, *13*(3), 14-16.

2518. Rucker, C. N., Howe, C. E., & Snider, B. The participation of retarded children in junior high academic and non-academic regular classes. *Exceptional Children,* 1969, *35,* 617-623.

2519. Schell, J. S. Some differences between mentally retarded children in special and in regular classes in the schools of Mercer County, Pennsylvania (Doctoral dissertation, The Pennsylvania State University, 1959). *Dissertation Abstracts,* 1959, *20,* 607. (University Microfilms No. 59-02913)

2520.   Schramm, B. J. *Case studies of two Down's Syndrome children functioning in a Montessori environment: Research project.* Dayton, OH: University of Dayton, School of Education, 1974. (ERIC Document Reproduction Service No. ED 111 120)

2521.   Schurr, K. T., & Brookover, W. B. *The effect of special class placement on the self-concept of ability of the educable mentally retarded child.* East Lansing, MI: Educational Publication Services, College of Education, Michigan State University, 1967. (ERIC Document Reproduction Service No. ED 027 658)

2522.   _____, Towne, R. C., & Joiner, L. M. Trends in self-concept of ability over 2 years of special-class placement. *Journal of Special Education,* 1972, *6,* 161-166.

2523.   Schwarz, R. H. Mental age as it relates to school achievement among educable mentally retarded adolescents. *Education and Training of the Mentally Retarded,* 1969, *4,* 53-56.

2524.   Scott, W. H. *The development and implementation of a plan for mainstreaming retarded educable students into regular classrooms in the comprehensive high school: Introductory practicum.* Fort Lauderdale, FL: Nova University, 1977. (ERIC Document Reproduction Service No. ED 157 216)

2525.   _____. *The development and implementation of a plan for mainstreaming retarded educable students into regular classrooms in the comprehensive high school: Phase II.* Fort Lauderdale, FL: Nova University, 1977. (ERIC Document Reproduction Service No. ED 168 262)

2526.   Segregation: I. The case for; segregation: II. The case against. *Australian Journal of Mental Retardation,* 1972, *2*(1).

2527.   Sellin, D. F. *Mental retardation 1984: Will the paradox end?* Paper presented at the 48th Annual Convention of the Council for Exceptional Children, Chicago, IL, April 1970. (ERIC Document Reproduction Service No. ED 039 383)

2528.   Shaw, S. F., & Gillung, T. B. Efficacy of a college course for regular class teachers of the mildly handicapped. *Mental Retardation,* 1975, *13,* 3-6.

2529.   Sheare, J. B. Social acceptance of EMR adolescents in integrated programs. *American Journal of Mental Deficiency,* 1974, *78,* 678-682.

2530.   Siegel, E. *Special education in the regular classroom.* New York, NY: John Day, 1969.

2531. Simek, R. *An investigation of the relationship between specific organizational variables and integration of emotionally disturbed and neurologically impaired students.* Paper presented at the 57th Annual International Convention of the Council for Exceptional Children, Dallas, TX, April 1979. (ERIC Document Reproduction Service No. ED 170 999)

2532. Sippel, H., Lazar, A. L., & D'Alonzo, B. J. *Changing attitudes toward TMR through an integrated recreation program.* Paper presented at the 100th Annual Meeting of the American Association on Mental Deficiency, Chicago, IL, May-June 1976. (ERIC Document Reproduction Service No. ED 123 860)

2533. Skindrud, K. In-service preparation for mainstreaming. A continuum of strategies for instructional planning (IEP) teams. *Teacher Education and Special Education,* 1978, *2*(1), 41-52.

2534. Smith, C. *Mainstreaming the handicapped in vocational education. Serving the mentally retarded.* Palo Alto, CA: American Institute for Research in the Behavioral Sciences, 1977. (ERIC Document Reproduction Service No. ED 142 767)

2535. Smith, J. E., Jr. A comparison of mainstreamed and special class educable mentally retarded pupils from two school systems in Virginia (Doctoral dissertation, University of Virginia, 1977). *Dissertation Abstracts International,* 1977 *38*, 4101A. (University Microfilms No. 77-28614)

2536. Smith, L. W. A study of retarded readers in special reading classes compared with retarded readers in regular classes (Doctoral dissertation, Oklahoma State University, 1967). *Dissertation Abstracts,* 1967, *29*, 188A. (University Microfilms No. 68-08499)

2537. Smith, M. F. Comparison of the reading and arithmetic progress of mainstreamed decertified educable mentally retarded students with slow learners within the same classrooms (Doctoral dissertation, University of Maryland, 1978). *Dissertation Abstracts International,* 1978, *39*, 3338A. (University Microfilms No. 78-24027)

2538. Smokoski, F., Blake, F., Hamlin, H., & Main, J. *The assimilation of two classes of T.M.H. children into a typical junior high school.* Paper presented at the 56th Annual International Convention of the Council for Exceptional Children, Kansas City, MO, May 1978. (ERIC Document Reproduction Service No. ED 153 425)

2539. Snapp, M. Resource classrooms or resource personnel? *Journal of Special Education,* 1972, *6*, 383-387.

2540. Sontag, E. (Ed.). *Educational programming for the severely and profoundly handicapped.* Boothwyn, PA: Council for Exceptional Children, Division on Mental Retardation, 1977.

2541. Stanton, J. E., & Cassidy, V. M. *A study of differences between children in residential school classes and special and regular classes in Ohio.* Columbus, OH: College of Education, Ohio State University, 1961.

2542. Steer, M. New chain for Fenrir: Supervising teachers of newly mainstreamed children. *Education and Training of the Mentally Retarded,* 1976, *11,* 262-268.

2543. Stein, J. U. Physical fitness in relation to intelligence quotient, social distance and physique of intermediate school mentally retarded boys (Doctoral dissertation, George Peabody College for Teachers, 1966). *Dissertation Abstracts,* 1966, *27,* 1253A. (University Microfilms No. 66-11235)

2544. _____. Physical fitness of mentally retarded boys relative to national age norms. *Rehabilitation Literature,* 1965, *26,* 205-208.

2545. Stend, D., Ragnes, S., & Lubansky, R. Normalization: Implementation in the public schools for T.M.R.s. *Journal for Special Educators of the Mentally Retarded,* 1977, *14,* 15-23.

2546. Stephens, W. E. Mainstreaming: Some natural limitations. *Mental Retardation,* 1975, *13,* 40-41.

2547. Stroud, M. B. The achievement of social studies objectives of a persisting life problems curriculum by educable mentally retarded pupils in four alternative mainstreaming settings in Ohio (Doctoral dissertation, Kent State University, 1976). *Dissertation Abstracts International,* 1977, *37,* 6411A. (University Microfilms No. 77-07839)

2548. _____. Do students sink or swim in the mainstream? *Phi Delta Kappan,* 1978, *60,* 316.

2549. Svebak, S. *Models for educational integration of retarded, normal and gifted children.* Bergen, Norway: University of Bergen, 1972.

2550. Swart, R. A secondary school resource room makes mainstreaming work. *Teaching Exceptional Children,* 1979, *11,* 77-79.

2551. Taylor, G. R. Special education at the crossroad: Class placement for the EMR. *Mental Retardation,* 1973, *11,* 30-33.

2552. _____, & Jackson, S. E. *Educational strategies and services for exceptional children.* Springfield, IL: C. C. Thomas, 1976.

2553. Thompson, M. National survey of community recreation services to the mentally retarded and physically handicapped. *Recreation,* 1965, *58,* 191-192.

2554. Thurstone, T. G. (Ed.). *An evaluation of educating mentally handicapped children in special classes and in regular classes.* Chapel Hill, NC: University of North Carolina Press, 1959. (ERIC Document Reproduction Service No. ED 002 798)

2555.   Tonn, M. The case for keeping mentally retarded children in your regular classrooms. *American School Board Journal*, 1974, *161*(8), 45.

2556.   Towne, R. C., & Joiner, L. M. *The effect of special class placement on the self-concept of ability of the educable mentally handicapped child*. East Lansing, MI: College of Education, Michigan State University, 1966. (ERIC Document Reproduction Service No. ED 024 160)

2557.   Trippi, J. A. Special-class placement and suggestibility of mentally retarded children. *American Journal of Mental Deficiency*, 1973, *78*, 220-222.

2558.   Urban, S. J. A study of the relationship of certain personality and situational variables to job satisfaction in regular elementary teachers and elementary level teachers of the educable mentally retarded in second class school districts in Michigan (Doctoral dissertation, Michigan State University, 1972). *Dissertation Abstracts International*, 1972, *33*, 2794A. (University Microfilms No. 72-30057)

2559.   Van Osdol, B. M. The sociometric status of educable mentally retarded students in regular school classes (Doctoral dissertation, University of Idaho, 1971). *Dissertation Abstracts International*, 1971, *32*, 3129A. (University Microfilms No. 72-02119)

2560.   _____, & Johnson, D. M. The sociometric status of educable mentally retarded students in regular school classes. *Australian Journal of Mental Retardation*, 1973, *2*, 200-203.

2561.   Walker, V. S. The efficacy of the resource room for educating retarded children. *Exceptional Children*, 1974, *40*, 288-289.

2562.   Warner, F., Thrapp, R., & Walsh, S. Attitudes of children toward their special class placement. *Exceptional Children*, 1973, *40*, 37-38.

2563.   Warren, S. A. Can education students' attitudes toward the retarded be changed? *Mental Retardation*, 1964, *2*, 235-242.

2564.   Watson, M. *Mainstreaming: The educable mentally retarded*. Washington, D.C.: National Education Association, 1975. (ERIC Document Reproduction Service No. ED 111 117)

2565.   Weber, M. B. *Attitudes of public school teachers toward mainstreaming the mentally retarded*. Preliminary draft. Paper presented at the Fall meeting of the Georgia Association of School Psychologists/Council for Exceptional Children, Atlanta, GA, October 1977. (ERIC Document Reproduction Service No. ED 150 817)

2566.   Weintraub, F. J. *Recent influences of law on the identification and placement of children in programs for the mentally retarded.* Paper presented at the Convention of Placement of Children in Special Education Programs for the Mentally Retarded, Lake Arrowhead, CA, March 1971. (ERIC Document Reproduction Service No. ED 048 685)

2567.   Where the bell rings for everyone. *Deficience Mentale/Mental Retardation,* 1975, *25*(1), 8-12.

2568.   Wilson, C. Intentionality judgement and adaptive behavior in mildly retarded children. *Slow Learning Child,* 1975, *22*(1), 5-12.

2569.   Wilson, M. L. T. *A comparative study of the speech responses and social ages of two selected groups of educable mental retardates.* Grambling, LA: Grambling College, 1960. (ERIC Document Reproduction Service No. ED 002 893)

2570.   Wilson, R. J. Characteristics of former special class (EMR) children who have been integrated into the regular classroom (Doctoral dissertation, University of Northern Colorado, 1973). *Dissertation Abstracts International,* 1973, *34*, 7080A. (University Microfilms No. 74-09770)

2571.   Winkelstein, E., Shapiro, B. J., Tucker, D. G., & Shapiro, P. P. Early childhood educational objectives for normal and retarded children. *Mental Retardation,* 1974, *12*, 41-45.

2572.   Winn, R. J., Jr. The survival of educable mentally retarded children in the regular classroom in science and social studies as related to academic deviation from normal children (Doctoral dissertation, The University of Texas at Austin, 1975). *Dissertation Abstracts International,* 1975, *37*, 230A. (University Microfilms No. 76-14535)

2573.   Winschel, J. F. Mainstreaming: No. *Exceptional Parent,* 1976, *6*(1), 8-10.

2574.   Wolfensberger, W. The future of residential services for the mentally retarded. *Journal of Clinical Child Psychology,* 1973, *2*, 19-20.

2575.   Wondergem, R. *A study of physical education participation and physical fitness development in trainable and educable mentally retarded children.* Master's thesis, Wisconsin State University, La Crosse, 1972.

2576.   Wyne, M. D. *Intervening with developmentally disabled children in a regular school setting.* Paper presented at the Annual Meeting of the American Educational Research Association, Toronto, Ontario, Canada, March 1978. (ERIC Document Reproduction Service No. ED 154 553)

2577. Yuill, R. D., & Bennett, M. Life skills orientation for EMR students. *School Shop,* 1978, *38*(3), 35, 37.

2578. Zawadzki, R. F. A study of what regular classroom teachers consider deterrents to teaching the educable mentally retarded child in regular classes (Doctoral dissertation, University of Pittsburgh, 1973). *Dissertation Abstracts International,* 1973, *35*, 292A. (University Microfilms No. 74-15613)

2579. Ziegler, S., & Hambleton, D. Integration of young TMR children into a regular elementary school. *Exceptional Children,* 1976, *42*, 459-461.

2580. _____, & Hambleton, D. *A study of the integration of trainable retarded students into a regular elementary school setting.* Toronto, Ontario, Canada: Research Department, Metropolitan Toronto School Board, 1974.

2581. Zito, R. J., & Bardon, J. I. Achievement motivation among negro adolescents in regular and special education programs. *American Journal of Mental Deficiency,* 1969, *74*, 20-26.

2582. Zneimer, L. Mainstreaming: A fad or a reality? *Journal for Special Educators of the Mentally Retarded,* 1976, *12*, 95-101.

2583. Zuckerman, D. G. The relationship of school factors to employment of intellectually similar persons formerly enrolled in educable mentally retarded and regular high school programs (Doctoral dissertation, University of California, 1973). *Dissertation Abstracts International,* 1973, *34*, 4901A. (University Microfilms No. 73-31400)

VI. PHYSICALLY HANDICAPPED

2584. Agron, G. A., & Donnelly, J. H. Cincinnati plans for special ed. *American School and University,* 1978, *51*(2), 50-52, 54.

2585. Ashcroft, S. C. The handicapped in the regular classroom. *Today's Education,* 1967, *56*(8), 33-48.

2586. Baldwin, C. P., & Baldwin, A. L. *Personality and social development of handicapped children.* Ithaca, NY: Cornell University, 1972. (ERIC Document Reproduction Service No. ED 079 895)

2587. Barkin, G. D., & McGovern, J. P. What the classroom teacher can do for . . . the asthmatic child. *Today's Education,* 1967, *56*(8), 40-41.

2588. Best, G. A. Mainstreaming characteristics of orthopedically handicapped students in California. *Rehabilitation Literature,* 1977, *38*, 205-209.

2589.	Billings, H. K. An exploratory study of the attitudes of non-crippled children toward crippled children in three selected elementary schools. *Journal of Experimental Education,* 1963, *31,* 381-387.

2590.	Blumberg, L. The case for integrated schooling. *Exceptional Parent,* 1973, *3*(4), 15-17 and 1981, *11*(4), 23-26.

2591.	Bothwell, H. Special feature on the physically handicapped: The aurally handicapped child. *Today's Education,* 1967, *56*(8), 33-48.

2592.	_____. What the classroom teacher can do for . . . the child with impaired hearing. *Today's Education,* 1967, *56*(8), 44-46.

2593.	Buchman, R., & Mullins, J. B. Integration of a spina bifida child in a kindergarten for normal children. *Young Children,* 1968, *23,* 339-344.

2594.	Calovini, G. *The principal looks at classes for the physically handicapped.* Reston, VA: The Council for Exceptional Children, 1969. (ERIC Document Reproduction Service No. ED 044 860)

2595.	Combs, R. H., & Harper, J. L. Effects of labels on attitudes of educators toward handicapped children. *Exceptional Children,* 1967, *33,* 399-403.

2596.	Condon, K., & Dahlstrom, M. *Development and implementation of an effective early childhood handicapped program.* Paper presented at the 58th Annual International Convention of the Council for Exceptional Children, Philadelphia, PA, April 1980. (ERIC Document Reproduction Service No. ED 187 079)

2597.	Conine, T., & Brennan, W. T. Orthopedically handicapped children in regular classrooms. *Journal of School Health,* 1969, *39,* 59-63.

2598.	Connor, F. P. What the classroom teacher can do for . . . crippled and health-impaired children. *Today's Education,* 1967, *56*(8), 37-39.

2599.	Cormack, E. O. *Considerations for integration of physically handicapped and non-handicapped preschool children.* Paper presented at the 57th Annual International Convention of the Council for Exceptional Children, Dallas, TX, April 1979. (ERIC Document Reproduction Service No. ED 171 024)

2600.	De Julio, E. L. Many happy returns. *Today's Education,* 1980, *69*(1), 72-73.

2601.	Dibner, S., & Dibner, A. *Integration or segregation for the physically handicapped child?* Springfield, IL: C. C. Thomas, 1973.

2602. Donaldson, J., & Martinson, M. C. Modifying attitudes toward physically disabled persons. *Exceptional Children,* 1977, *43,* 337-341.

2603. Duke, K. *Realistic approaches to writing individual education programs for homebound/hospitalized.* Paper presented at the 58th Annual International Convention of the Council for Exceptional Children, Philadelphia, PA, April 1980. (ERIC Document Reproduction Service No. ED 187 054)

2604. Edgington, D. *The physically handicapped child in your classroom: A handbook for teachers.* Springfield, IL: C. C. Thomas, 1976.

2605. Federlein, A. C. *A study of play behaviors and interactions of preschool children in mainstreamed and segregated settings.* Paper presented at the 57th Annual International Convention of the Council for Exceptional Children, Dallas, TX, April 1979. (ERIC Document Reproduction Service No. ED 171 048)

2606. _____. *A year long study of the frequency of play interactions of handicapped preschoolers in mainstreamed and segregated classrooms.* Paper presented at the 58th Annual International Convention of the Council for Exceptional Children, Philadelphia, PA, April 1980. (ERIC Document Reproduction Service No. ED 188 426)

2607. Fox, J. Personal perspectives on educating handicapped children. *Journal of Teacher Education,* 1978, *29*(6), 15-17.

2608. Friedman, R. S. *The peer-peer program: A model project for the integration of severely physically handicapped youngsters with non-disabled peers.* Albertson, NY: Human Resources School, 1975. (ERIC Document Reproduction Service No. ED 142 004)

2609. Goodman, G., & Yasumura, K. *Physically handicapped children in the mainstream: A transdisciplinary application of physical management techniques.* Paper presented at the 58th Annual International Convention of the Council for Exceptional Children, Philadelphia, PA, April 1980. (ERIC Document Reproduction Service No. ED 187 069)

2610. Graham, N. Making it in the mainstream. *Pointer,* 1978, *23*(1), 10-14.

2611. Grandstaff, C. L. *Creative approaches to compliance with P.L. 94-142 for H/H programs: Under the law, who is to be served and by whom.* Paper presented at the 58th Annual International Convention of the Council for Exceptional Children, Philadelphia, PA, April 1980. (ERIC Document Reproduction Service No. ED 187 053)

2612. Gromek, I., & Scandary, J. Considerations in the educational placement of the physically or otherwise health impaired child. *DOPHHH Journal*, 1976, *3*(1), 8-11.

2613. Grosse, S. J. *Mainstreaming the physically handicapped student for team sports.* Washington, D.C.: American Alliance for Health, Physical Education and Recreation, 1978. (ERIC Document Reproduction Service No. ED 165 350)

2614. *Guidance services for the physically disabled two-year college student. A counselor's manual.* Albany, NY: State University of New York, Coordinating Area No. 4, 1978. (ERIC Document Reproduction Service No. ED 161 490)

2615. Hanna, R. L. *Physically handicapped child: Facilitating regular classroom adjustment.* Austin, TX: Learning Concepts, 1977.

2616. Haskell, S. H., & Anderson, E. M. Physically handicapped children: Special or normal schooling? *Slow Learning Child,* 1969, *16*(3), 150-161.

2617. Healy, A., McAreavey, P., Saaz von Hippel, C., & Jones, S. H. *Mainstreaming preschoolers: Children with health impairments. A guide for teachers, parents, and others who work with health impaired preschoolers.* Belmont, MA: Contract Research Corp., 1978. (ERIC Document Reproduction Service No. ED 164 104)

2618. Hendrickson, B. Teachers make mainstreaming work. *Learning,* 1978, *7*(2), 104-110.

2619. Hennon, M. L. *Identifying handicapped children for child development programs.* Atlanta, GA: Humanics Press, 1973.

2620. Higgs, R. W. Attitude formation—contact or information? *Exceptional Children,* 1975, *41*, 496-497.

2621. Hoggan, I. M. David mainstreams himself. *Teacher,* 1978, *96*(4), 49-50.

2622. _____. Mainstreaming: A sequel to David's story. *Teacher,* 1979, *96*(5), 75.

2623. Ingold, J. Where handicaps are forgotten; vocational-technical schools. *American Education,* 1972, *8*(2), 25-28.

2624. Jackson, R. The education of the physically handicapped child. *Aspects of Education,* 1975, *20*, 92-98.

2625. James, H. *The physically handicapped child: Facilitating regular classroom adjustment.* Austin, TX: Learning Concepts, 1977.

2626. Jones, R. L. Correlates of orthopedically disabled children's school achievement and interpersonal relationships. *Exceptional Children,* 1974, *41*, 191-192.

2627.   Kieran, S. S., Connor, F. P., Saaz von Hippel, C., & Jones, S. H. *Mainstreaming preschoolers: Children with orthopedic handicaps. A guide for teachers, parents, and others who work with orthopedically handicapped preschoolers.* Belmont, MA: Contract Research Corp., 1978. (ERIC Document Reproduction Service No. ED 164 107)

2628.   Kim is handicapped, but . . . *Today's Education,* 1980, 69(1), 76.

2629.   Kloepping, K. B. The prediction of academic achievement of physically disabled students (Doctoral dissertation, The University of Arizona, 1972). *Dissertation Abstracts International,* 1972, *33,* 2735A. (University Microfilms No. 72-31837)

2630.   Lauder, C. E., Kanthor, H., Myers, G., & Resnick, J. Educational placement of children with spina bifida. *Exceptional Children,* 1979, *45,* 432-437.

2631.   Lord, F. E. Education of the physically handicapped: Review and implications. *PRISE Reporter,* May 1974, pp. 1-2.

2632.   Mayer, C. A. *Understanding young children: The handicapped child in the normal preschool class.* Anchorage, AK: Treatment Center for Crippled Children and Adults, 1974. (ERIC Document Reproduction Service No. ED 092 257)

2633.   Mitchack, J. A. Empathic understanding related to manifest disability and cognitive style (Doctoral dissertation, University of Illinois, Urbana-Champaign, 1972). *Dissertation Abstracts International,* 1973, *33,* 5497A. (University Microfilms No. 73-10004)

2634.   Mullins, J. B. Integrated classrooms. *Journal of Rehabilitation,* 1971, *37*(2), 14-16.

2635.   Nebelung, R. G. *The value of segregated classes versus regular classroom instruction for post rheumatic fever children in the San Francisco Public Schools.* Unpublished doctoral dissertation, University of Oregon, 1953.

2636.   Nelson, D. H. Mainstreaming a child with spina bifida. *Instructor,* 1979, *88*(8), 134-136.

2637.   Newman, J. Faculty attitudes toward handicapped students. *Rehabilitation Literature,* 1976, *37,* 194-197.

2638.   Owen, B. H. Mainstreaming at Dae Valley Camp. *Journal of Physical Education and Recreation,* 1978, *49*(5), 28-30.

2639.   Pell, D. M. Teacher acceptance and perception of behavior of physically handicapped pupils transferred from special to regular classes (Doctoral dissertation, Brigham Young University, 1973). *Dissertation Abstracts International,* 1973, *33,* 4209A. (University Microfilms No. 73-02865)

2640. Podietz, L. Activity group therapy for adolescents with orthopedic handicaps. *Annual Proceedings of the American Psychological Association,* 1971, *6*(pt.2), 639-640.

2641. Puhek, L. Hooray we passed! *Exceptional Parent,* 1972, *1*(5), 9-10.

2642. Rapier, J., Adelson, R., Carey, R., & Croke, K. Changes in children's attitudes toward the physically handicapped. *Exceptional Children,* 1972, *39,* 219-223.

2643. Ratchick, I., & Koenig, F. G. *Guidance and the physically handicapped child.* Chicago, IL: Science Research Assoc. 1963.

2644. Redlick, S. S. *The physically handicapped student in the regular home economics classroom: A guide for teaching grooming and clothing.* Danville, IL: Interstate Printers & Pub., 1976.

2645. _____. *The physically handicapped student in the regular home economics classroom: A guide for teaching housing and home care.* Danville, IL: Interstate Printers & Pub., 1976.

2646. _____. *Physically handicapped student in the regular home economics classroom: A guide for teaching nutrition and foods.* Danville, IL: Interstate Printers & Pub., 1976.

2647. Robb, G. M. Camping for the physically handicapped: A rationale and approach. *Rehabilitation Literature,* 1973, *34,* 130-133.

2648. Robison, R. For the handicapped: Renovation report card. *American School and University,* 1980, *52*(8), 28-30.

2649. Schliefer, M. J. Mainstreaming: Entering junior high. "He's had a difficult fall, and now he wants to go back to his old school." *Exceptional Parent,* 1979, *9*(1), A20, A22, A24-A26.

2650. Schoen, L. R. A study of practices and problems in the integration of physically handicapped children in regular school programs (Doctoral dissertation, University of Southern California, 1965). *Dissertation Abstracts,* 1965, *26,* 2083A. (University Microfilms No. 65-11245)

2651. Smith, D. B., & Larson, P. A. Adolescent attitudes toward disabled persons in an integrated and nonintegrated school setting. *Education,* 1980, *100,* 390-394.

2652. Smoot, S. L. *Physical education for kids who can't move.* Paper presented at the 57th Annual International Convention of the Council for Exceptional Children, Dallas, TX, April 1979. (ERIC Document Reproduction Service No. ED 171 084)

2653. Swisher, J. D. Developmental restaging: Meeting the mental health needs of handicapped students in the schools. *Journal of School Health,* 1978, *48*(9), 548-550.

2654. Thompson, M. National survey of community recreation services to the mentally retarded and physically handicapped. *Recreation,* 1965, *58,* 191-192.

2655. Wechsler, H., Suarez, A. C., & McFaden, M. Teachers' attitudes toward the education of physically handicapped children: Implications for the implementation of Massachusetts Chapter 766. *Journal of Education,* 1975, *157*(1), 17-24.

2656. Weisgerber, R. *Mainstreaming the handicapped in vocational education. Serving the orthopedically handicapped.* Palo Alto, CA: American Institutes for Research in the Behavioral Sciences, 1977. (ERIC Document Reproduction Service No. ED 142 748)

2657. Weishahn, M. W., & Mitchell, R. Educational placement practices with visually disabled and orthopedically disabled children—a comparison. *Rehabilitation Literature,* 1971, *32,* 263-266, 288.

2658. Welsh, E. Preparing a school for the multiple handicapped. *Instructor,* 1973, *83*(3), 90-92.

2659. Wyne, M. D. *Intervening with developmentally disabled children in a regular school setting.* Paper presented at the Annual Meeting of the American Educational Research Association, Toronto, Ontario, Canada, March 1978. (ERIC Document Reproduction Service No. ED 154 553)

VII. SPEECH HANDICAPPED

2660. Ainsworth, S. The speech clinician in public schools: Participant or separatist? *Journal of Speech and Hearing Research,* 1965, *7,* 495-503.

2661. Battle, D. E. *Mainstreaming from plan to program: The speech and language component of a mainstream program.* Paper presented at the 55th Annual International Convention of the Council for Exceptional Children, Atlanta, GA, April 1977. (ERIC Document Reproduction Service No. ED 139 229)

2662. Blanchard, M., & Nober, E. H. *Mainstreaming and its effects on the delivery of services to the handicapped: The speech, language and hearing special educator.* Paper presented at the 54th Annual International Convention of the Council for Exceptional Children, Chicago, IL, April 1976. (ERIC Document Reproduction Service No. ED 126 636)

2663. Condon, K., & Dahlstrom, M. *Development and implementation of an effective early childhood handicapped program.* Paper presented at the 58th Annual International Convention of the Council for Exceptional Children, Philadelphia, PA, April 1980. (ERIC Document Reproduction Service No. ED 187 079)

2664. Freeman, G. G. Solve speech-language problems with a team effort. *Teacher,* 1978, *95*(9), 52, 54.

2665. _____. *Speech and language services and the classroom teacher.* Minneapolis, MN: University of Minnesota, National Support Systems Project, 1977. (ERIC Document Reproduction Service No. ED 152 040)

2666. Fudala, J. B. Applied awareness: Speech improvement in an elementary classroom. *Teaching Exceptional Children,* 1973, *5,* 190-194.

2667. Green, R. A. *Development and implementation of procedures to maximize instructional time in an itinerant special education setting.* Ft. Lauderdale, FL: Nova University, 1978. (ERIC Document Reproduction Service No. ED 166 878)

2668. Liebergott, J., Favors, Jr., A., Saaz von Hippel, C., & Needleman, H. L. *Mainstreaming preschoolers: Children with speech and language impairments. A guide for teachers, parents, and others who work with speech and language impaired preschoolers.* Belmont, MA: Contract Research Corp., 1978. (ERIC Document Reproduction Service No. ED 164 106)

2669. McCartan, K. W. *The communicative disordered child.* Austin, TX: Learning Concepts, 1977.

2670. Maloney, P., & Weisgerber, R. *Mainstreaming the handicapped in vocational education. Serving the communication impaired.* Palo Alto, CA: American Institutes for Research in the Behavioral Sciences, 1977. (ERIC Document Reproduction Service No. ED 142 749)

2671. Mayer, C. A. *Understanding young children: Language development and language disabilities.* Anchorage, AK: Alaska Treatment Center for Crippled Children and Adults, 1974. (ERIC Document Reproduction Service No. ED 092 260)

2672. Miller, M. D. *Research design and results: Demonstration center for language-handicapped children.* Houston, TX: Education Service Center, Region 4, n.d. (ERIC Document Reproduction Service No. ED 096 792)

2673. Moody, J. B., & Bozeman, R. *Integration and mainstreaming of communicatively disordered children.* Paper presented at the 57th Annual International Convention of the Council for Exceptional Children, Dallas, TX, April 1979. (ERIC Document Reproduction Service No. ED 171 043)

2674. Perrin, E. The social position of the speech defective child. *Journal of Speech and Hearing Disorders,* 1954, *19,* 250-252.

2675. Scofield, S. J. The language-delayed child in the mainstreamed primary classroom. *Language Arts,* 1978, *55,* 719-723.

2676. Zedler, E. Y. Educating programming for pupils with neurologically based language disorders. *Journal of Learning Disabilities,* 1970, *3,* 618-628.

VIII. VISUALLY HANDICAPPED

2677. Akkerman, C., & Clark, J. F. Field experience: Working with the visually handicapped. *Education of the Visually Handicapped.* 1978, *10*(3), 91-94.

2678. Alonso, L. What the classroom teacher can do for . . . the child with impaired vision. *Today's Education,* 1967, *56*(8), 42-43.

2679. _____, Moor, P. M., Raynor, S., Saaz von Hippel, C., & Baer, S. *Mainstreaming preschoolers: Children with visual handicaps. A guide for teachers, parents, and others who work with visually handicapped preschoolers.* Belmont, MA: Contract Research Corp., 1978. (ERIC Document Reproduction Service No. ED 164 105)

2680. Barrage, N. C. *Visual handicaps and learning: A developmental approach.* Belmont, CA: Wadworth Pub., 1976.

2681. Bateman, B. Sighted children's perceptions of blind children's abilities. *Exceptional Children,* 1962, *29,* 42-46.

2682. _____, & Wetherell, J. L. Some educational characteristics of partially seeing children. *International Journal for the Education of the Blind,* 1967, *17*(2), 33-40.

2683. Boninger, W. B. (Ed.). *Proceedings of the special demonstration workshop for integrating blind children with sighted children into on-going physical education and recreation programs, Cleveland, OH, October 1969:* Cleveland Society for the Blind, 1970. (ERIC Document Reproduction Service No. ED 046 147)

2684. Buell, C. How to include blind and partially seeing children in public secondary school vigorous physical education. *The Physical Educator,* 1972, *29*(1), 6-8.

2685. Calovini, G. (Ed.). *Mainstreaming the visually impaired child.* Springfield, IL: BEH Instructional Materials Center, Office of the Superintendent of Public Instruction, State of Illinois, 1977. (ERIC Document Reproduction Service No. ED 140 540)

2686. Computerized Braille helps mainstream the blind. *American School and University,* 1978, *50*(10), 26.

2687. Corn, A. L., & Martinez, I. *When you have a visually handicapped child in your classroom: Suggestions for teachers.* New York, NY: American Foundation for the Blind, 1977.

2688. Crawford, G. B., Dvorak, C. C., Mastre, L. L., & Ulvin, J. L. *Clothing construction: An instructional package with adaptations for visually impaired individuals.* Grand Forks, ND: University of North Dakota, Dept. of Home Economics and Nutrition and School for the Blind, 1976. (ERIC Document Reproduction Service No. ED 159 393).

2689. _____, Dvorak, C. C., Mastre, L. L., & Ulvin, J. L. *Food preparation: An instructional package with adaptations for visually impaired individuals.* Grand Forks, ND: North Dakota School for the Blind and the University of North Dakota, 1976. (ERIC Document Reproduction Service No. ED 156 924)

2690. Dean, M. *Teacher-pupil package. Visually handicapped handbook.* Lansing, MI: Michigan State Department of Education, 1972. (ERIC Document Reproduction Service No. ED 089 512)

2691. De Lucchi, L., Malone, L., & Thier, H. D. Science activities for the visually impaired: Developing a model. *Exceptional Children,* 1980, *46,* 287-288.

2692. Dillman, C. M., & Maloney, P. *Mainstreaming the handicapped in vocational education; serving the visually handicapped.* Palo Alto, CA: American Institutes for Research in the Behavioral Sciences, 1977. (ERIC Document Reproduction Service No. ED 142 766)

2693. Eaglestein, A. S. The social acceptance of blind high school students in an integrated school. *New Outlook for the Blind,* 1975, *69,* 447-451.

2694. Freund, C. Teaching art to the blind child integrated with sighted children. *New Outlook for the Blind,* 1969, *63,* 205-210.

2695. Gottlieb, D., & Shorkey, C. A. *Jo-Ann—working together to help her see.* Paper presented at the 55th Annual International Convention of the Council for Exceptional Children, Atlanta, GA, April 1977. (ERIC Document Reproduction Service No. ED 139 231)

2696. Gray, D. L. *Pre-reading and beginning reading materials for the blind child in the regular school.* Unpublished doctoral dissertation, Columbia University, 1958.

2697. Green, R. A. *Development and implementation of procedures to maximize instructional time in an itinerant special education setting.* Ft. Lauderdale, FL: Nova University, 1978. (ERIC Document Reproduction Service No. ED 166 878)

2698. Hadary, D. C., & Cohen, S. H. *Laboratory science and art for blind, deaf, and emotionally disturbed children: A mainstreaming approach.* Baltimore, MD: University Park Press, 1978.

2699. Hanninen, K. A. *Teaching the visually handicapped.* Columbus, OH: C. E. Merrill, 1975.

2700. Hapeman, L. Reservations about the effect of P.L. 94-142 on the education of visually handicapped children. *Education of the Visually Handicapped,* 1977, 9(2), 33-36.

2701. Hulsey, S. Liberating the blind student. *American Education,* 1973, 9(6), 18-22.

2702. Johnson, I. *A blind child becomes a member of your class.* New York: American Foundation for the Blind, n.d.

2703. Jones, R. L., Lavine, K., & Shell, J. Blind children integrated in classrooms with sighted children: A sociometric study. *New Outlook for the Blind,* 1972, 66, 75-80.

2704. Levine, H. G. *A proposed program of personal adjustment for visually handicapped pupils.* Cincinnati, OH: Cincinnati Public Schools, Divison of Special Education, 1969. (ERIC Document Reproduction Service No. ED 048 715)

2705. Lombana, J. H. Career planning with visually handicapped students. *Vocational Guidance Quarterly,* 1980, *28,* 219-224.

2706. Lowenfeld, B. *The changing status of the blind: From separation to integration.* Springfield, IL: C. C. Thomas, 1975.

2707. _____. (Ed.). *The visually handicapped child in school.* New York, N.Y.: John Day, 1973.

2708. *Mainstreaming preschoolers: Children with visual handicaps.* Belmont, MA: Contract Research Corp., 1977. (ERIC Document Reproduction Service No. ED 148 083)

2709. Mangold, S. The importance of precision teaching in the education of visually impaired students being mainstreamed into public schools: Part I. *Education of the Visually Handicapped,* 1978, *10*(1), 1-9.

2710. _____. The importance of precision teaching in the education of visually impaired students being mainstreamed into public schools: Part II. *Education of the Visually Handicapped,* 1978, *10*(2), 50-56.

2711. *A manual for the classroom teacher of a blind student. Catholic Charities.* Chicago, IL: Vision-Hearing Services, 1969.

2712. Martin, G. J., & Hoben, M. *Supporting visually impaired students in the mainstream: The state of the art.* Reston, VA: Council for Exceptional Children, 1977.

2713. Masoodi, B., & Ban, J. R. Teaching the visually handicapped in regular classes. *Educational Leadership,* 1980, *37,* 351-355.

2714. Mayer, C. A. *Understanding young children: The handicapped child in the normal preschool class.* Anchorage, AK: Treatment Center for Crippled Children and Adults, Inc., 1974. (ERIC Document Reproduction Service No. ED 092 257)

2715. Meyer, H. J. Joint agreement program in Illinois: Another effort to meet the needs of visually handicapped children. *International Journal for the Education of the Blind,* 1966, *15*(3), 83-85.

2716. Miller, O. O. Programs for the handicapped: Blind bowling. *Journal of Health, Physical Education and Recreation,* 1971, *42*(4), 59-61.

2717. Miller, P. W. Industrial arts—an education for the visually impaired. *Man/Society/Technology,* 1978, *38*(1), 8-11.

2718. Milnes, Jane. *Integrating the visually impaired student into the classroom.* Fairfax, VA: Special Education Division, Fairfax County Public Schools, 1976.

2719. Moor, P. M. *A blind child, too, can go to nursery school.* New York, American Foundation for the Blind, 1962.

2720. Morris, Q. F. Reading performance of normally sighted and partially sighted third-grade and fourth-grade students using regular print and large print (Doctoral dissertation, University of Minnesota, 1973). *Dissertation Abstracts International,* 1973, *34,* 7076A. (University Microfilms No. 74-10552)

2721. National Society for the Prevention of Blindness. *Helping the partially seeing child in the regular classroom.* New York: Author, 1965.

2722. New York City Board of Education. *Educating visually handicapped pupils.* New York: Author, 1967. (ERIC Document Reproduction Service No. ED 017 106)

2723. Niederer, M., & Reguly, B. A program to enable visually impaired students in Illinois to realize their full potential. *Illinois Libraries,* 1977, *59.* 495-497.

2724. O'Brien, R. The integrated resource room for visually impaired children. *New Outlook for the Blind,* 1973, *67,* 363-368.

2725. Olson, M. R. Orienting the blind student. *Learning,* 1978, 7(2), 110-111.

2726.   Orlansky, M. D. *Mainstreaming the visually impaired child: Blind and partially sighted students in the regular classroom.* Austin, TX: Learning Concepts, 1977.

2727.   Pelone, A. J. *Handbook for use by school personnel in New York state to help the visually handicapped child adjust in regular classes.* Unpublished doctoral dissertation, Columbia University, 1956.

2728.   _____. *Helping the visually handicapped child in a regular classroom.* New York: Teachers College Press, Columbia University, 1957.

2729.   Perlman, M., & Dubrovin, V. Kevin's a typical child . . . and blind. *Instructor,* 1979, *88*(7), 175-177.

2730.   Pfeiffer, E. *Study of Joe—a blind child in a sighted group.* New York, Bank Street College of Education, 1958.

2731.   Porter, E. Mainstreaming: Visually handicapped students. *Journal of Home Economics,* 1978, 70(2), 34-38.

2732.   Porter, J., & Holzberg, B. The changing role of the school psychologist in the age of P.L. 94-142: From conducting testing to enhancing instruction. *Education of the Visually Handicapped,* 1978, 10(3), 71-74.

2733.   Rogow, S. Mainstreaming: Can it work for blind children. *Education Canada,* 1978, *18*(2), 18-21, 48.

2734.   Salt, J. P. The integration of visually handicapped children into normal schools. *Education for Teaching,* 1972, *89,* 57-60.

2735.   Schatz, D. Hands-on science for the blind. *Science and Children,* 1976, *13*(6), 21-22.

2736.   Schindele, Rudolf. The social adjustment of visually handicapped children in different educational settings. *Research Bulletin,* 1974, *28,* 125-144.

2737.   Scholl, G. T. *The principal works with the visually impaired.* Reston, VA: Council for Exceptional Children, 1968.

2738.   _____. Visually handicapped children in the regular classroom. *Teacher,* 1978, *95*(6), 79-80.

2739.   Scott, E. Visually impaired students in public schools. *British Columbia Journal of Special Education.* 1978, *2,* 245-251.

2740.   Shumway, H. S. The highway of the future. *Rehabilitation Teacher,* 1974, *6*(11), 3-8.

2741.   Simon, E. P., & Gillman, A. E. Mainstreaming visually handicapped preschoolers. *Exceptional Children,* 1979, *45,* 463-464.

2742.   Skinner, D. E. The partially sighted child in the regular classroom. *Special Education in Canada*, 1970, *44*(3), 26-28.

2743.   Stephens, T. M., & Birch, J. W. Merits of special class, resource, and itinerant plans of teaching partially seeing children. *Exceptional Children*, 1969, *35*, 481-485.

2744.   Stratton, J. *The blind child in the regular kindergarten.* Springfield, IL: C. C. Thomas, 1977.

2745.   Sullivan, M. G. *Understanding children who are partially seeing: A classroom teacher's guide.* Seattle, WA: Special Child Pub., Bernei Straub, 1974.

2746.   Tait, P. E. Believing without seeing: Teaching the blind child in a "regular" kindergarden. *Childhood Education*, 1974, *50*, 285-291.

2747.   Thier, M. Utilizing science experiences for developing visual perception skills. *Science and Children*, 1976, *13*(6), 39-40.

2748.   Thurman, D. Mainstreaming the visually impaired: A report from Atlantic Canada. *Education of the Visually Handicapped*, 1978, *10*(2), 35-37.

2749.   Ward, M. E., & Peabody, R. L. *Education of visually handicapped children, computer assisted remedial education report No. R-50.* University Park, PA: Pennsylvania State University, Computer Assisted Instruction Lab, n.d. (ERIC Document Reproduction Service No. ED 077 164)

2750.   Weisgerber, R. A. Individualizing for the handicapped child in the regular classroom. *Educational Technology*, 1974, *14*(11), 33-35.

2751.   Weishahn, M. W., & Mitchell, R. Educational placement practices with visually disabled and orthopedically disabled children—a comparison. *Rehabilitation Literature*, 1971, *32*, 263-266, 288.

2752.   Westaway, D. L. Alternatives to the blindness system in Australia. *New Outlook for the Blind*, 1973, *67*, 66-71.

2753.   Wilson, J. D. Early intervention: The right to sight. *Education of the Visually Handicapped*, 1976, *8*(3), 83-90.

2754.   Woodcock, C. C. A sensory stimulation center for blind children. *Phi Delta Kappan*, 1974, *55*, 541.

SUPPLEMENT

GENERAL

2755.   Abbott, A. A. Durkheim's theory of education: A case for mainstreaming. *Peabody Journal of Education*, 1981, *58*, 235-241.

2756.   Abend, A. Design criteria for educational facilities for special education services. *Journal of Research and Development in Education*, 1979, *12*(4), 23-35.

2757.   Alexander, C., & Strain, P. S. Review of educators' attitudes toward handicapped children and the concept of mainstreaming. *Psychology in the Schools*, 1978, *15*, 390-396.

2758.   Allen, K. E. Least restrictive environment: Implications for early childhood education. *Educational Horizons*, 1977, *56*, 34-41.

2759.   Amerson, G. T., & Kachur, D. S. Preparing regular classroom educators for teaching handicapped students. *Illinois School Research and Development*, 1981, *17*(2), 33-37.

2760.   Antonak, R. F. Hierarchy of attitudes toward exceptionality. *Journal of Special Education*, 1980, *14*, 231-241.

2761.   Arends, R. I., Sivage, C. A., & Reinhard, D. L. *The educational dean: An examination of behaviors associated with special products.* Paper presented at the Annual Meeting of the American Association of Colleges for Teacher Education, 1981. (ERIC Document Reproduction Service No. ED 199 217)

2762.   Aufderheide, S. K., Knowles, C. J., & McKenzie, T. L. Individualized teaching strategies and learning time: Implications for mainstreaming. *Physical Educator*, 1981, *38*, 20-26.

2763.   Auxter, D. Equal educational opportunity for the handicapped through physical education. *Physical Educator*, 1981, *38*, 8-14.

2764.   Barclay, J. R., & Kehle, T. J. The impact of handicapped students on other students in the classroom. *Journal of Research and Development in Education*, 1979, *12*(4), 80-92.

2765.   Bassore, D. A voice from the back row. *School and Community*, 1980, 66(9), 30-31.

2766.   Bateman, B. *So you're going to a hearing.* Northbrook, IL: Hubbard, 1980.

2767.   Berkey, A. L. Mainstreaming: There's more involved than teaching students. *Agricultural Education*, 1980, *53*, 6-8.

2768.   Bersoff, D. N., & Veltman, E. S. Public law 94-142: Legal implications for the education of handicapped children. *Journal of Research and Development in Education*, 1979, *12*(4), 10-22.

2769.   Berstein, J. Kim is handicapped, but . . . *Today's Education*, 1980, 69(1), 76.

2770.   Bloom, M., & Garfunkel, F. Least restrictive environments and parent-child rights: A paradox. *Urban Education*, 1981, *15*, 379-401.

2771.   Boas, E. E., Jr. Special-needs learner in industrial arts: Are you prepared? *Man/Society/Technology*, 1981, *40*, 19-20.

2772.   Boileau, D. M., & Boileau, J. L. *Teaching competencies for mainstreamed students: A format for the next fifty years.* Unpublished manuscript, n.d. (ERIC Document Reproduction Service No. ED 199 784)

2773.   Borg, W. R., & Ascione, F. R. Changing on-task, off-task, and disruptive pupil behavior in elementary mainstreaming classrooms. *Journal of Educational Research*, 1979, *72*, 243-252.

2774. Boyle, M., & Sleeter, C. E. Inservice for a federally-mandated educational change: A study of P.L. 94-142. *Journal of Research and Development in Education*, 1981, *14*(2), 79-91.

2775. Brennan, R. Reading and the mainstreamed child. *Early Years*, 1978, *8*, 30-31.

2776. Bright, L., & Mullendore, J. A private university's approach to faculty and curriculum development for implementation of P.L. 94-142. *Illinois School Research and Development*, 1981, *17*(2), 39-42.

2777. Britton, E. Warnock and integration. *Educational Research*, 1978, *21*, 3-9.

2778. Broadhead, G. D. Integrating handicapped children by opening doors. *Scottish Educational Journal*, 1974, *57*, 1020-1021.

2779. _____. Integrating special children in Scotland: A P.L. 94-142 is needed. *Journal of Special Education*, 1979, *13*, 91-98.

2780. _____. Keys to integrating handicapped children. *Scottish Educational Journal*, 1974, *57*, 1046-1047.

2781. Bryan, E., Warden, M. G., Berg, B., & Hauck, G. R. Medical considerations for multiple-handicapped children in the public schools. *Journal of School Health*, 1978, *48*, 84-89.

2782. Buttery, T. J. Pre-service teachers' affective perceptions on mainstreamed children. *College Student Journal*, 1981, *15*, 74-78.

2783. _____. Reading readiness for mainstreamed exceptional children in early childhood education. *Reading Improvement*, 1979, *16*, 118-123.

2784. Bybee, R. W. Helping the special student fit in. *Science Teacher*, 1979, *46*, 22-24.

2785. Candler, A., & Sowell, V. *Mainstreaming special educators: Interface between regular and special education*. Paper presented at the 58th Annual International Convention of the Council for Special Education, Philadelphia, PA, April 1980. (ERIC Document Reproduction Service No. ED 187 076)

2786. Carlberg, C., & Kavale, K. Efficacy of special versus regular class placement for exceptional children: A meta-analysis. *Journal of Special Education*, 1980, *14*, 295-309.

2787. Carpenter, W. Why mainstreaming will succeed while some other special education will fail. *Education*, 1979, *99*, 368-369.

2788. Carvell, R., & Kerr, M. A self-appraisal survey of reading specialists: Education in the least restrictive environment. *Journal of Educational Research*, 1980, *74*, 120-124.

2789. Cavallaro, S. A., & Porter, R. H. Peer preferences of at-risk and normally developing children in a preschool mainstream classroom. *American Journal of Mental Deficiency*, 1980, *84*, 357-366.

2790. Christiansen, K. M. Is recess(ion) over for teachers. *Kappa Delta Pi Record*, 1981, *17*(3), 77-78, 80.

2791. *Clarification of P.L. 94-142 for the classroom teacher*. Rolling Hills Estates, CA: B. L. Winch & Associates, n.d.

2792. Clark, E. J. Integrating skills, knowledge, and attitudes for teaching the handicapped into regular teacher education. *Illinois School Research and Development*, 1981, *17*(2), 13-17.

2793. Collins, C. The left-handed notebook. *Language Arts*, 1981, *58*(1), 63-67.

2794. *A common body of practice for teachers: The challenge of public law 94-142 to teacher education*. Washington, D.C.: American Association of Colleges for Teacher Education, and Minneapolis, MN: University of Minnesota, National Support Systems Project, 1980. (ERIC Document Reproduction Service No. ED 186 399)

2795. Cone, W. H., & Hyatt, J. A. Principal: Key manager in mainstreaming. *Compact*, 1980, *14*, 13-15.

2796.   Cooper, J. A., & Bjorling, B. J. Individualized education programs for multiply hand-
         icapped students. *Viewpoints in Teaching and Learning*, 1981, *57*(1), 21-25.

2797.   Corder, B. Secondary teachers' perceptions toward the handicapped. *American
         Secondary Education*, 1981, *11*, 29-31.

2798.   Coursen, D. *Administration of mainstreaming*. Burlingame, CA: Association of Cali-
         fornia School Administrators, 1981.

2799.   Creighton, C. A common sense guide to reasonable accommodation. *VocEd*, 1981,
         56(3), 55-58.

2800.   Dahl, P. R. Practical guide to mainstreaming. *School Shop*, 1978, *37*, 66-69.

2801.   Davis, C. G. Mainstreaming versus an appropriate education. *Yearbook of Special
         Education*, 1980-81, *6*, 29-35.

2802.   Davis, R. E. Mainstreaming special needs students in DE classes. *Business Education
         Forum*, 1979, *33*, 28.

2803.   Davis, W. E. Principal's attitudes toward placement of mildly and moderately handi-
         capped pupils. *Journal for Special Educators*, 1981, *17*, 265-269.

2804.   DeChiara, E., & Kaplan, V. Viewpoint: Mainstreaming in art. *School Arts*, 1981,
         80(8), 62-63.

2805.   Degler, L. S., & Risko, V. J. Teaching reading to mainstreamed sensory impaired
         children. *Reading Teacher*, 1979, *32*, 921-925.

2806.   DeJulio, E. L. Many happy returns; Developmental Learning Center, Fairmont
         School, Downers Grove, Ill. *Today's Education*, 1980, 69(1), 72-73.

2807.   Deno, S. L., & Mirkin, P. K. Data based IEP development: An approach to substan-
         tive compliance. *Teaching Exceptional Children*, 1980, *12*, 94-97.

2808.   Dillard, J. M., Kinnison, L. R., & Peel, B. Multicultural approach to mainstreaming:
         A challenge to counselors, teachers, psychologists, and administrators. *Peabody Jour-
         nal of Education*, 1980, *57*, 276-290.

2809.   DiRocco, P. Preparing for the mainstreamed environment: A necessary addition to
         preservice curriculums. *Journal of Physical Education and Recreation*, 1978, *49*(1),
         24-25.

2810.   Dodd, J. Mainstreaming. *English Journal*, 1980, *69*, 51-55.

2811.   Dougherty, J. W. Implementing IEP's: Implications for the principal. *National Asso-
         ciation for Secondary School Principals Bulletin*, 1969, *63*, 49-54.

2812.   Dunlop, K. H., Stoneman, Z., & Cantrell, M. L. Social interaction of exceptional and
         other children in a mainstreamed preschool classroom. *Exceptional Children*, 1980,
         47, 132-141.

2813.   Dunn, R. S., & Cole, R. W. Enter into the world of the handicapped; P. L. 94-142
         opens the door. *Clearinghouse*, 1980, *53*, 241-243.

2814.   Dybwad, G. Avoiding misconceptions of mainstreaming, the least restrictive environ-
         ment and normalization. *Exceptional Children*, 1980, *47*, 85-88.

2815.   Dykman, R. A. In step with 94-142, two by two. *Music Educators Journal*, 1979,
         65(5), 58-63.

2816.   Dyson, L. L., & Kubo, H. R. *Attitudes of preschool teachers toward the integration of
         handicapped children*. Paper presented at the 58th Annual International Convention
         of the Council for Exceptional Children, Philadelphia, PA, April 1980. (ERIC Docu-
         ment Reproduction Service No. ED 187 043)

2817.   Educating handicapped individuals; symposium. *Journal of Teacher Education*, 1978,
         29(6), 7-47.

2818.   Edwards, L. L. Curriculum modification as a strategy for helping regular classroom
         students. *Focus on Exceptional Children*, 1980, *12*, 1-11.

2819. Eschuk, B. One experience in mainstreaming. *American Secondary Education*, 1979, 9, 20-25.

2820. Federlein, A. C. *A year long study of the frequency of play interactions of handicapped preschoolers in mainstreamed and segregated classrooms.* Paper presented at the 58th Annual International Convention of the Council for Exceptional Children, Philadelphia, PA, April 1980. (ERIC Document Reproduction Service No. ED 188 426)

2821. Feirer, J. L. Is mainstreaming the answer to serving special needs students? *Industrial Education*, 1978, 67, 2.

2822. Fern's doing, not talking, mainstreaming. *Instructor*, 1977, 87(5), 12.

2823. Filer, P. S. Preparing for IEP conferences. *School Counselor*, 1981, 29, 46-50.

2824. Fink, W. T., & Sandall, S. R. One-to-one vs. group academic instruction with handicapped and nonhandicapped preschool children. *Mental Retardation*, 1978, 16, 236-240.

2825. Flygare, T. J. Disciplining special education students. *Phi Delta Kappan*, 1981, 62, 670-671.

2826. Folio, M. R., & Norman, A. Toward more success in mainstreaming: A peer teacher approach to physical education. *Teaching Exceptional Children*, 1981, 13, 110-114.

2827. Forness, S. R. Clinical criteria for mainstreaming mildly handicapped children. *Psychology in the Schools*, 1979, 16, 508, 514.

2828. Freeman, R. N. Mainstreaming in the high school: Some problems and solutions. *American Secondary Education*, 1980, 10, 15-18.

2829. Frith, G. H. "Advocate" vs. "professional employee," a question of priorities for special educators. *Exceptional Children*, 1981, 47, 486-492.

2830. Gage, K. H. Principal's role in implementing mainstreaming. *Educational Leadership*, 1979, 36, 575-577.

2831. Gallent, B. L. Out of the frying pan, into the fire: A teacher's view. *Clearinghouse*, 1981, 54, 345-348.

2832. Garrett, J. P. Mainstreaming for every child. *Clearinghouse*, 1978, 51, 294-296.

2833. Garrison, L. L. Are you ready for mainstreaming? *Business Education Forum*, 1978, 32, 9-10.

2834. Gazda, G. M., Crisler, J., & Hunt, J. (Eds.). Public education and the handicapped; symposium. *Journal of Research and Development in Education*, 1979, 12(4), 1-108.

2835. Gear, G. H., & Gable, R. K. Educating handicapped children in the regular classroom: Needs assessment in teacher preparation. *Journal of Research and Development in Education*, 1979, 12(4), 36-45.

2836. Gerler, E. R., Jr. Preventing the delusion of uniqueness: Multi-modal education in mainstreamed classrooms. *Elementary School Journal*, 1979, 80, 34-40.

2837. Getting art into the mainstream. *Early Years*, 1981, 11, 23-25.

2838. Gilbert, J. P., & Asmus, E. P., Jr. Mainstreaming: Music educators' participation and professional needs. *Journal of Research in Music Education*, 1981, 29, 31-37.

2839. Glazzard, P. Adaptations for mainstreaming. *Teaching Exceptional Children*, 1980, 13, 26-29.

2840. _____. Building self-concepts. *Early Years*, 1981, 12, 74.

2841. _____. Mainstreaming is more than a definition. *Early Years*, 1980, 10, 28-30.

2842. _____. Simulation of handicaps as a teaching strategy for preservice and inservice training. *Teaching Exceptional Children*, 1979, 11, 101-104.

2843. _____. Training students to work independently in the classroom. *Teaching Exceptional Children*, 1981, 13, 66-70.

2844.   Glick, H. M., & Schubert, M. Mainstreaming: An unmandated challenge. *Educational Leadership*, 1981, *38*, 326-329.

2845.   Goldman, N. Mainstreaming procedures at an exemplary school. *Phi Delta Kappan*, 1980, *62*, 263.

2846.   de Grandpré, B. B., & Messler, J. M. Helping mainstreamed students stay in the mainstream. *Yearbook of Special Education*, 1980-81, *6*, 27-28.

2847.   Guerin, G. R. Regular teacher concerns with mainstreamed learning handicapped children. *Psychology in the Schools*, 1979, *16*, 543-545.

2848.   Guldager, L. The Oak Hill model for severely handicapped persons. *Viewpoints in Teaching and Learning*, 1981, *57*(1), 26-32.

2849.   Gunderson, L. Who is that stranger? *Academic Therapy*, 1978, *14*, 99-102.

2850.   Haisley, F. B., Tell, C. A., & Andrews, J. Peers as tutors in the mainstream: Trained "teachers" of handicapped adolescents. *Journal of Learning Disabilities*, 1981, *14*, 224-226, 238.

2851.   Hall, S. Catholic education becomes special. *Momentum*, 1979, *10*, 18-23.

2852.   _____. The parish school as "least restrictive environment." *Momentum*, 1981, *12*, 40-41.

2853.   Hamilton, W. M. Hazardous course; practical problems of integration. *Times Educational Supplement (London)*, September 26, 1980, no. 3353, p. 33.

2854.   Handicapped child in school: the seventh annual Schering symposium. *Journal of School Health*, 1979, *49*, 137-167.

2855.   Hannah, E. P., & Parker, R. M. Mainstreaming vs the special setting. *Academic Therapy*, 1980, *15*, 271-278.

2856.   Hansen, K. H. Implications of P.L. 94-142 for higher education. In *Regional mainstreaming conference, Kansas City, MO, December 12-13, 1976*. Minneapolis, MN: Leadership Training Institute, 1976.

2857.   Hansen, P. A., & Hansen, S. B. Mainstreaming across nations. *Claremont Reading Conference Yearbook*, 1979, *43*, 39-47.

2858.   Harvey, J., & Siantz, J. Public education and the handicapped. *Journal of Research and Development in Education*, 1979, *12*(4), 1-9.

2859.   Hauser, C. Evaluating mainstream programs: Capitalizing on A VICTORY. *Journal of Special Education*, 1979, *13*, 107-129.

2860.   Hedberg, S. Outdoor education can help the handicapped; program at Miramonte High School, Orinda, Calif. *Today's Education*, 1980, *69*(2), 54G-55G, 83G.

2861.   Hegarty, S. Every child is special, no child exceptional: Great Britain. *Times Educational Supplement (London)*, September 22, 1978, no. 3299, pp. 41-42.

2862.   Heisler, V. *Handicapped child in the regular classroom*. New York, NY: Grune & Stratton, 1976.

2863.   Helge, D. I. Problems in implementing comprehensive special education programing in rural areas. *Exceptional Children*, 1981, *47*, 514-520.

2864.   Henderson, R. A., & Hage, R. E. Economic implications of public education of the handicapped. *Journal of Research and Development in Education*, 1979, *12*(4), 71-79.

2865.   Henson, J. Public law 94-142; mainstreaming. *Physical Educator*, 1979, *36*, 162-165, 215-217.

2866.   Herlihy, J. G., & Herlihy, M. T. (Eds.). Mainstreaming in elementary social studies: The least restrictive environment. *Social Education*, 1979, *43*, 57-68.

2867.   Hirshoren, A., & Almy, S. W. Mandatory special education and mainstreaming across the Atlantic. *Journal of Special Education*, 1978, *12*, 315-319.

2868. _____, & Burton, T. Willingness of regular teachers to participate in mainstreaming handicapped children. *Journal of Research and Development in Education,* 1979, *12*(4), 93-100.

2869. Hoben, M. Toward integration in the mainstream. *Exceptional Children,* 1980, *47,* 100-105.

2870. Houck, C., & Sherman, A. Mainstreaming current flows two ways. *Academic Therapy,* 1979, *15,* 133-140.

2871. Huckaby, H., & Daly, J. Got those PL 94-142 blues. *Personnel and Guidance Journal,* 1979, *58,* 70-72.

2872. Huttar, E. Put on a handicap. *Early Years,* 1978, *8,* 46-49.

2873. Ito, H. R. After the resource room—then what. *Academic Therapy,* 1981, *16,* 283-287.

2874. Jackson, A. A case for mainstreaming: First contact with handicapped students. *American Music Teacher,* 1979, *29,* 18.

2875. Jacobs, N. C. Helping student teachers learn more about mainstreaming. *Teacher Educator,* 1980, *16,* 36-38.

2876. Johnson, A. B. Effects of in-service training in preparation for mainstreaming. *Journal for Special Educators,* 1980, *17,* 10-13.

2877. _____. Teachers' attitudes toward mainstreaming: Implications for inservice training and program modifications in early childhood. *Child Care Quarterly,* 1981, *10,* 137-147.

2878. _____, & Cartwright, C. A. Roles of information and experience in improving teachers' knowledge and attitudes about mainstreaming. *Journal of Special Education,* 1979, *13,* 453-462.

2879. _____, & Fiscus, E. D. Media and mainstreaming: Partners in providing appropriate education for the handicapped. *Educational Technology,* 1980, *20,* 15-17.

2880. _____, & Gold, V. Principal's role in implementing Public Law 94-142. *Clearinghouse,* 1980, *54,* 32-35.

2881. Johnson, D. W., & Johnson, R. T. Integrating handicapped students into the mainstream. *Exceptional Children,* 1980, *47,* 90-98.

2882. Johnson, R., Rynders, J., Johnson, D. W., Schmidt, B., & Haider, S. Interaction between handicapped and non-handicapped teenagers as a function of situational goal structuring: Implications for mainstreaming. *American Educational Research Journal,* 1979, *16,* 161-167.

2883. Kameen, M. C. (Ed.). Creating least restrictive environments for handicapped children; symposium. *Elementary School Guidance and Counseling,* 1979, *13,* 150-228.

2884. Karagianis, L. D., & Nesbit, W. C. The Warnock report: Britain's preliminary answer to public law 94-142. *Exceptional Children,* 1981, *47,* 332-336.

2885. Karnes, M. B. Use of volunteers and parents in mainstreaming. *Viewpoints in Teaching and Learning,* 1979, *55*(1), 44-56.

2886. Kehle, T. J., & Guidubaldi, J. Do too many cooks spoil the broth? Evaluation of team placement and individual educational plans on enhancing the social competence of handicapped students. *Journal of Learning Disabilities,* 1980, *13,* 552-556.

2887. Kennedy, Z. M. Mainstream in all classes except social studies. *Volta Review,* 1980, *82,* 161-162.

2888. Kierscht, M. S., & DuHoux, M. A. Preparing the mainstream: Changing children's attitudes toward the disabled. *School Psychology Review,* 1980, *9,* 279-283.

2889. Kingsley, R. F., Szweda, G. A., & Klein, D. W. Practices and trends in outdoor education for exceptional children: A look at mainstreaming. *Education,* 1978, *98,* 353-358.

2890.   Kinnison, L. R., Hayes, C., & Acord, J. Evaluating student progress in mainstream classes. *Teaching Exceptional Children*, 1981, *13*, 97-99.

2891.   Klemencic, G. Individualized instruction and mainstreaming. *Industrial Education*, 1981, *70*, 36.

2892.   Klesius, S. E. Measurement and evaluation: The neglected element in physical education for the handicapped. *Physical Educator*, 1981, *38*, 15-19.

2893.   Knapp, R. A. Choir for total communication. *Music Educators Journal*, 1980, *66*, 54-55.

2894.   Knowles, C. J. Concerns of teachers about implementing individualized instruction in the physical education setting. *Research Quarterly*, 1981, *52*, 48-57.

2895.   Kratoville, B. L. Dealing with public schools. *Academic Therapy*, 1977, *13*, 225-232.

2896.   Kunzweiler, C. E. Mainstreaming; will it really work? *Education*, 1979, *99*, 233-235.

2897.   Lapidus, H. P. Let's get serious about mainstreaming. *Journal of Learning Disabilities*, 1980, *13*, 500.

2898.   Larew, L. A. Mainstreaming perceptually handicapped children in Rochester, New York. *Hispania*, 1980, *63*, 736-738.

2899.   Larrivee, B. Effect of inservice training intensity on teachers' attitudes toward mainstreaming. *Exceptional Children*, 1981, *48*, 34-39.

2900.   _____, & Cook, L. Mainstreaming: A study of the variables affecting teacher attitude. *Journal of Special Education*, 1979, *13*, 315-324.

2901.   Least restrictive environment: Getting there; symposium. *VocEd*, 1981, *56*, 21-33.

2902.   Leonard, J. 180 day barrier: Issues and concerns. *Exceptional Children*, 1981, *47*, 246-253.

2903.   Leone, P., & Retish, P. Handicapped kid in my class? *Social Studies*, 1978, *69*, 18-20.

2904.   Leyser, Y., & Heinze, A. Training teachers for mainstreaming: An inservice model for developing behavior management skills. *Teacher Educator*, 1980, *16*, 30-37.

2905.   _____, & Lipscomb, E. Keeping up with the law of the land: Mainstreaming elementary education program at Northern Illinois University. *Illinois School Research and Development*, 1981, *17*(2), 25-31.

2906.   Liddell, M. B. *AACTE state associations and Public Law 94-142*. Washington, D.C.: American Association of Colleges for Teacher Education, 1981. (ERIC Document Reproduction Service No. ED 200 583)

2907.   Lieberman, L. M. Mainstreaming for the eighties. *Academic Therapy*, 1980, *16*, 111-114.

2908.   Lietz, J., & Kaiser, J. S. Principal's role in administering programs for exceptional children. *Education*, 1979, *100*, 31-40.

2909.   Litton, F. W. Materials for educating nonhandicapped students about their handicapped peers. *Teaching Exceptional Children*, 1980, *13*, 39-43.

2910.   Lovitt, T. New ways to handle old problems; mainstreaming children and discipline problems. *Early Years*, 1979, *9*, 34-36.

2911.   McClenaghan, B. A. Normalization in physical education: A reflective review. *Physical Educator*, 1981, *38*, 3-7.

2912.   _____. (Ed.). Equal physical education opportunities for all; symposium. *Physical Educator*, 1981, *38*, 2-41.

2913.   McGill, J. Special children; symposium. *Journal of Education*, 1979, *14*, 259-385.

2914.   MacGugan, K. First steps in mainstreaming. *Media & Methods*, 1979, *15*(8), 46-48.

2915.   McIntosh, D. K. Mainstreaming: Too often a myth, too rarely a reality. *Academic Therapy*, 1979, *15*, 53-59.

2916. McKalip, K. J. Developing acceptance toward the handicapped. *School Counselor,* 1979, *26,* 293-298.

2917. Macy, D. J., & Carter, J. L. Comparison of a mainstream and self-contained special education program. *Journal of Special Education,* 1978, *12,* 303-313.

2918. Mahan, T., & Mahan, A. *Assessing children with special needs.* New York, NY: Holt, Rinehart & Winston, 1981.

2919. Mainstream update: Planning, problems and programs; symposium. *Exceptional Parent,* 1979, 9(4), E1-32.

2920. Mainstreaming; symposium. *Curriculum Review,* 1978, *17,* 251-284.

2921. Mainstreaming; symposium. *Journal of Teacher Education,* 1979, *30*(6), 11-32.

2922. Mainstreaming; symposium. *Learning,* 1978, 7(2), 104-117.

2923. Mainstreaming: Texts and supplements. *Curriculum Review,* 1978, *17,* 260-284.

2924. Mainstreaming; the readiness of the child and the school; symposium. *Exceptional Parent,* 1979, 9(5), R1-32.

2925. Mallinson, G. G. Do I have to eat the bill and legs, too? *School Science and Mathematics,* 1980, *80,* 181-182.

2926. Markus, E. J. Mapping the social structure of a class: A practical instrument for assessing some effects of mainstreaming. *Journal of Special Education,* 1980, *14,* 311-324.

2927. Martin, M. J. Mainstreaming and teaching in the public high school. *English Journal,* 1980, *69,* 9-11.

2928. Megginson, N. L. Regular vs. specially designed programs: Use of least restrictive environment in the clarification of physical education services to be extended to handicapped children. *Physical Educator,* 1980, *37,* 206-207.

2929. Melton, G. B. Preparing normal children for mainstreaming. *Journal for Special Educators,* 1980, *16,* 198-204.

2930. Messages from the mainstreaming scene. *Early Years,* 1980, *10,* 24-27.

2931. Meyen, E. L., & Lehr, D. H. Least restrictive environments: Instructional implications. *Focus on Exceptional Children,* 1980, *12,* 1-8.

2932. Michaelis, C. T. Two teachers and one child. *Early Years,* 1980, *10,* 56-57.

2933. _____. Welcome to the mainstream. *Early Years,* 1980, *10,* 54-55.

2934. _____. When is a child ready for mainstreaming? *Exceptional Parent,* 1979, 9(5), R4-R5.

2935. Miller, P. W., & D'Amore, A. Mainstreaming: Implications for the industrial education teacher. *Man/Society/Technology,* 1979, *39,* 10-12.

2936. Moller, B. Mainstreaming: Who? What? When? Where? Why? *Early Years,* 1978, 9, 48-50.

2937. Monson, D. Mainstreaming, we're almost there. *Early Years,* 1979, 9, 38-39.

2938. Moore, C. Problems the handicapped will encounter as a result of mainstreaming. *Journal of Business Education,* 1980, *56,* 22-24.

2939. Moore, E. A. Serving special needs students. *Agricultural Education,* 1980, *53,* 10-11.

2940. Morgan, D., & York, M. E. Ideas for mainstreaming young children. *Young Children,* 1981, 36(2), 18-25.

2941. Mori, A. A. Handicapped child in the mainstream; new roles for the regular educator. *Education,* 1979, 99, 243-249.

2942. _____. Mildly handicapped children in the mainstream—implications for the health educator. *Journal of School Health,* 1981, *51,* 119-122.

2943. MSU researchers say mainstreaming of handicapped children can begin early. *Journal for Special Educators,* 1980, *16,* 278-279.

2944.   Murphy, L. C., & Banta, T. W. Career education for the handicapped: A model of cooperative programming for effective mainstreaming. *Journal of Career Education,* 1981, *7,* 236-242.

2945.   Murphy, T. J. (Ed.). Looking at special education; symposium. *Thrust,* 1979, *9,* 4-19.

2946.   Nadler, B., & Merron, M. Collaboration: A model for survival for schools of education; New Jersey mainstream inservice project. *Journal of Education,* 1980, *162,* 55-62.

2947.   Naor, M., & Milgram, R. M. Two preservice strategies for preparing regular class teachers for mainstreaming. *Exceptional Children,* 1980, *47,* 126-129.

2948.   Newberger, D. A. Situational socialization: An affective interaction component of the mainstreaming reintegration construct. *Journal of Special Education,* 1978, *12,* 113-121.

2949.   Nuce, D. E. Technology and special education. *Man/Society/Technology,* 1980, *39,* 18-19.

2950.   Orlansky, M. D. Teasing and name-calling: What can a special educator teacher do? *Journal for Special Educators,* 1980, *16,* 127-129.

2951.   Otey, J. W. *The sociometric IEP.* Paper presented at the Annual Meeting of the Southwest Educational Research Association, Dallas, TX, January 1981. (ERIC Document Reproduction Service No. ED 199 230)

2952.   Ottman, R. A. Before a handicapped student enters the classroom: What the special educator can do. *Teaching Exceptional Children,* 1981, *14,* 41-43.

2953.   Owens, J. Physical education activity for everyone. *Viewpoints in Teaching and Learning,* 1981, *57*(1), 94-98.

2954.   Palmer, D. J. Factors to be considered in placing handicapped children in regular classes. *Journal of School Psychology,* 1980, *18,* 163-171.

2955.   Palomaki, M. J. (Ed.). *Teaching handicapped students vocational education. A resource handbook for K-12 teachers.* Washington, D.C.: National Education Association, 1981. (ERIC Document Reproduction Service No. ED 199 568)

2956.   Parrish, L. H., & Kok, M. R. Misinterpretation hinders mainstreaming; individualized educational plan. *Phi Delta Kappan,* 1980, *61,* 685. Also in Yearbook of Special Education, 1980-81, *6,* 24.

2957.   Pate, J. Defining the child's world. *Early Years,* 1978, *8,* 44-45.

2958.   Patryla, V. M., & Seevers, K. Views on special education vs. mainstreaming. *Lutheran Education,* 1979, *114,* 278-284.

2959.   Paul, R. R. Approach to mainstreaming at the middle school level; improved class program, Oakville Junior High School, St. Louis. *National Association for Secondary School Principals Bulletin,* 1981, *65,* 119-121.

2960.   Perry, H. W. (Ed.). Handicapped child in the least restrictive environment; symposium. *Journal of Research and Development in Education,* 1980, *13,* v-vi, 1-73.

2961.   Pettit, N., & Robinson, R. D. Mainstreaming: Implications for reading inservice education. *Reading Improvement,* 1977, *14,* 286-288.

2962.   Phillip, G., Cartwright, C. A., & Ward, M. E. *Educating special learners.* Belmont, CA: Wadsworth, 1981.

2963.   Platt, J. M., & Platt, J. S. Volunteers for special education: A mainstreaming support system. *Teaching Exceptional Children,* 1980, *13,* 31-34.

2964.   Point of view: Including the handicapped in junior high general music classes; discussion. *Music Educators Journal,* 1981, *67,* 56-57.

2965.   Poorman, C. Mainstreaming in reverse with a special friend. *Teaching Exceptional Children,* 1980 *12,* 136-142.

2966.   Powell, T. H. Mainstreaming: A case for the consulting teacher. *Journal for Special Educators*, 1981, *17*, 183-188.

2967.   Procci, L., Magary, J. F., & Tucker, A. S. Meeting the challenges of PL 94-142 through a continuing education program for the school nurse. *Journal of School Health*, 1981, *51*, 154-156.

2968.   Pugach, Marleen C. Preparation for mainstreaming in teacher education programs at the University of Illinois. *Illinois School Research and Development*, 1981, *17*(2), 7-11.

2969.   Ravers, S. A. Preschool integration: Experiences from the classroom. *Teaching Exceptional Children*, 1979, *12*, 22-26.

2970.   Redefining the handicapped; Warnock report. *Times Educational Supplement (London)*, May 26, 1976, no. 3283, p. 5.

2971.   Reynolds, M. C., & Birch, J. W. Teacher preparation for mainstreaming. *Momentum*, 1978, *9*, 40-45.

2972.   Rieber, L. Industrial arts education and special-needs students. *Man/Society/Technology*, 1981, *40*, 6-8.

2973.   Riley, S. Joey comes to class. *Early Years*, 1977, *8*, 42-43.

2974.   Ringlaben, R. P., & Price, J. R. Regular classroom teachers' perceptions of mainstreaming effects. *Exceptional Children*, 1981, *47*, 302-304.

2975.   Roberson, J. B. Preservice changes in teacher education relative to mainstreaming. *Yearbook of Special Education*, 1980-81, *6*, 387-390. Also in *Teacher Education and Special Education*, 1980, *3*(2).

2976.   _____. Research note: Teacher education and mainstreaming: A status report for the South. *Phi Delta Kappan*, 1979, *61*, 70.

2977.   Robie, D. E., Pierce, M. M., & Burdett, C. Implementing a special education, mainstreaming, competency-based teacher-training program. *Educational Technology*, 1979, *19*(2), 36-38.

2978.   Rodrigues, R. J., & White, R. H. *Mainstreaming the non-English speaking student.* Urbana, IL: ERIC Clearinghouse on Reading and Communication and National Council of Teachers of English, 1981. (ERIC Document Reproduction Service No. ED 197 382)

2979.   Rupley, W. H., & Blair, T. R. Mainstreaming and reading instruction; ERIC/RCS report. *Reading Teacher*, 1979, *32*, 762-765.

2980.   Sabatino, D. A. Are appropriate educational programs operationally achieveable under mandated promises of P.L. 94-142? Symposium lead article. *Journal of Special Education*, 1981, *15*, 9-23.

2981.   _____. (Ed.). P.L. 94-142: Popular welfare bandwagon or a non-too-stable educational ship? Symposium rebuttal. *Journal of Special Education*, 1981, *15*, 47-54.

2982.   Salend, S. J. Active academic games: The aim of the game is mainstreaming: *Teaching Exceptional Children*, 1979, *12*, 3-6.

2983.   _____. Cooperative games promote positive student interactions. *Teaching Exceptional Children*, 1981, *13*, 76-79.

2984.   Sapon-Shevin, M. Mainstreaming: Implementing the spirit of the law. *Journal of Negro Education*, 1979, *48*, 364-381.

2985.   Sargent, L. K., Swartzbaugh, T., Sherman, P. Teaming up to mainstream in English: A successful secondary program. *Teaching Exceptional Children*, 1981, *13*, 100-103.

2986.   Savage, C. A. Breaking down the barriers to mainstreaming: A perspective for administrators. *Journal for Special Educators*, 1980, *17*, 71-77.

2987.   Scheetz, J., & Hudak, B. *Strategies and techniques for mainstreaming.* Rev. ed. Lansing, MI: AEGIS, Inc., 1981.

2988.   Scherer, M. Taking the special out of special education; educational resource teachers. *School and Community*, 1978, *64*, 8-10.

2989.   Schleifer, M. J. Entering junior high. *Exceptional Parent*, 1979, *9*(1), A20, A22, A24-26.

2990.   _____ (Ed.). Teacher and mainstreaming; I'm ashamed to admit how angry I can feel. *Exceptional Parent*, 1978, *8*(5), S3-6.

2991.   Schmelkin, L. P. Teachers' and nonteachers' attitudes toward mainstreaming. *Exceptional Children*, 1981, *48*, 42-47.

2992.   Semones, T. Walk in my shoes. *Exceptional Parent*, 1980, *10*(1), 33-34.

2993.   Shaver, J. P., & Curtis, C. K. Handicapism: Another challenge for social studies. *Social Education*, 1981, *45*, 208-211.

2994.   Shulman, B. Accessibility: A practical approach to mainstreaming. *Exceptional Parent*, 1978, *8*(6), E30-32.

2995.   Simpson, R. L. Modifying the attitudes of regular class students toward the handicapped. *Focus on Exceptional Children*, 1980, *13*(3), 1-11.

2996.   Smart, R., Wilton, K., & Keeling, B. Teacher factors and special class placement. *Journal of Special Education*, 1980, *14*, 217-229.

2997.   Smith, D. B., & Larson, P. A. Adolescent attitudes toward disabled persons in an integrated and nonintegrated school setting. *Education*, 1980, *100*, 390-394.

2998.   Smith, T. E. C. Attitudes of principals and teachers toward mainstreaming handicapped children. *Journal for Special Educators*, 1979, *16*, 89-95.

2999.   Solomon, E. Promising a rose garden? *Times Educational Supplement (London)*, April 7, 1978, no. 3275, pp. 16-17.

3000.   Sorgman, M. Least restrictive environment; social studies goals and practices. *Social Studies*, 1979, *70*, 108-111.

3001.   Souers, M. E. (Ed.). Perspectives on mainstreaming; symposium. *Educational Horizons*, 1981, *59*, 102-153.

3002.   Special education; symposium. *Delta Kappa Gamma Bulletin*, 1981, *47*(3), 6-54.

3003.   Spell, J., & Carlson, N. Mainstreaming at the preschool level? *Early Years*, 1981, *11*, 70-71.

3004.   Spencer, D. Pressure group to push for integration of handicapped; Great Britain. *Times Educational Supplement (London)*, November 10, 1978, no. 3306, p. 5.

3005.   Stoner, M. Education in mainstreaming. *Clearinghouse*, 1981, *55*, 39-42.

3006.   Stagich, T. M. Mainstreaming in education: Rights, barriers, and administrative alternatives. *Educational Horizons*, 1980, *58*, 217-221.

3007.   Stainback, W., Stainback, S., & Jaben, T. Providing opportunities for interaction between severely handicapped and nonhandicapped students. *Teaching Exceptional Children*, 1981, *13*, 72-75.

3008.   Switzky, H. N., & Miller, T. L. Least restrictive alternative. *Mental Retardation*, 1978, *16*, 52-54.

3009.   Taylor, B. Back into the mainstream. *Times Educational Supplement (London)*, May 26, 1978, no. 3283, p. 2.

3010.   Teacher training in mainstreaming; integrating handicapped children into the regular classroom. *EPIE Materials Report*, 1978, *12*, 5-107.

3011.   Thibodeau, G. P., & Kennedy, S. J. PL 94-142 and questions parents should be asking. *Academic Therapy*, 1981, *16*, 415-423.

3012.   This principal keeps opening new doors for kids. *Instructor*, 1978, *87*(9), 38.

3013.   Thole, J. P. Reading needs of mainstreaming children; interview; edited by D. McClenathan. *Early Years*, 1981, *11*, 59.

3014.   Thomas, W. V. Mainstreaming: Handicapped children in the classroom. *Editorial Research Reports*, 1981, *2*, 533-552.

3015.   Thornburg, J. Into the mainstream. *Contemporary Education*, 1980, *51*, 161-162.

3016.   Todd, T. W., & Lazear, J. B. Mainstreaming: Getting out the word. *Yearbook of Special Education*, 1980-81, *6*, 25-26.

3017.   Tuckwell, P., & Beresford, P. An end to isolation? Schools for all by Patience Tuckwell and Peter Beresford; report. *Times Educational Supplement (London)*, April 7, 1978, no. 3275, p. 15.

3018.   Tunick, R. H., Platt, J. S., & Bowen, J. Rural community attitudes toward the handicapped: Implications for mainstreaming. *Exceptional Children*, 1980, *46*, 549-550.

3019.   Turnbull, A. P., & Leonard, J. Parent involvement in special education: Emerging advocacy roles. *School Psychology Review*, 1981, *10*(1), 37-44.

3020.   Umansky, W., & Cryan, J. R. Mainstreaming of young children: Unanswered questions. *Childhood Education*, 1979, *55*, 186-191.

3021.   Valett, R. E. Mainstreaming exceptional children by functional achievement grouping. *Journal of Learning Disabilities*, 1981, *14*, 123, 171.

3022.   Vandivier, S. S., & Vandivier, P. L. Mainstreaming exceptional teachers. *Clearinghouse*, 1979, *52*, 458-459.

3023.   Vlasak, J. W. Mainstreaming handicapped children: The underlying legal concept. *Journal of School Health*, 1980, *50*, 285-287.

3024.   *Vocational education for handicapped, limited English proficiency and disadvantaged persons.* Springfield, IL: Illinois State Board of Education, 1981. (ERIC Document Reproduction Service No. ED 198 355)

3025.   Voeltz, L. M., & Appffel, J. A. A leisure activities curricular component for severely handicapped youth: Why and how. *Viewpoints in Teaching and Learning*, 1981, *57*(1), 82-93.

3026.   Wang, M. C. Mainstreaming exceptional children: Some instructional design and implementation considerations. *Elementary School Journal*, 1981, *81*, 195-221.

3027.   Warren, S. A., & Gardner, D. C. Correlates of class rank of high school handicapped students in mainstream vocational education programs. *Adolescence*, 1981, *16*, 335-344.

3028.   Weil, J. Learning is a partnership. *Journal of Current Social Issues*, 1979, *16*, 63-64.

3029.   Weiss, R., & Karper, W. B. Teaching the handicapped child in the regular physical education class. *Journal of Physical Education and Recreation*, 1980, *51*(2), 32-35, 77.

3030.   White, E. P.L. 94-142's touchiest topics: Health care, discipline, summer school. *American School Board Journal*, 1981, *168*(2), 19-23.

3031.   Williams, R. J., & Algozzine, B. Teachers' attitudes toward mainstreaming. *Elementary School Journal*, 1979, *80*, 63-67.

3032.   Witters, L. A. Mainstreaming the mildly handicapped secondary student; another view. *American Secondary Education*, 1977, *7*, 30-33.

3033.   Yard, G. J. Managing seizures in mainstream education. *Journal for Special Educators*, 1980, *17*, 52-56.

3034.   Yates, J. R. Financing of public law 94-142. *Education and Training of the Mentally Retarded*, 1977, *12*, 396-401.

3035.   Zeigler, A. Mainstreaming can be fun, profitable. *Thrust*, 1980, *10*(1), 16-17.

GIFTED

3036.   Peterson, J. S. *Teaching the novel: Mainstreaming the gifted and jetstreaming the average.* Paper presented at the 19th Annual Meeting of the Conference on English Education, Anaheim, CA, March 1981. (ERIC Document Reproduction Service No. ED 199 764)

HEARING IMPAIRED

3037.   Bevilacqua, T., & Osterlink, E. Components of a service program for the mainstreaming of hearing-impaired students into regular university programs. *American Annals of the Deaf,* 1979, *124,* 400-402.

3038.   Conway, A. Mainstreaming from a school for the deaf. *Volta Review,* 1979, *81,* 237-241.

3039.   _____. A "support" curriculum for mainstreamed students. *Volta Review,* 1980, *82,* 380-385.

3040.   Froelinger, V. (Ed.). *Today's hearing impaired child: Into the mainstream.* Washington, D.C.: Alexander Graham Bell Association for the Deaf, 1981.

3041.   Hein, R. D., & Bishop, M. E. *An annotated bibliography on mainstreaming the hearing impaired, the mentally retarded, and the visually impaired in the regular classroom.* 2 vols. Rochester, NY: National Technical Institute for the Deaf, 1978.

3042.   James, P., & James C. Benefits of art for mainstreamed hearing-impaired children. *Volta Review,* 1980, *82,* 103-108.

3043.   Jensema, C. K. Paraprofessionals working with deaf-blind children: Why we need them; what training they need. *American Annals of the Deaf,* 1978, *123,* 914-917.

3044.   Kindred, E. M. Mainstream teenagers with care. *American Annals of the Deaf,* 1980, *125,* 1053-1056.

3045.   Libbey, S. S., & Pronovost, W. Communication practices of mainstreamed hearing-impaired adolescents. *Volta Review,* 1980, *82,* 197-219.

3046.   Maisel, C. G. NEST for hearing-impaired children in the schools; network of educational support services team. *Volta Review,* 1979, *81,* 441-443.

3047.   Mollick, L. B., & Etra, K. S. Poor learning ability . . . or poor hearing. *Teacher,* 1981, *98*(7), 42-43.

3048.   Mothner, H. Promoting independent study skills for the mainstreamed hearing-impaired student. *Volta Review,* 1980, *82,* 291-293.

3049.   Murray, J. Comments on the least restrictive environments for deaf-blind severe and profoundly handicapped children. *Viewpoints in Teaching and Learning,* 1981, *57*(1), 8-13.

3050.   Pflaster, G. A factor analysis of variables related to academic performance of hearing-impaired children in regular classes. *Volta Review,* 1980, *82,* 71-84.

3051.   _____. A second analysis of factors related to the academic performance of hearing-impaired children in the mainstream. *Volta Review,* 1981, *83,* 71-80.

3052.   Stoefen, J. M. Instructional alternatives for teaching content reading to mainstreamed hearing impaired students. *Journal of Reading,* 1980, *24,* 141-143.

3053.   Thompson, M., & Thompson, G. Mainstreaming: A closer look. *American Annals of the Deaf,* 1981, *126,* 395-401.

3054.   Vernon, M. The decade of the eighties: Significant trends and developments for hearing impaired individuals. *Rehabilitation Literature,* 1981, *42,* 2-7.

3055.   _____. Deinstitutionalization and mainstreaming. *American Annals of the Deaf*, 1979, *124*, 348-349.

3056.   Wood, F., & Hirshoren, A. Hearing impaired in the mainstream: The problem and some successful practices. *Journal for Special Educators*, 1981, *17*, 291-302.

LEARNING DISABLED AND EMOTIONALLY DISTURBED

3057.   Abidin, R. R., & Seltzer, J. Special education outcomes: Implications for implementation of Public Law 94-142. *Journal of Learning Disabilities*, 1981, *14*, 28-31.

3058.   Abkarian, G. G. Non-verbal child in a regular classroom. *Journal of Learning Disabilities*, 1981, *14*, 138-139.

3059.   Blankenship, C., & Lilly, M. S. *Mainstreaming students with learning and behavior problems*. New York: Holt, Rinehart & Winston, 1981.

3060.   Carberry, H., Waxman, B., & McKain, D. An in-service workshop model for regular class teachers concerning mainstreaming of the learning disabled child. *Journal of Learning Disabilities*, 1981, *14*, 26-28.

3061.   Demers, L. A. Effective mainstreaming for the learning disabled student with behavior problems. *Journal of Learning Disabilities*, 1981, *14*, 179-188, 203.

3062.   Diamond, B. Myths of mainstreaming. *Journal of Learning Disabilities*, 1979, *12*, 246-250.

3063.   Egel, A. L., Richman, G. S., & Koegel, R. L. Normal peer models and autistic children's learning. *Journal of Applied Behavior Analysis*, 1981, *14*, 3-12.

3064.   Frostig, M. Meeting individual needs of all children in the classroom setting. *Journal of Learning Disabilities*, 1980, *13*, 158-161.

3065.   Harrington, A. M., & Morrison, R. A. Modifying classroom exams for secondary LD students. *Academic Therapy*, 1981, *16*, 571-577.

3066.   Hedberg, S. Integrating LD students into a regular high school. *Academic Therapy*, 1981, *16*, 559-562.

3067.   Kokoszka, R., & Drye, J. Toward the least restrictive environment: High school L. D. students. *Journal of Learning Disabilities*, 1981, *14*, 22-23, 26.

3068.   Parish, T. S., & Copeland, T. F. Teachers' and students' attitudes in mainstreamed classrooms. *Psychological Reports*, 1978, *43*(1), 54.

3069.   Phipps, P. M. Mainstreaming and the learning disabled child. *Claremont Reading Conference Yearbook*, 1979, *43*, 48-53.

3070.   Prillaman, D. Acceptance of learning disabled students in the mainstream environment: A failure to replicate. *Journal of Learning Disabilities*, 1981, *14*, 344-346, 368.

3071.   Ramsey, R. W., & Ramsey, R. S. Educating the emotionally handicapped child in the public school setting. *Adolescence*, 1978, *13*, 537-541.

3072.   Richey, D. D., Miller, M., & Lessman, J. Resource and regular classroom behavior of learning disabled students. *Journal of Learning Disabilities*, 1981, *14*, 163-166.

3073.   Russo, D. C., & Koegel, R. L. Method for integrating an autistic child into a normal public-school classroom. *Journal of Applied Behavior Analysis*, 1977, *10*, 579-590.

3074.   Sabatino, D. A. The learning disabled secondary student: Traditional vs. alternative programming. *Momentum*, 1981, *12*, 10-12, 52-53.

3075.   Schiff, G., Scholom, A., Swerdlik, M., & Knight, J. Mainstreamed vs. self-contained classes; a two-year study of their effects on the personal adjustment and academic achievement of children with learning disabilities. *Education*, 1979, *99*, 397-405.

3076.   Scholom, A., Schiff, G., Swerdlik, M. E., & Knight, J. Three year study of learning disabled children in mainstreamed and self contained classes. *Education*, 1981, *101*, 231-238.

3077.   Scranton, T. R., & Ryckman, D. B. Sociometric status of learning disabled children in an integrative program. *Journal of Learning Disabilities*, 1979, *12*, 402-407.

3078.   Wilkes, H. H., Bereley, M. K., & Schultz, J. J. Criteria for mainstreaming the learning-disabled child into the regular classroom; editorial. *Journal of Learning Disabilities*, 1979, *12*, 251-256.

MENTALLY HANDICAPPED

3079.   Buttery, T. J., & Mason, G. E. Reading improvement for mainstreamed children who are mildly mentally handicapped. *Reading Improvement*, 1979, *16*, 334-337.

3080.   Childs, R. E. Drastic change in curriculum for the educable mentally retarded child. *Mental Retardation*, 1979, *17*, 299-301; discussion, 1979, *17*, 301-306.

3081.   Davis, W. E. Public school principals' attitudes toward mainstreaming retarded pupils. *Education and Training of the Mentally Retarded*, 1980, *15*, 174-178.

3082.   Downing, C. J. TMR class and the open space school. *Education and Training of the Mentally Retarded*, 1978, *13*, 64-66.

3083.   Gottlieb, J., Semmel, M. I., & Veldman, D. J. Correlates of social status among mainstreamed mentally retarded children. *Journal of Educational Psychology*, 1978, *70*, 396-405.

3084.   Hee, J., & McClennen, S. Comparison of severely retarded students from homes and institutions integrated in a public school setting. *Journal for Special Educators*, 1981, *17*, 213-223.

3085.   Hein, R. D., & Bishop, M. E. *An annotated bibliography on mainstreaming the hearing impaired, the mentally retarded, and the visually impaired in the regular class room. 2 vols.* Rochester, NY: National Technical Institute for the Deaf, 1978.

3086.   Kavale, K., & Rossi, C. Regular class teachers' attitudes and perceptions of the resource specialist program for educable mentally retarded pupils. *Education and Training of the Mentally Retarded*, 1980, *15*, 195-198.

3087.   Kesselman-Turkel, J., & Peterson, F. Taking the tough route of fairness. *American Education*, 1981, *17*(1), 6-13.

3088.   MacMillan, D. L., & Borthwick, S. The new educable mentally retarded population: Can they be mainstreamed? *Mental Retardation*, 1980, *18*, 155-158.

3089.   Mosley, J. L. Integration: The need for a systematic evaluation of the socioadaptive aspect. *Education and Training of the Mentally Retarded*, 1978, *13*, 4-8.

3090.   Murray, J. Comments on the least restrictive environments for deaf-blind severe and profoundly handicapped children. *Viewpoints in Teaching and Learning*, 1981, *57*(1), 8-13.

3091.   Peck, C. A., Apolloni, T., Cooke, T. P., & Raver, S. A. Teaching retarded preschoolers to imitate the free-play behavior of nonretarded classmates: Trained and generalized effects. *Journal of Special Education*, 1978, *12*, 195-207.

3092.   Powers, D. A. Mainstreaming EMR pupils at the secondary level: A consideration of the issues. *High School Journal*, 1979, *63*, 102-108. Also in *Education Digest*, 1980, *45*, 46-49.

3093.   Rider, R. A. Mainstreaming moderately retarded children in the elementary physical education program. *Teaching Exceptional Children*, 1980, *12*, 150-152.

3094. Santomier, J., & Kopczuk, W. Facilitation of interactions between retarded and non-retarded students in a physical education setting. *Education and Training of the Mentally Retarded*, 1981, *16*, 20-23.

3095. Spewock, M. A. Color cues help EMR mainstreaming production of a model airplane. *School Shop*, 1979, *39*, 38.

3096. Stager, S. F., & Young, R. D. Intergroup contact and social outcomes for mainstreamed EMR adolescents. *American Journal of Mental Deficiency*, 1981, *85*, 497-503.

3097. Thurman, S. K. Least restrictive environments; another side of the coin. *Education and Training of the Mentally Retarded*, 1981, *16*, 68-70.

PHYSICALLY HANDICAPPED

3098. Huth, R. Special class; with cerebral palsy. *Early Years*, 1980, *10*, 54-55.

3099. Parish, T. S., & Copeland, T. F. Teachers' and students' attitudes in mainstreamed classrooms. *Psychological Reports*, 1978, *43*(1), 54.

3100. Silverman, M. Beyond the mainstream: The special needs of the chronic child patient. *American Journal of Orthopsychiatry*, 1979, *49*, 62-68.

3101. Stearns, S. E. Understanding the psychological adjustment of physically handicapped children in the classroom. *Children Today*, 1981, *10*(1), 12-15.

3102. Van Putte, A. W. Relationship of school setting to self concept in physically disabled children. *Journal of School Health*, 1979, *49*, 576-578.

3103. Venn, J., Morganstern, L., & Dykes, M. K. Checklists for evaluating the fit and function of ortheses, protheses, and wheelchairs in the classroom. *Teaching Exceptional Children*, 1979, *11*, 51-56.

3104. Volkmann, C. S. Integrating the physically disabled student into the elementary school. *Education*, 1978, *99*, 25-30.

SPEECH HANDICAPPED

3105. Edelsky, C., & Rosegrant, T. J. Language development for mainstreamed severely handicapped non-verbal children. *Language Arts*, 1981, *58*(1), 68-76.

3106. Liebergott, J., Favors, Jr., A. F., Saaz von Hippel, C., & Liftman, H. Mainstreaming children with speech and language impairments; excerpts. *Yearbook of Special Education*, 1979-80, *5*, 188-201.

3107. Navratil, K., & Petrasek, M. Approach to mainstreaming language-disabled children in the elementary school. *Language, Speech and Hearing Services in Schools*, 1978, *9*, 17-23.

VISUALLY HANDICAPPED

3108. Alsin, M. L. He sees with his fingers. *Early Years*, 1977, *8*, 46-47.

3109. Billy: Mainstreaming a five-year old who is blind. *Exceptional Parent*, 1978, *8*(1), 28-29.

3110. Davis, P. A. Teaching partially sighted children. *Teacher*, 1981, *98*(7), 39-41.

3111. Forman, E. The inclusion of visually limited and blind children in a sighted physical education program. *Education of the Visually Handicapped*, 1969, *1*, 113-115.

3112.   Gale, G. S. Ink-a-dink; mainstreaming a blind child in art class. *Arts and Activities,* 1978, *83*(4), 30-31. Also in *Yearbook of Special Education,* 1979-80, *5*, 221.

3113.   Gorman, E. J. Blind boy in my metalshop? *School Shop,* 1978, *37*, 38-39.

3114.   Hein, R. D., & Bishop, M. E. *An annotated bibliography on mainstreaming the hearing impaired, the mentally retarded, and the visually impaired in the regular classroom. 2 vols.* Rochester, NY: National Technical Institute for the Deaf, 1978.

3115.   Johnson, P. Physical education for blind children in public elementary schools. *New Outlook for the Blind,* 1969, *1*, 264-271.

3116.   Kearney, S., & Copeland, R. Goal ball; a sports idea for mainstreaming visually impaired children. *Journal of Physical Education and Recreation,* 1979, *50*, 24-26.

3117.   Kersten, F. Music as therapy for the visually impaired. *Music Educators Journal,* 1981, *67*, 63-64.

3118.   Mulhern, K. Among the sighted. *Times Educational Supplement (London),* September 22, 1978, no. 3299, p. 46.

3119.   Murray, J. Comments on the least restrictive environments for deaf-blind severe and profoundly handicapped children. *Viewpoints in Teaching and Learning,* 1981, *57*(1), 8-13.

3120.   Vermeij, G. J. On teaching the blind student. *Today's Education,* 1978, *67*, 77-78.

3121.   Ward, M., & McCormick, S. Reading instruction for blind and low vision children in the regular classroom. *Reading Teacher,* 1981, *34*, 434-444.

3122.   Wienke, P. Blind children in an integrated physical education program. *New Outlook for the Blind,* 1966, *59*, 73-76.

SUBJECT INDEX

(Numbers refer to citations)